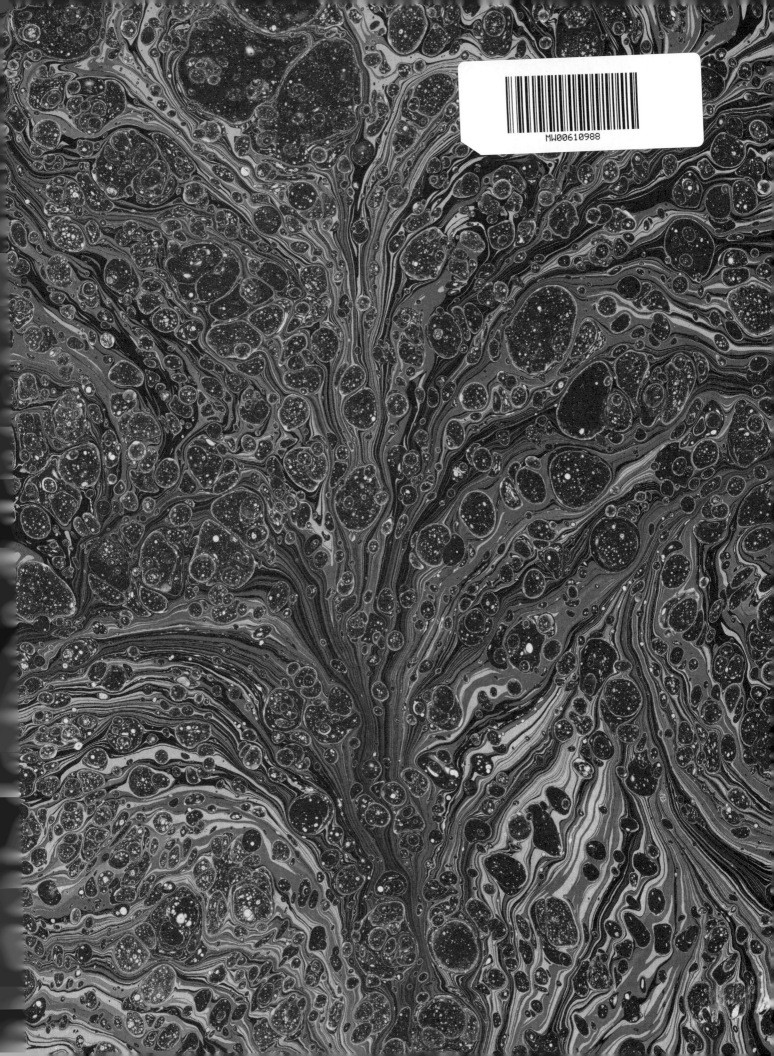

Rations
of the German Wehrmacht
in World War II

Volume II

Braunkohl

Herstellung 11 43

H. C. Jentsch & Sohn, Braunschweig

RATIONS
OF THE GERMAN WEHRMACHT
IN WORLD WAR II

VOLUME II

Lieutenant Colonel (Retired) Jim Pool

Schiffer Military History
Atglen, PA

I want to thank my wife Deborah, without whose support and encouragement this project would not have materialized. I love you.

To Ripley, Dallas, Diz, and Rico; thank you for making me laugh when I hit those all too frequent brick walls.

Book Design by Stephanie Daugherty.

Copyright © 2012 by Lieutenant Colonel (Retired) Jim Pool.
Library of Congress Control Number: 2010926366

Printed in the United States of America.
ISBN: 978-0-7643-4265-3

We are interested in hearing from authors with book ideas on related topics.

Published by Schiffer Publishing Ltd.
4880 Lower Valley Road
Atglen, PA 19310
Phone: (610) 593-1777
FAX: (610) 593-2002
E-mail: Info@schifferbooks.com.
Visit our web site at: www.schifferbooks.com
Please write for a free catalog.
This book may be purchased from the publisher.
Try your bookstore first.

In Europe, Schiffer books are distributed by:
Bushwood Books
6 Marksbury Avenue
Kew Gardens
Surrey TW9 4JF, England
Phone: 44 (0) 20 8392-8585
FAX: 44 (0) 20 8392-9876
E-mail: Info@bushwoodbooks.co.uk.
Visit our website at: www.bushwoodbooks.co.uk
Try your bookstore first.

TABLE OF CONTENTS

ACKNOWLEDGMENTS

Any serious research project is a collaborative effort involving many individuals. The following persons, organizations, and firms provided invaluable assistance in bringing this project to life. Hooah!

Bill Petz Collection

Jim Haley Collection

Thomas Bock Collection

Tim O'Gorman, Director, USA Quartermaster Museum

Luther Hanson, Curator, USA Quartermaster Museum

Sammlung Zeugmeister

Kerstin Schindler-Brock, Bahlsen GmbH & Co. KG

Clay W. Chambers of **Bunker Militaria**

Ed Stroh Collection

Chris Mason Collection

Peter Whamond of the **Collector's Guild**

Klaus Peter Emig of **Militaria-Versand Emig**

Chris Karr Collection

Todd Gylsen Collection

Kevin Barrett Collection

George W. Cone Collection

Leon DeSpain (Photographer for George W. Cone)

Colonel Douglas Nash (Retired)

Mike Hamady Collection

Ruelle Frėdėric Collection

Rich Prandoni Collection

Henrik Rask of **RASKANTIK**

Mike Gilbert Collection

Stanislav Kramsky Collection

Thomas Salazar of **OSTFRONT Militaria**

Maciej Tylec Collection

Paul Gromkowski Collection

Marcin Jonczyk Collection

Bundesarchiv - Federal Archives, Potsdamer Str. 1, D-56075 Koblenz

Andreas Grote Collection

Jens Kattner Collection

Chris Pittman Collection

M. Sc. Stephan Haase Collection

Nikolay Konovalov of **Demyansk Battlefield Militaria and Collectibles**

FOREWORD

In this follow-up to his first book, *Wehrmacht Rations of WWII, LTC (Ret.)* Jim Pool has done successfully what few authors manage to pull off – write a companion volume on the same subject using completely new material that sheds a wholly different light on the topic. Though his first book was an eye-opening survey on German military rations of that conflict, replete with photographs, contemporary advertisements, and technical specifications, his second book brings it down to earth in a more accessible style that will appeal to both military historians and World War II reenactors alike. Drawing on hitherto unknown British military studies on German rations that were not available when he wrote his first book, the author uses this immense trove of technical information and troop surveys to recreate what it must have been like to prepare and consume a wide variety of ingeniously designed and produced foodstuffs, ranging from arctic survival rations to tank troop rations, and even more exotic rations, such as those issued to the Fallschirmjäger, Germany's elite parachute force. Lavishly illustrated with color pictures of original and recreated German rations, the author takes it one step further by grouping photos of various food items into what visually constituted a certain type of ration, a novel approach that readers will immediately appreciate. It almost makes one want to conduct a taste test! But throughout, Jim Pool has woven a fascinating story that combines a lively writing style with bits of technical information and Wehrmacht jargon that is never dull, frequently entertaining, and always informative. With this latest work, our understanding of the ordinary German soldier has been greatly increased, for to know what the average Landser ate and what it took to get the food to his mess kit is to know one important aspect of what it was like to serve in one of history's premier military organizations.

Colonel Douglas E. Nash, U.S. Army Retired

Author of
Hell's Gate:
The Battle of the Cherkassy Pocket
January to February 1944
and
Victory Was Beyond Their Grasp:
with the 272nd Volks-Grenadier Division from
the Huertgen Forest to the Heart of the Reich

INTRODUCTION

R *ations of the German Wehrmacht in World War II: Vol. II* is the continuing story of German rations during the Second World War. Since its publication in 2010, *Rations of the German Wehrmacht in World War II*, hereafter referred to as "Volume I", has found an eager audience among collectors and students of the German military in WWII. For the reenacting community it provides the first accurate picture of the German ration system beyond the field kitchen. As long time collectors, Tom and I wrote the book with the collector in mind. *German Rations and Subsistence Items*, Quartermaster Food and Container Institute for the Armed Forces, May 1947, which I refer to as the *U.S. Army Ration Report*, was chosen as the foundation for the book. This allowed us to provide the best overview of the German ration system, but placed certain restrictions on how we presented the information. The *U.S. Army Ration Report* focused on individual food items segregated by food groups, which were the building blocks from which Germany's Special and Emergency rations were built.

In Volume I, the Special and Emergency rations were discussed in a single chapter, as originally formatted in the *U.S. Army Ration Report*. Realistically, many of these specialized rations deserved individualized treatment in their own chapter or annex. So after Volume I was published I decided to write articles on specific Emergency and Special rations for the reenactor website "Der Erste Zug". Those articles served as the inspiration for this project. This approach provides the reader with a clearer understanding of why certain rations were developed, who they were issued to, and what components made up each ration. Even though collecting the individual food components is rewarding, the ultimate goal for any collector would be a display of one or more of the Special/Emergency rations available to the German soldier. I hope this book will make it easier for the collector to define his/her collecting goals.

The challenge in taking this approach was how to avoid rehashing all the information found in Volume I. Tom and I thought we located most of the wartime English language references when we wrote Volume I, which meant there wouldn't be a lot of new information to add to this project. Either through fate or luck, a large volume of British Intelligence reports on the German wartime food industry suddenly surfaced; information not available when we wrote the first book. The most important reference was *A Survey of German Wartime Food Processing, Packaging and Allocation*, Parts I and II, 27 September 1945. In addition, numerous field reports and interviews were also consulted and woven into this volume. It's important to note that the British reports are actually joint endeavors between the United States and the United Kingdom. The U.S. intelligence of the period was focused on the information needs of the individual G.I., while the British reports were geared to the needs of U.S. and British Industry. The intent of these investigations was to provide a detailed look at German industry and pass that information on to Allied companies. While the Soviets dismantled complete factories and shipped them back to "Mother Russia" after the war, the western Allies were more

likely to confiscate and ship selected pieces of machinery back home to evaluate. Intellectual properties in the form of persons or written reports were exploited by all of the victors. The Allied exploitation of German rocket technology is well known, but every German technological, manufacturing, or scientific innovation in every field was seized upon by the Allies. In the 1950s, the U.S. Government made these reports available to American industry and the general public. Over time they were largely forgotten, until now. Taken together, the *U.S. Army Ration Report* and the British reports present a pretty thorough picture of the German wartime food industry from factory to individual product.

So while the search for new information proved successful, attempts to locate additional wartime or contemporary pictures of issue rations proved more difficult. Since many of the issue items shown in Volume I are "one of a kind" I couldn't avoid using them again. So while some of the text and about 25% of the photographs come from Volume I, this should not be viewed as an attempt to repackage the first book. This volume builds upon, clarifies, and expounds on the success of the first book, and taken together they provide the most detailed accounting of German rations possible. I am hopeful that the reader will be pleased with this approach and that the new information, topics, and pictures will compensate for having to duplicate information between the two works. Since reports from the British Intelligence Objectives Sub Committee are such an important part of this project it's fitting that I include this foreword from *A Survey of German Wartime Food Processing, Packaging and Allocation*, Part II 27 September 1945:

> This story about what and how the German Army ate was written largely by those who had been directly responsible to the Berlin Headquarters for keeping the ever present stew pots simmering in the field. Quartermaster records were destroyed to a considerable extent, but the available remains which survived the fall of Berlin were carefully examined. Alleged contents of several pertinent memos between high command Generals about the growing food distribution nightmare contributed further information. Here the stupendous Stalingrad revival of Napoleon's original Russian ambition caught the German without the proper emergency rations because 'to intimate that the Wehrmacht might be encircled is treason'. This is said to have been an important factor in the Stalingrad rout.

> Sketchy records were fortified in part, at least, by a series of interviews with former German Quartermaster officers and with prisoners of war recently released. The courtesies extended by our Third Army and Seventh Army Intelligence Officers were most helpful in those investigations.

> A large numbers of further interrogations were made on all phases of this subject in various parts of Germany during the course of other technical investigations by this group. American combat troops who had tasted German

rations, displaced persons who were being fed in part with captured enemy food stuffs, former civilian employees of the Wehrmacht, returning German soldiers and food technologists at several universities were included in this group. Their views are included with others in this report.

The German Quartermaster General, food-wise, often was described as running a 'two pot outfit'. Obviously his food activities were not that simple but the German habit of eating thick foods and stews placed great favor upon that technique. It had the advantage of providing hot foods under almost every field condition, as the glycerin bath surrounding the cooking pot held the temperature without burning. Unexpected combat conditions could delay the mess four or five hours without the troops having to eat cold food. Some variety was achieved by mixing in different combinations of fresh or dehydrated vegetables, meats, cereals, and potatoes being the base in many cases. The daily weighed quantities of food per man could be consumed by the unit at most convenient times and in combinations as preferred.

Another feature of the Quartermaster activities was planned foraging during the campaign. Platoons of skilled butchers equipped to slaughter animals which had been captured or shipped in, were an important segment of every regiment. When foraging was poor, larger withdrawals were made from quartermaster stocks. The German combat plan of fast movement was counted upon, apparently to assure the capture of supplies, and special foraging units were trained for this purpose.

The regular distribution of stimulating drugs to flyers and combat troops should be mentioned because of the general attitude of the soldier and his family on that procedure. 'Better a live soldier full of caffeine than a dead one who hadn't moved fast enough', seemed to be the universal conclusion. One explanation for this view was the fact that many German civilians took caffeine tablets or other stimulants during the war years to offset fatigue from excessive working hours. The shortage of coffee was said to have contributed to the use of these drugs. The soldier received his stimulants largely in the chocolate cola paste disc known as Scho-ka-kola. Vitamin C was also considered as a necessary addition to special combat or panzer troop rations. Fruit bars or hard candies were the vehicle for it.

Another development in German Army feeding which was forced forward because raw materials were limited was the training and follow up program for field cooks. The pre war German habit of eating four or five times a day gave a real incentive toward qualification for the position of cook. He alone controlled the eternally bubbling coffee and stew pots. Specialists from Berlin carried on demonstrations regularly at the individual company kitchen, and popularly written bulletins came directly from Berlin to the cooks. Humorous cartoons often were used to illustrate the major points in the "Goulash Cannon", the exclusive newspaper which the cooks prized as their own special line to the High Command.

Special rations in cans or other individual packages were distributed only to particular combat organizations whose service involved unusual physical exertion or hazards. Among the canned rations, the German canned meats, canned boned hams, cheese and sausage can be classed as unusually good in quality. German Army chocolate was considered superior to the American by some of our troops. Its keeping quality was without doubt better than ours. The absence of milk was said to enhance its keeping quality.

The Oberkommando des Heeres (OKH) or Army High Command directed a vigorous effort toward greater variety in the field mess by providing accessory attachments for the 'two pot outfit'. These accessories were to provide means of cooking meat and potatoes separately and to create other variations beyond the heavy soups and stews. Meat stretchers, crisp breads, cheese powder, dehydrated preserves, meat baked into a bread loaf, salt free meat to be cooked with salt water at sea, powdered vegetable oils, dried egg pancakes, powdered butter, a belated 300 gram emergency ration, and various canned mixtures of meats, poultry, rice, and noodles were introduced experimentally late in the war. OKH also sponsored the synthetic fat program which resulted in reasonably tasty butter substitutes being made from coal. A substantial quantity of synthetic fat was purchased by the Wehrmacht as practical tests convinced them that these fats were assimilated satisfactorily.

The growing shortage of certain essential raw materials during the later war years taxed the ingenuity of the research staffs. German soldiers, according to eating habits and standards in the Reich, were well fed until these shortages developed.

1

THE HALF IRON RATION

As you read through the book you'll notice comments by analysts, soldiers, and others concerning the quality and likability of certain items of food. It's important that the reader view these comments with a grain of salt and pay particular attention to the source of the comments. Where a person grew up and what they ate while growing up are the most important factors influencing a person's judgment, and soldiers certainly have their own perspective on "Army Chow". I found this paragraph in one of the intelligence reports to be most enlightening:

> Every soldier brings with him the food habits and tastes of his home and country. In the Army he had to eat what was set before him and when it was set before him. It was impossible to satisfy his individual food preferences and he soon became tired of Army food. This situation naturally made him a sharp critic of all Army rations. By his criticisms he wished to indicate to his associates that he was eating better foods at home. This characteristic is a weakness of the German people. The satisfaction of the troops was further complicated by the fact there are different sections in Germany. On a basis of food habits and tastes Germany can be divided into more than ten different geographical areas. In the minds of all soldiers foods were listed as good or bad depending upon his previous customs and his likes and dislikes.

While geared towards the German soldier, those comments likely apply to anyone in the world who has served in uniform. With that being said, let's continue with the story of Germany's rations during WWII.

From the perspective of the German WWII collector or reenactor, the single most important ration has to be the Half Iron Ration (Halb Eiserne Portionen). It was the only ration required by regulation to be carried by the individual frontline soldier at all times. It was strictly for emergency use when the tactical situation prohibited the bringing up of hot food for 24 hours or more. The authority to consume the ration was given to Company Commander, Platoon Leader, or independent Squad Leader when the unit was cut off or isolated. Once the Half Iron Ration was consumed it was to be immediately reported, so replacements could be requisitioned and the soldiers replenished.

The Half Iron Ration consisted of the following components:

A. **Hard Crackers.** The daily allowance was for 250 grams of hard crackers (Zwieback, Hartkeks, or Knäckebrot).

B. **Preserved Meat.** The daily allowance called for 200 grams of preserved meat (Fleischkonserve).

It should be noted that the Half Iron Ration was a component of certain Air Force Emergency Flight Rations, and was also issued to certain shore based naval units. It's possible that some of the ad hoc units raised towards the end of the war like Naval Infantry units, Volkssturm, etc., were at least authorized the Half Iron Ration.

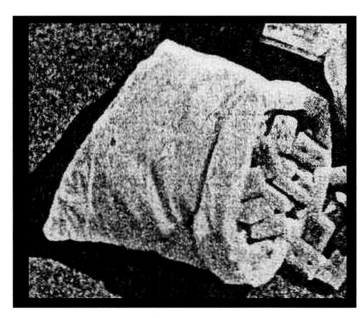

This is how Zwieback was delivered from the Field Bakery.

There were three types of bread products distributed to the soldier as part of the Half Iron Ration, each of which are discussed. Zwieback was described in the *U.S. Army Ration Report* as: "a miniature loaf of bread, with a very slightly rounded top. Two docker holes penetrated each bread piece. The average dimensions were 1 x 0.625 x 0.437 inches. The top was a shiny brown, indicating that some wash was used on top of the pieces. The internal color was creamy and slightly dark. Three or four caraway seeds were evident in each piece. The texture was quite hard, flinty, and difficult to bite through. The moisture content was three to four percent higher than that for the U. S. Army 'C' ration biscuits, but the texture was harder, because of the low fat content. It had a flat dry taste and would not appeal to the American soldier." Commercially baked Zwieback was manufactured in various shapes. The proximate analysis follows:

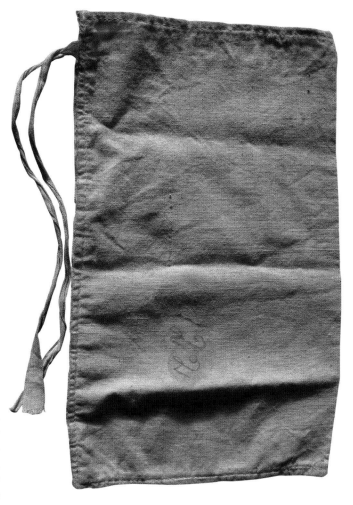

Moisture %	10.80
Fat %	1.60
Protein %	8.70
Ash %	1.60
Thiamin mg. /lb.	0.70
Niacin mg. /lb.	6.50
Riboflavin mg. /lb.	0.43
Iron mg. /lb.	22.10

The majority of the military's supply of Zwieback was provided by the Field Bakery Companies. After it was baked it was placed into 250 gram bags (Zwiebackbeutel). There were essentially four types of bags/sacks used to package Zwieback. The style most often seen in wartime pictures was of a simple two piece construction, with two closure ties, all done in a white material. According to *H.Dv. 320/4*, the Zwiebackbeutel was also manufactured from plastic/synthetic materials (aus kunststoffen) and was also packed into viscose foil (Zellglass) and paper sacks by the Field Bakeries. The reference to synthetic (aus kunststoffen) fabric is most likely rayon. Rayon was widely used in

Various views of a Zwiebackbeutel manufactured from lightweight linen or cotton. *Courtesy Ed Stroh.*

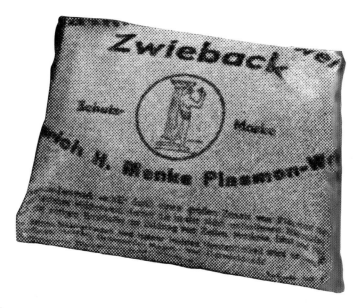

A package of Zellglas, more commonly known as Cellophane. *Courtesy Zeugmeister.*

This photograph of commercially supplied Zwieback came from a German wartime publication on rations. Other firms probably used packaging that reflected the firm's name or brand.

A similar style of clear cellophane bag was probably used to pack Zwieback. *Courtesy Thomas Bock.*

This bakery specialized in Friedrichsdorfer Zwieback. Zwieback was also supplied to the troops in paper bags.

The Brandt Firm was the largest commercial Zwieback factory in Germany. It's likely they supplied Zwieback to the military. This "Keep Fresh" waxed paper bag held "235 grams to 250 grams" of Zwieback, or the daily allowance for one soldier. *Courtesy Zeugmeister.*

Wrapping Zwieback in paper was an accepted commercial practice. It's possible the military adopted this practice when more acceptable packaging was unavailable. *Courtesy Zeugmeister.*

the clothing and equipment industry. Rayon took dyes easily, and it's possible that Zwiebackbeutels came in other colors, but only if there was no potential of dyes bleeding over into the bread. Zellglass/viscose foil is essentially cellophane. We know that cellophane bags marked as "Supplementary Rations for Frontline Infantry" were used to pack Knäckebrot. It's possible that a similar style of bag was also used for Zwieback. The paper sacks were probably just standard off the shelf commercial sacks. Recycled Zwiebackbeutels manufactured from fabric were thoroughly cleaned and disinfected before they were reutilized. The viscose foil and paper sacks were destroyed. Commercial firms like the Bahlsen Company also supplied Zwieback to the military.

Hartkeks, or simply Keks, are crunchy, sweet biscuits or cookies. From the information contained in the *U.S. Army Ration Report*, various brands of Keks were supplied to the military. The most common shapes were square, rectangular, tubular, and round. Keks were supplied in bulk containers, paper bags, cardstock containers, and wrapped in paper or Zellglass. Wartime pictures show that Keks were also packed into Zwiebackbeutels. Hartkeks packaged for military use, as well as standard commercial packages, were probably all distributed to the soldier. The proximate analysis of XOX Kraft Keks and U.S. Biscuits Type V follows:

This picture shows what appears to be Hartkeks packed for military use. They appear to be wrapped in some type of paper.

Topic	XOX Kraft Keks	U.S. Biscuits Type V
Calories/100 g.	396.00	440.00
Moisture %	5.60	6.30
Protein %	10.50	10.60
Fat %	6.00	14.70
Ash %	3.00	unk
Carbohydrates %	75.00	66.00
Thiamin mcg. /g.	1.29	11.60
Niacin mcg. /g.	3.27	8.70
Riboflavin mcg. /g.	19.60	26.30

This picture shows Hartkeks packed inside a Zwiebackbeutel. *Courtesy Chris Mason.*

A carton of Bahlsens Leibniz Keks, which the firm produced till the end of the war.

In the *U.S. Army Ration Report* these XOX Kraft Keks were described as resembling in texture the regular sweet dog biscuit.

Bahlsen Duve Keks were mentioned by name in the *U.S. Army Ration Report*.

A carton of Bahlsens Heimatgrüss Keks, which the firm produced till the end of the war.

A package of Pecher Keks wrapped in paper. *Courtesy Thomas Bock.*

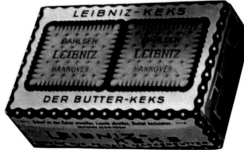

Wartime picture of two Bahlsens Leibniz Keks cartons.

The final bread product that was prescribed for the Half Iron Ration was Knäckebrot. The description in the *U.S. Army Ration Report* was "Four rectangular pieces approximately 5.375 x 4.5 x 0.25 inches, were packaged together in a light cardboard carton. Knäckebrot had the appearance of the typical whole rye Swedish hard bread, sold in the U.S. It was somewhat darker in color than the similar American product. It was hard and brittle, with a strong rye taste." The majority of the military's Knäckebrot appears to have been manufactured by commercial firms. Knäckebrot was generally shipped already packaged in cardstock cartons or wrapped in paper. It's likely that Knäckebrot was bulk shipped without any wrapping, or baked by Field Bakery Companies and packaged in Zellglass or paper bags. The proximate analysis follows:

Calories/100 g.	348.00
Moisture %	9.50
Protein %	9.30
Carbohydrate %	76.10
Ash %	2.40
Thiamin mg. /lb.	1.12
Niacin mg. /lb.	10.20
Riboflavin mg. /lb.	1.30
Iron mg. /lb.	16.80

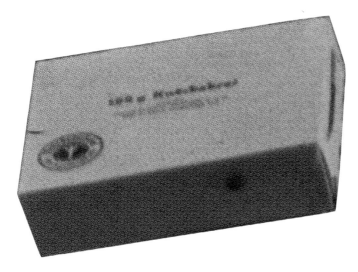

This picture shows Knäckebrot in a side locking cardstock carton.

A carton of Knäckebrot from the firm of Hecke and Co. Hamburg.

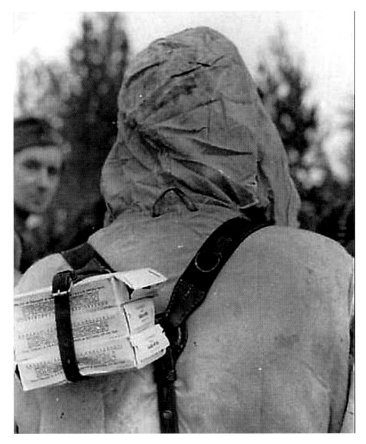

A soldier carrying side locking Knäckebrot cartons attached to his Y-Straps.

The front of a package of Heinis Knäckebrot wrapped in paper. *Courtesy Chris Mason.*

The other component of the Half Iron Ration was the 200 gram can of meat. Meat products were packaged for the military in the following four styles of sanitary cans: Weißblechdosen, Sparverzinntdosen, Schwarzblechdosen WEHRM, and Schwarzblechdosen Lötrand. All of these cans were covered in detail in Volume I. The use of drawn aluminum and steel cans to pack meat products is discussed later on in the book. Pork was the most prevalent type of meat packed in the 200 gram can. From the *U.S. Army Ration Report* we also know that beef was available in 200 gram cans. Products from Axis allies or captured from the enemy in bulk were used to augment the German supply. There is still a question whether fish products were substituted for canned meat as part of the Half Iron Ration. Fish and meat were interchangeable on the normal ration tables, so technically speaking it was allowed. Wartime pictures of soldiers laying out rations show numerous fish products. As a rule I believe that the canned meat was preferred, but it's likely that fish in cans was a viable substitute.

This 200 gram can of pork measured 3 inches wide and 2.625 inches high. This style of can was described in the *U.S. Army Ration Report. Courtesy Thomas Bock.*

Italian canned meat was widely distributed to the German soldier. The can measures 2.81 inches in diameter and 2.68 inches high. It held 200 grams of product.

Erroneously identified as being Polish in Volume I, this can is actually German. This 200 gram Sparverzinntdosen pork can measures 3 inches wide and 2.3125 inches high, and was described in the *U.S. Army Ration Report* (see Volume I page 77, item 13.A).

A nice layout of rations showing one 200 gram can, three 400-500 gram cans, and front fresh bread wrapped in paper, along with a selection of other accessories.

125 g Knäckebrot

A Half Iron Ration consisting of two cartons of Knäckebrot and a can of pork.

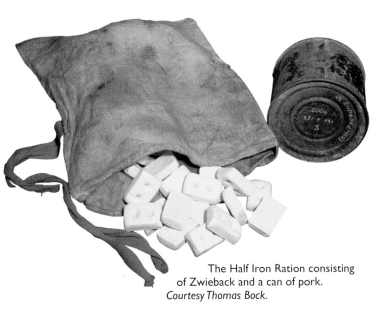

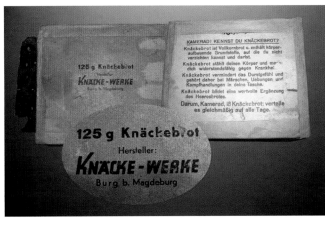

All the evidence suggests this carton of Knäckebrot manufactured by Knäcke-Werke is of wartime construction..

The Half Iron Ration consisting of Zwieback and a can of pork.
Courtesy Thomas Bock.

SS personnel putting some type of spread on their bread. *Courtesy Todd Gylsen Collection.*

Waffen SS troops taking a break. *Bundesarchiv Bild 1011-024-3535-22, Foto:Vorpahl 1944/ Licence CC-BY-SA 3.0.*

The Half Iron Ration consisting of a commercial package of Zwieback and a can of pork.

Air Force ground personnel conferring over a map. Notice the bread and small cans of food. *Bundesarchiv Bild 1011-394-1499-27, Foto: Leo 1942 / Licence CC-BY-SA 3.0.*

2

THE FULL IRON RATION

Under normal conditions, a tactical unit would carry three days of rations for the day to day feeding of the troops in the field. Additionally they were supplied with two types of Iron Rations for emergency use. The Half Iron Ration was issued to the soldier (see Chapter 1). The Full Iron Ration was a back up supply for the field kitchen, when rations for the day to day feeding of the troops were exhausted. It was stored with the field kitchen or on other support vehicles until required.

The Full Iron Ration consisted of the following components:

A. **Hard Crackers.** The daily allowance was for 250 grams of hard crackers (Zwieback, Hartkeks, or Knäckebrot).

B. **Preserved Meat.** The daily allowance called for 200 grams of preserved meat (Fleischkonserve). If possible issue two portions (400 grams) or one large can (850 grams).

C. **Vegetables.** The daily allowance was 150 grams of preserved or dehydrated vegetables (Gemüse) or pea sausage (Erbswurst).

D. **Coffee.** The allowance called for 25 grams of artificial substitute coffee (Kaffe- ersatz).

E. **Salt.** The daily allowance called for 25 grams of salt (Salz).

Once the unit's normal food rations were exhausted, the unit Commander would analyze the tactical and logistic situation to determine how the troops would be fed and what portions to allocate. The major consideration would be "how long will it take before normal ration resupply occurs?" In the book *Der Feldkochunteroffizier* (*The Field Cook NCO*), the author states that when the regular food supply was exhausted the (full) iron rations could be distributed. However, it was not issued in accordance with the standard ration tables, but at a reduced rate. Instead of the standard 200 grams of canned meat, only 60 to 100 grams would be issued; 100 grams of Wehrmacht Suppenkonserven instead of 150 grams; and 10 grams of coffee (roasted) instead of 20 grams. The actual allocation would be based on the Commander's assessment of the overall tactical and logistic situation.

In Volume I the picture shown below is misleading. The Full Iron Ration was not segregated and stored by individual soldier. The unit Commander would requisition the required rations based on the unit ration strength and store them until required. All of the ration items were packaged in a manner which facilitated long term storage, e.g. canned, jarred, or dehydrated. The salt and select dehydrated items were probably issued in bulk to the unit. The cooks would utilize the components of the Full Iron Ration to prepare meals for the troops. Certainly the Commander could issue the components of the ration by individual soldier. However, certain items like the dehydrated vegetables, which had a prep time of 2-3 hours before cooking, were not soldier friendly.

The majority of the bread components of the Full Iron Ration are discussed in Chapter 1. One item not mentioned was canned bread. The information available on Iron Rations came from *H. DV. 86/1* dated 1940. Canned bread probably didn't see large scale distribution, except within the Navy, until 1943/44, which explains why it wasn't mentioned in the regulation. In the book *The HG Panzer Division* by Alfred Otte, the author has captioned a photograph on page 87 "Let's go! Rations for the march have already been issued. Completely new to us is canned

This picture shows the amount of food, minus the salt, that a unit might have set aside for one soldier as part of the Full Iron Ration. *Courtesy Thomas Bock.*

bread, standard in the Navy, which was issued to us." The timeframe was November 1942-May 1943. With its long shelf life and convenient storage container, it had to be a strong candidate for use as an Emergency Ration. From the evidence available, it appears that canned bread was packaged in Schwarzblechdosen WEHRM and Schwarzblechdosen Lötrand style cans. The only portion weight that can be verified is approximately 800-850 grams. Based on the Full Iron Rations daily portion weight of 250 grams per soldier, a single 850 gram can could feed 3+ soldiers.

Unlike the Half Iron Ration, there were several portion weights of meat products that the unit commander could choose to stock as a component of the Full Iron Ration. *H. DV. 86/1* allows the commander to stock a single 200 gram can, two (200 gram cans), or a single 850 gram can per soldier. The 850 gram can was recommended. Obviously the larger can would allow the unit to extend its feeding time or increase the individual portion size. The 200 gram can was discussed in Chapter 1. Four hundred gram cans were also available, which would have been easier to store than two individual 200 gram cans.

Bread packed inside an 850 gram Schwarzblechdosen Lötrand can.

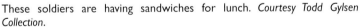

These soldiers are having sandwiches for lunch. *Courtesy Todd Gylsen Collection.*

A standard 850 gram can coded "S" for pork.

A 400 gram can of pork, possibly of wartime manufacture. The lack of a date and the side seam so common on postwar cans makes a definitive call impossible. *Courtesy Andreas Grote.*

Storage case for canned pork as part of the Full Iron Ration. *Courtesy Chris Mason.*

Three sizes of canned meats which could have been stocked as part of the Full Iron Ration.

A 850 gram can of cured pork spiced much like American pork luncheon meat.

As the vegetable component of the Full Iron Ration, the unit could stock 150 grams of preserved or dehydrated vegetables or pea sausage per soldier. Pea sausage is actually a soup, and also goes by the name Wehrmacht Suppenkonserven or Erbsen-suppe. While the Pea flavored soup is the most prevalent, other flavors are discussed in the *U.S. Army Ration Report*. Both the preserved/dehydrated vegetables and Pea soup were packaged in a variety of weights. Vegetables and soups were also available in cans and jars. Obviously the dehydrated products were preferred, since they weighed less and took up less space.

This 600 gram package of dehydrated cabbage would feed four soldiers.

A 850 gram can of kale.

A 150 gram package of Wehrmacht Suppenkonserven.
Courtesy Thomas Bock.

A large container of Knorr Ox tail soup. Note the term
"Kriegspackung". *Courtesy OSTFRONT Militaria.*

Soups were also
available in cans. Three
of these 200 gram cans
would fulfill the daily
requirement for four
soldiers. By turning the
top you could open or
close the can.

This crate held 210 packages of Wehrmacht
Suppenkonserven (150 grams each).
Courtesy Zeugmeister.

Fresh bread was a staple of the German soldier's diet.
Courtesy Todd Gylsen Collection.

Fig. 29.- Three types of German dehydrated noodle soup: left, alphabet; center, star-shaped; and right, plain.

A selection of Maggi dehydrated soups as shown in the *U. S. Army Ration Report.*

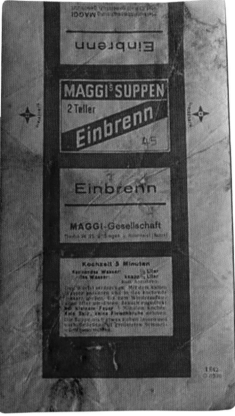

Two Maggi soup wrappers. *Courtesy Militaria-Versand Emig.*

A label for a 300 gram package of Wehrmacht Suppenkonserven manufactured by the C.H. Knorr firm. *Courtesy Zeugmeister.*

Labels for 300 gram packages of Wehrmacht Suppenkonserven manufactured by the Schüle-Hohenlohe firm. *Courtesy Zeugmeister.*

The Coffee allowance called for 25 grams of artificial substitute coffee (Kaffe-ersatz) or 20 grams of roast coffee. Coffee was available in many different portion sizes and packaging. *H.DV. 320/4* dated 1939 states that coffee products were packaged in individual portion sizes: Raw Coffee (25 grams in a bag), Roast Coffee (20 grams in a bag), and Roast Coffee (20 grams in a can). Unfortunately, very few pictures exist of the various types of individual packaging for issue coffee. Coffee was issued to the unit wrapped in paper and cellophane or delivered in bulk, which would have required that it be individually packaged before issuing it to the soldier. During the war coffee was also packaged in drawn aluminum tubes or cans. The unit Commander would take the ration strength of the unit multiplied by the portion size to determine how much coffee to stock as part of the Full Iron Ration.

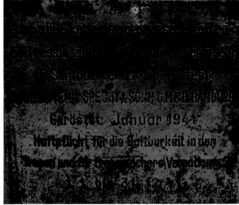

A tin container for 5 Kilograms of pressed coffee. The can is dated 1941 and contains fifty (100 gram) packages of pressed coffee; enough for two hundred, 25 gram portions. *Courtesy Militaria-Versand Emig.*

Supply NCO inventorying rations.
Notice the large paper sack of coffee.

Fig. 8.- German coffee compound, which had been pressed into bricks and packed in cellophane.

Pressed coffee wrapped in cellophane.

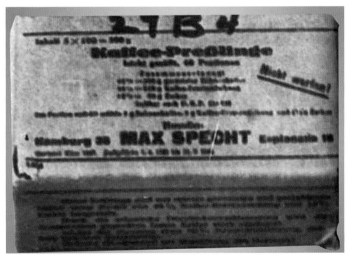

Pressed coffee wrapped in paper.

One hundred grams of pressed coffee wrapped in cellophane. It was divided into eight, 12.5 gram portions. *Courtesy Thomas Bock.*

A small, drawn aluminum can containing 3.5 grams of coffee; enough for two cups. The *U.S. Army Ration Report* makes mention of a 4 oz. can of Nescafe coffee. *Courtesy Zeugmeister.*

Commercial package of Ersatz coffee. It's not known if the stamps are period. *Courtesy Chris Karr.*

The daily allowance called for 25 grams of salt (Salz). *H.DV. 320/4* dated 1939 states that salt was packaged in individual portion sizes of 15 grams (in a bag). Some medicinal salts were packed in 20 gram cardstock containers, which was a viable though costly option for table salts. Unfortunately, there are no pictures or detailed information about the packaging. It's assumed that the majority of the salt was shipped to the unit in bulk and divided into individual portion sizes if required.

A front row seat at the Reindeer Olympics! *Courtesy Todd Gylsen.*

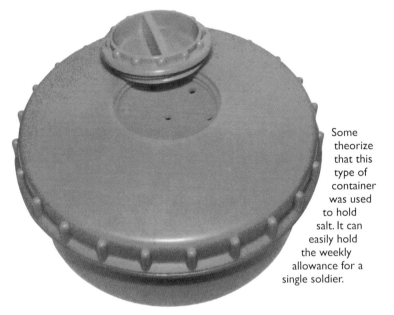

Some theorize that this type of container was used to hold salt. It can easily hold the weekly allowance for a single soldier.

Waffen SS soldiers sharing a mess kit. *Bundesarchiv Bild 1011-695-0405-16A Foto: Möller 1944 / Licence CC-BY-SA 3.0.*

A healthy breakfast of jam, bread, butter, coffee, and probably honey.

German NCO in Stalingrad preparing a meal. *Bundesarchiv Bild 183-J18808 Foto: Herber November 1942 / Licence CC-BY-SA 3.0.*

What a great day to eat outside. *Courtesy Paul Gromkowski.*

3

Special Rations for Mountain Troops, Ski Troops, and Patrols

A. Mountain Troops: During the war, the United States War Department printed numerous publications on enemy forces. One such publication was Special Series No. 21 dated 29 February, 1944, *German Mountain Warfare*. This publication covered all aspects of German mountain warfare to include a general discussion on rations, which is explained below:

The problem of supply becomes extremely acute in mountains, and the proportion of supply troops to combat troops increases. Supply routes are few; food, forage, and ammunition must be carried over narrow roads and mountain trails as far as possible by motor transport, then on mules and mountain horses, and finally on the backs of the soldiers. Economy of supplies is necessary because the danger of extending a unit beyond reach of its supply column is great, and furthermore, it is impossible for an overextended unit to live off the country in mountains.

As there is no food in high mountains the men depend entirely on transported supplies, which are difficult to bring up. Supplies usually go through valleys in motor vehicles, and by animal or porter columns in pathless terrain; but when snow, ice, and bad weather seriously hamper regular movement, caterpillar tractors and snow plows may be put to use. For supply purposes, mountain troops require a valley echelon as well as a mountain echelon. The valley echelon is responsible for all horse drawn and motorized vehicles including the second rations train. Besides ammunition the valley echelon carries food for 2 days, forage for 2 days, reserve clothing and mountaineering equipment, and baggage. The mountain echelon consists of pack animal columns which may be supplemented by porter columns. It should be able to carry ammunition for 1 to 2 days, food for 2 days, oats for 3 days, and a part of the baggage. It includes the pack animals carrying medical and veterinary equipment, the mountain kitchen, and pioneer and mountaineering equipment. Extra mules may be needed to carry water. The number of pack animals necessary will depend on the weight of the food, ammunition, equipment, and baggage, and the carrying capacity of the animals. Ordinarily the mountain units will have food for 4 to 5 days. If the distance from the troops to the valley echelon is greater than a day's march, the mountain echelon must be reinforced in order to set up new distributing points closer to

the troops and to keep them constantly supplied. When position warfare starts, some of the pack animals of the combat units should be used for supply purposes. The use of aerial railways takes a great burden from the pack animals and porter columns. In difficult rocky terrain and in snow-covered high mountains, improvised rope elevators or airplanes are often the only means for supplying large units regularly. When non-mountain troops fight in high mountains they should be equipped if possible, with pack animals and light trucks, or with the usual local vehicles. Since these troops will generally be used near roads, they may be allowed to keep their regular baggage vehicles.

The Germans have worked out a special emergency ration for mountain troops. Its precise content is unknown, but it is probably high in fats. It was reported shortly before the outbreak of the present war that the ration was palatable, light, and nourishing. Among the items were pemmican, dried eggs, powdered milk, frozen green vegetables, dried and smoked meats, biscuits, and coffee concentrate. *(Author's note: These emergency rations were discussed in other intelligence reports which are discussed below).* Extensive use was made of pills, probably vitamin concentrates. The German mountain soldier uses the regular Army meat can, which has less surface area and is much deeper than the U. S. meat can. Moreover, the inverted top of the can will nest in the bottom section, in which hot liquids can be placed to keep the food in the top warm. *(Author's note: I believe that the authors are discussing the German mess kit instead of a standard meat can.)*

In the U.S. Army Intelligence report entitled *German Clothing, Equipment and Rations*, dated 5 September 1945, the following additional information was provided on mountain troop rations: "At the beginning of the war, considerable emphasis had been placed on supplying troops in the high mountains with a supplementary ration. Generalstabsintendant (Major General of the Quartermaster Corps) Fritsch, Chief Quartermaster of the Commander in Chief of the West, said that this supplementary ration, like all other similar ones, became less important and was less often supplied as the war progressed. A mountain troop officer with the 4th Mountain Division in the Caucasus said that they had received supplements at about 1,200 meters (4,750 feet). Another from the 2nd Mountain Division said that they had received supplements above the Arctic Circle. These, they said, came in packages with one (1) man's daily ration in each. They received the following: 250 grams bacon or fat meat, 1 to 2 packages of Dextro Energen, or vitamin candy, 150 grams dried fruit, 100 grams biscuits, 200 grams Scho-ka-kola, and 6 cigarettes."

H. Dv. 86/1 (*Regulations for the Rations of the Armed Forces with Specific Deployment*) was somewhat vague in its description about the supplement used above 1,200 meters. It basically states:

units that operate in mountain regions (over 1200 meters), will receive a mountain allowance of a third beverage serving and a chocolate or sweets serving, above the normal ration rate or as available a similar supplement of (dried fruit, sour grape sugar, crackers, lemon powder).

In addition to the supplementary rations, there was a special mountain ration which existed until the very end of the war. This consisted of a specially packaged ration packed for one man for four days or four men for one day. This was said to provide each man with 4,500 calories per day, and so the package could be used by as many as 6 men per day, under unusual circumstances, since that would not reduce each man to a diet of less than 3,000 calories. There were three different menus of this ration, of which Ration A is reproduced below. The list was received from a document in the possession of an officer of the 5th Mountain Division. The packages had been authorized for use in Northern Italy by troops in strong points in late April 1945.

The standard German mess kit with the top nested in the bottom as described above. *Courtesy Rich Prandoni.*

The High Mountain Supplement as described in *German Clothing, Equipment and Rations* dated 5 September 1945.

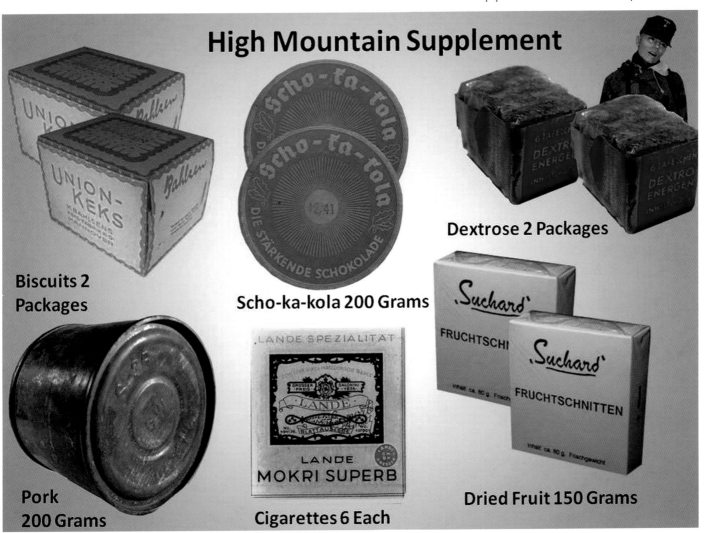

High Mountain Supplement

Biscuits 2 Packages

Scho-ka-kola 200 Grams

Dextrose 2 Packages

Pork 200 Grams

Cigarettes 6 Each

Dried Fruit 150 Grams

Grams	Pounds	Item
1200	2.64	Preserved Bread B (Dauerbrot)
1000	2.20	Field Rusk's (Zwieback)
800	1.76	Canned Meat
400	.88	Flat Cakes
1000	2.20	Oatmeal
170	.37	Butter Biscuits (in two packages)
400	.88	Preserved Sausages (Wurst)
200	.44	Fatty Meat
240	.53	Marmalade Powder
400	.88	Sugar
200	.44	Apple Flakes
100	.22	Compressed Coffee
10	.02	Compressed Tea
400	.88	Dried Fruit
32	.07	Salt
16 Each		Bouillon Cubes
200	.44	Chocolate
24 Each		Cigarettes
1 Each		ESBIT Cooker with 3 packages of ESBIT fuel
1 Each		Cooking Instructions
6752	14.85	Total weight minus bouillon cubes, fuel and cigarettes
1688	3.71	Weight per ration minus bouillon cubes fuel and cigarettes

The contents of the special mountain ration as described in the *U.S. Army Ration Report*.

Grams	Item
1200	Dauerbrot
1000	Feldzwieback
800	Canned Meat
400	Flädle (Noodles)
1000	Haferflocken (Oatmeal)
170	Butter Bisquits (2 Packages: 85 grams each)
400	Dauerwurst (Preserved Sausages)
200	Fatty Meat
240	Jam Powder
400	Sugar
100	Pressed Coffee
10	Pressed Tea
400	Dried Fruit
32	Salt
	16 Bouillon Cubes
200	Chocolate
200	Apple Powder
	24 Cigarettes
	Esbit cooker with 7 packages of fuel
	Cooking Instructions

A variation menu for the special mountain ration, or Gebirgsjagerkost.

B. Ski Troops: German Ski Jägers were Light Infantry specially trained for movement on skis. The U.S. Army Special Series No. 290 January 31, 1944, *German Ski Training and Tactics*, provides some insight into the methods of supplying ski troops:

"(1). **Typical Organization of a Raiding Party**. A typical organization for a raiding party consists of one platoon, reinforced by one heavy mortar squad and one engineer detachment. It is assumed, for purposes of illustration, that the party will be gone for 2 days.

(2). **Equipment**.
  a. Carried on person: Shoes, semi-waterproof and large enough so that 2 or 3 pairs of socks may be worn, socks (2 or 3 pairs), winter combat suit (quilted trousers, fur-lined jacket, fur cap), white camouflage suit, gloves (1 pair), fur-lined leather mittens (1 pair, worn over gloves), wristlets and knee

protectors, woolen underclothing, skis and ski poles (1 pair of each), sheath knife (1 each) and First-aid packets (2 each).

  b. Carried in the rucksack: Shelter half, woolen socks (2 pairs), personal cooking and mess equipment, rations for 1 1/2 days, (additional rations for one and a half day on hand sled), newspaper, candies, matches, and a portable gasoline cook stove (1 for each squad).

(3). **Means of Supply**. Methods of supplying ski units depend largely on the situation, the terrain, the condition of the winter roads, and snow and weather conditions. They may be different for each undertaking; hence the manner in which the troops will be supplied will be stated precisely in every tactical order. The motor vehicles of the second echelon of the ration train of the ski battalion can take care of the supply of the fighting unit only so far as the enemy situation and the condition of winter roads

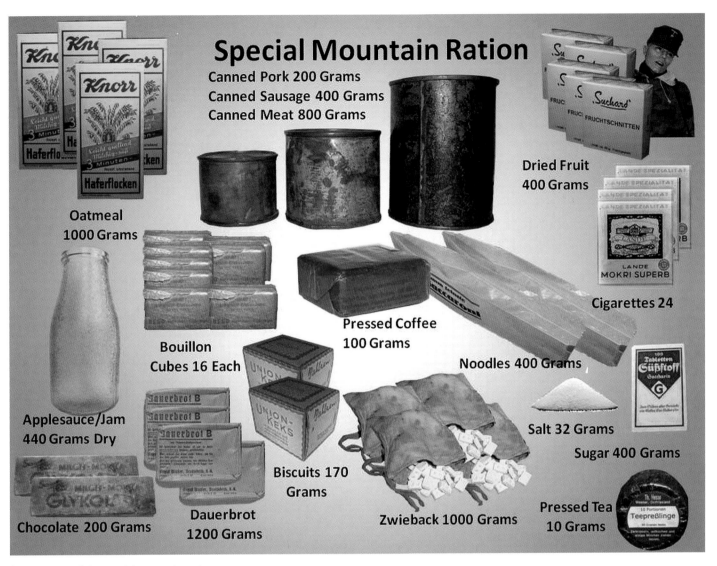

Special Mountain Ration

Canned Pork 200 Grams
Canned Sausage 400 Grams
Canned Meat 800 Grams

Oatmeal 1000 Grams

Applesauce/Jam 440 Grams Dry

Chocolate 200 Grams

Dauerbrot 1200 Grams

Bouillon Cubes 16 Each

Biscuits 170 Grams

Pressed Coffee 100 Grams

Zwieback 1000 Grams

Dried Fruit 400 Grams

Cigarettes 24

Noodles 400 Grams

Salt 32 Grams

Sugar 400 Grams

Pressed Tea 10 Grams

A recreation of the special mountain ration.

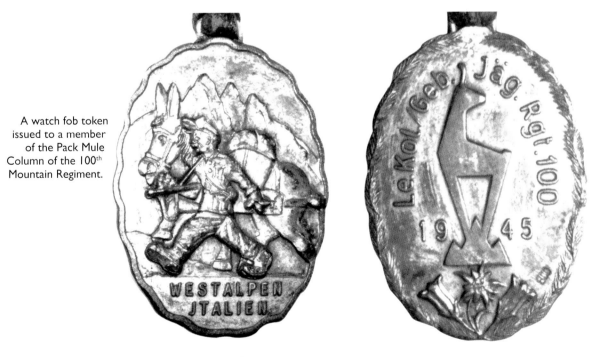

A watch fob token issued to a member of the Pack Mule Column of the 100th Mountain Regiment.

Mountain troops using a rope tram to move supplies in difficult terrain. *Bundesarchiv Bild 183-B22462 Foto: Kintscher Oktober 1942 / Licence CC-BY-SA 3.0.*

Mules and horses were an indispensable means of moving rations. *Courtesy Todd Gylsen Collection.*

This soldier is dividing treats among his comrades.

Sleds being used to move supplies. *Bundesarchiv Bild 1011-287-0872-32 Foto: Koll 1941/ 1942 Dezember-Januar / Licence CC-BY-SA 3.0.*

permit. As a rule, it will be necessary to establish a distribution point for companies in the forward area for supplies drawn from ration and ammunition depots. This may necessitate the use of horse-drawn sleds. The company, as a rule, uses the first-echelon ration train, equipped with horse-drawn sleds, for its supply. If, because of the tactical situation or terrain or snow conditions, horse-drawn sleds cannot be used, an adequate number of hand sleds will be substituted. Dog teams may prove particularly useful. Sled echelons supplying companies must be in a position to defend themselves against hostile attack. They will always be equipped with light machine guns and submachine guns. When necessary, they will be further protected by guard details.

(4). **Supply Dumps**. The establishment of supply dumps between receiving and distributing points depends on the length of the supply lines as well as on the difficulties of terrain and snow conditions. Often supply dumps must be set up even by small units (raiding parties and patrols), which, being absent for several days from their units while on special missions, cannot be supplied through regular supply channels and are unable to take the necessary supply of rations and ammunition along. Dumps must be prepared along the route of approach at such intervals that the distance between dumps, or between dump and receiving or distributing point, is not more than a day's march. If sufficient means of transportation are available, supply can be accelerated by shuttle traffic between dumps, and between dumps and receiving and distributing points, in which case the distance between the individual dumps should not exceed half a day's march. In the selection of dump sites, attention must be given to the storage of supplies in places which are well camouflaged and protected as well as possible from frost. Best suited are shacks and small woods which are a short distance off the route of approach. Wind shelters for horses may have to be provided. In terrain threatened by the enemy, conditions may arise when dumps will have to be guarded continually and in adequate strength. If no special snow-shoveling details have been organized, guards will keep open the supply and approach routes in the vicinity of the supply dumps." *(Author's note: Menus were probably similar to Patrol Ration menus).*

C. **Jadgsatz (Patrol Ration)**: The ability to conduct patrols was a critical task that all front line combat units had to master. I decided to address the topic in this chapter since Gebirgsjäger, Jäger, and Ski Jägers routinely operated in small units, often behind enemy lines, a major characteristic of patrols. Types of patrols can generally be grouped into two categories: Reconnaissance to acquire intelligence and Combat to inflict casualties on the enemy. The mission dictated the size and duration of the actual patrol. Patrol rations were only briefly mentioned in Volume I. It appears that the Germans developed a number of special menus for troops involved in Patrol activities. *Oberkommando des Heeres, GenStdH / Ausb.Abt. (I) Nr. 10/44: Supplement to Fighting in Forests*, dated February 2, 1944, provides a menu for patrols lasting not longer than one day. Special menus developed specifically for patrols lasting two day and five days were provided in *A Survey of German Wartime Food Processing, Packaging and Allocation* Part II dated 27 September 1945.

(1). Here is the composition of the one-day patrol ration according to *Oberkommando des Heeres, GenStdH / Ausb.Abt. (I) Nr. 10/44: Supplement to Fighting in Forests*, dated February 2, 1944:

ONE DAY PATROL RATION
150 grams Smoked Bacon or 180 grams Preserved Meat
100 grams Preserved Sausage *(Author's note: Canned sausage, sausage packed in aluminum, and fresh sausage were probably issued.)*
450 grams Knäckebrot
75 grams Butter or Lard
Coffee or Bouillon Cubes *(Author's note: The amount wasn't specified, but I believe 25 grams of Pressed Coffee or 2 Bouillon Cubes was fairly standard.)*
50 grams Scho-ka-kola if possible
50 grams Dextro-Energen
12 Cigarettes

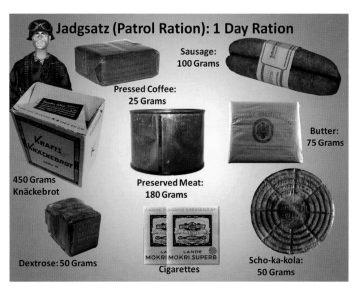

The menu for the one day patrol ration.

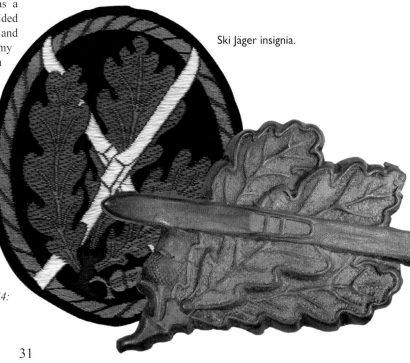

Ski Jäger insignia.

(2). Here is the composition of the two day ration according to *A Survey of German Wartime Food Processing, Packaging and Allocation* Part II dated 27 September 1945:

Two Day Patrol Ration	
Day 1 Dinner	*Day 2 Dinner*
180 grams Bacon or 180 grams Preserved Meat or 200 grams Canned Pork	*Same as on Day 1*
Day 1 Supper	*Day 2 Supper*
110 grams Preserved Sausage or 120 grams Preserved Meat or 120 grams Canned Sausage or 150 grams Canned Fish	125 grams Tube Cheese or 120 grams Preserved Meat or 120 grams Canned Sausage
375 grams Knäckebrot	375 grams Knäckebrot
3 grams Tea Tablet	3 grams Tea Tablet
10 grams Sugar	10 grams Sugar
50 grams Scho-ka-kola	50 grams Scho-ka-kola
2 Cubes of broth	2 Cubes of Dehydrated broth
	100 grams Dehydrated fruit

Recreation of the Day 1 supper menu of the 5 Day Patrol Ration.

(3). Here is the composition of the five day ration according to *A Survey of German Wartime Food Processing, Packaging and Allocation* Part II dated 27 September 1945:

Five Day Patrol Ration				
Day 1 Dinner	*Day 2 Dinner*	*Day 3 Dinner*	*Day 4 Dinner*	*Day 5 Dinner*
200 grams Canned Pork	50 grams Soup ready for cooking 200 grams Canned Beef or Pork	*same as Day 2*	*same as Day 2*	*same as Day 1*
Day 1 Supper	*Day 2 Supper*	*Day 3 Supper*	*Day 4 Supper*	*Day 5 Supper*
110 grams Preserved Sausage or 120 grams Preserved Meat or 120 grams Canned Sausage or 125 grams Tube Cheese or 90 grams Lard Meat or 150 grams Canned Fish	110 grams Preserved Sausage or 120 grams Preserved Meat or 120 grams Canned Sausage or 125 grams Tube Cheese or 150 grams Canned Fish	*same as Day 2 except*	*same as Day 2*	*same as Day 1 plus*
375 grams Knäckebrot	600 grams Dauerbrot	375 grams Knäckebrot instead of 600 grams Dauerbrot		
	40 grams Lard Spread			
25 grams Pressed Coffee	25 grams Pressed Coffee			
10 grams Sugar	40 grams Sugar			
50 grams Scho-ka-kola	25 grams Dextro-Energen or 30 grams Drops			
	50 grams Tartaric Acid Bon-bons			200 grams Dehydrated fruit

4

SPECIAL RATIONS FOR FALLSCHIRMJÄGER

The *U.S. Army Ration Report* discussed Fallschirmjäger rations in the following terms:

Membership in German parachute units (as in the case of U. S. Army parachute units) was on a voluntary basis and in this connection the Germans put out a good deal of propaganda about special rations to attract volunteers. The truth is that enemy paratroops received special rations only just before actual parachute operations. When these soldiers were to go into combat as ordinary infantrymen, no additional rations were issued. However, the specially planned rations that were given to German paratroopers prior to jumping (both in training and in combat), had a significance the importance of which did not escape the intelligent U. S. fighting men. These rations included items which were not only attractive to the Germans, thereby building morale, but actually increased the physical stamina of the paratroop personnel. Incidentally, the special rations, creating a heartier appetite, led to greater consumption of ordinary foods, which, although less attractive, were energy giving and naturally helped to improve physical fitness. White bread and dairy products, such as milk and fresh eggs, were considered real luxuries by the German soldiers; these items normally were not issued to troops of the other arms and services as part of the regular diet. On the day that a jump was to be made, German paratroopers were given the following, in addition to their normal ration:

Jump Ration
approximately **.25 pounds crackers (113 grams)**
approximately **.06 pounds butter (27 grams)**
approximately **1 pint fresh milk (.47 liters)**
1 fresh egg

"A ration of an entirely different kind was issued on days when long flights were to be made. The Germans studied the nutritional benefits of specialized rations and concluded that on long flights regular rations would sit too heavily on the stomach. The rations described below were issued only when two flights of two hours duration were to be made or a single flight lasting four hours or more":

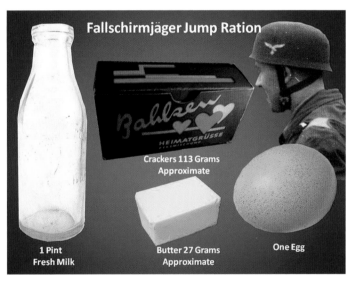

A recreation of the supplemental paratrooper ration issued on days when a jump was made.

A recreation of the paratrooper supplemental ration issued when long flights were made.

Flight Ration
approximately **.18 pounds crystallized fruits (comfiture or candied fruit) (81 grams)**
approximately **.25 pounds crackers (113 grams)**
approximately **.08 pounds sugar (36 grams)**
approximately **.04 pounds butter (18 grams)**
1 bar of chocolate substitute

"Analysis of this ration indicated that it contained an abundance of energy giving foods, which would sustain the individual without causing gastric discomfort. The Germans adopted an iron ration which was intended to last for a three day period during operations. A ration of this bulk could easily be carried on the person and provided the necessary 'lift' for a man to carry out the most arduous tasks."

It consisted of:

Fallschirmjäger 3 Day Iron Ration
2 cans of sausage
2 cans of cheese
1 bar of chocolate substitute
1 package of crackers
6 packages of chewing gum
1 package of lemonade powder
1 package of coffee mixed with sugar
1 tablet of solid fuel for heating

"The iron rations were intended to make the German paratrooper self sufficient for a limited period of time. Inclusion of the fuel tablet allowed him to prepare a hot beverage and yet maintain individual security precautions. This tablet burned for about five minutes, yielding a smokeless white flame of two or three inches."

The mention of chewing gum as part of the ration has been a point of contention. It has been argued that the U.S. intelligence report was wrong and that German paratroops were never issued chewing gum. Since the

3 day Fallschirmjäger Iron Ration, with Dextrose substituted for chewing gum. *Army Ration Report.*

Prewar German advertising sign (reproduction) from the Wrigley firm. PK stands for *Philip Knight* Wrigley.

Air Force personnel getting ready to set up the Field Kitchen.

publication of Volume I, I've come to believe that chewing gum was indeed issued to the paratroopers. There are far too many references to chewing gum as part of various Special or Emergency rations to be a mistake. Chewing gum was certainly being produced in Germany, as in 1929 there were three manufacturers of chewing gum in the country: the Wrigley's firm in Frankfurt a.M., the American Chewing Gum Company in Berlin, and the Laufer chewing gum factory in Hannover. It also seems unlikely that Allied intelligence personnel would not recognize chewing gum if they saw it.

A 48 hour Paratrooper Iron Ration was identified in Part II of *A Survey of German Wartime Food Processing, Packaging and Allocation* dated 27 September 1945. There were two types of rations designated as Paratroop Provisions: North and South.

THE 48 HOUR FALLSCHIRMJÄGER PROVISIONS SOUTH
250 grams of fresh sausage (beer or hunting) in 4 aluminum bags
150 grams of cheese in 2 aluminum tubes *(Author's note: I believe this should read 250 grams).*
250 grams of Zwieback in 2 linen bags
500 grams Soya-meat-bread in 5 packages
200 grams Schoka-Tropa in 4 bars
150 grams Dextro-Energen in 3 packages
1 bag of Chewing Gum

THE 48 HOUR FALLSCHIRMJÄGER PROVISIONS NORTH
400 grams smoked bacon in cellophane
200 grams preserved sausage (Landjäger)
250 grams of Zwieback in 2 linen bags
500 grams Soya-meat-bread in 5 packages
200 grams Glykolade in 4 packages
100 grams Marzipan in 2 cubes
100 grams Dextro-Energen in 2 portions
1 bag of Chewing Gum

In *German Clothing, Equipment and Rations*, dated 5 September 1945, they make light of a jump ration designed to last 5 to 6 days. There were two different packagings for this ration: a Northern and a Southern one. Most of the food in the Southern Ration was canned. The ration was designed to sustain a soldier for 5 or 6 days and was said to consist of the following:

THE 6 DAY FALLSCHIRMJÄGER IRON RATION
1500 grams of meat or sausage
2000 grams of preserved bread (Dauerbrot)
750 grams of Zwieback or biscuits
100 cigarettes
6 packages of lemonade powder
1200 grams Chocolate (Scho-ka-kola) (6 packages) *(Author's note: This probably should read 12 packages, unless there was a 200 gram package not yet identified).*
900 grams Dextro-Energen (18 packages)
200 grams of sugar
600 grams of Cognac
18 packages of Soluble coffee

This ration was usually carried in two small canvas field bags. Esbit cookers and three packages of fuel were also usually carried with it.

In Volume I we provided a broad overview of Luftwaffe rations. One of the ration containers discussed was the reusable 300 gram waterproof can for pilots and aircrew. It was finished in two colors, depending on the type of terrain the aircraft operated over: green for flights over land and blue for flights over water. Mick Prodger put forth the color premise in his

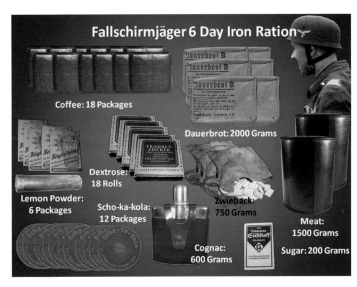

The 6 day Iron Ration as described in *German Clothing, Equipment and Rations.*

excellent book *Luftwaffe vs. RAF: Flying Equipment of the Air War, 1939-45*. However he does not cite a reference to support his statement.

I believe that the finish on the 300 gram container has nothing to do with operating enviroment. In *Die Seenotfibel* or the *Luftwaffe Guide to Survival at Sea*, there is a color illustration of the 300 gram can, which appears to be painted a standard Luftwaffe blue-grey color. The paint on the blue-grey and green Luftwaffe 300 gram cans, as well as the Navy blue-grey 300 gram can all appear to be standard factory finishes; which were used on all types of equipment. The Luftwaffe did distribute at least two containers clearly identified for flights over water; the blue Scho-ka-kola and Zwieback containers. These containers are painted a different shade of blue then the 300 gram cans and are clearly marked as "SEENOTPACKUNG" or "Packed for Emergencies over Water". I believe that the 300 gram *Absprungverpflegung* cans were simply multipurpose ration cans manufactured to Luftwaffe specification, to fill a number of requirements. The main purpose was obviously as an Emergency Ration container for Luftwaffe pilots, aircrews, and paratroopers. Chris Mason, renowned expert on German paratroopers, provided the following justification for their use by paratroopers.

> The critical element to assessing this item is the German language itself, which in comparison to English is extraordinarily precise. The Germans have seven words for "party," for example, while we have just one, each defining a very specific kind of social event with specific expectations. The same principle is at work with the terminology for parachute jumps. The word "*Absprung*" in German means a deliberate, planned parachute jump from an aircraft - something you meant to do when you first got in the airplane. A "*Notsprung*" on the other hand is an emergency evacuation, an unplanned bailout from a damaged aircraft. The ration tin is clearly marked as a ration for a deliberate, planned parachute jump - and therefore is a paratrooper special ration can. If it were an emergency ration can, it would be labeled a *Notabsprungverpflegung*, an emergency jump ration. There is really zero ambiguity or doubt here. To a native German speaker or a fluent German speaker there is no question.

While Mr. Mason's argument makes perfect sense, it isn't supported by a wartime reference. One of the pictures shown below is believed to be of German paratroopers carrying this style of ration can. If I had to guess I would say that German paratroopers were issued the 300 gram (color immaterial) can as required by mission. The Luftwaffe and Navy containers were identical except for the wording on the bottom.

According to Mr. Prodger the contents of the Luftwaffe 300 gram cans were similar, regardless of color: Scho-ka-kola, chewing gum, Pervitin tablets, Dextrose, and sunburn/frostbite ointment. Again, there was no reason to color code the cans. Mr. Prodger also mentions a special high calorie ration for flights over wilderness/sparsely populated areas which consisted of high protein soy bread, dried meat, and additional caffeine tablets. He doesn't mention if this ration was packed inside the 300 gram can.

As far as the contents are concerned, I am not aware of any unopened 300 gram cans in any collection or of the existence of a standardized packing list. It's likely there were numerous packing lists. Don't forget, Notverpflegung Süß was manufactured in 300 gram portions and was designated as a component of an air-droppable ration. Was this a coincidence or was Notverpflegung Süß also packed inside 300 gram cans? See Chapter 10.

This illustration in *Die Seentfibel* is the only one known of the 300 gram emergency ration can.

The 300 gram emergency ration can issued to the German Air Force. *Courtesy OSTFRONT Militaria.*

This picture appears to show two German paratroopers that have been issued the emergency ration tin. *Courtesy Chris Mason.*

Fallschirmjäger taking a break. *Courtesy Bill Petz.*

These German paratroopers appear to have been issued the Front Line Infantry Assault Ration.

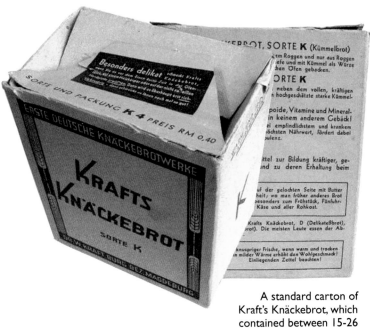

The bread cartons used by these Fallschirmjäger appear to be commercial off the shelf items. *Courtesy Bill Petz.*

A standard carton of Kraft's Knäckebrot, which contained between 15-26 pieces depending on the flavor.[1]

German paratroopers checking the tactical situation. Note the loaves of bread. *Bundesarchiv Bild 1011-5844-2161-36, Foto: Reich 1944 Sommer / Licence CC-BY-SA 3.0.*

A package of Knäckebrot wrapped in paper manufactured by Dr. Wilhelm Kraft, Erste Deutsche Knäckebrot-werke.

These Fallschirmjäger have confiscated a cart to haul supplies. Bundesarchiv Bild 1011-570-1619-06, Foto: Haas September 1943/ Licence CC-BY-SA 3.0.

This is pretty good stuff. *Bundesarchiv Bild 183-J15764, Foto: o Ang. Oktober 1943/ Licence CC-BY-SA 3.0.*

A ground dug chewing gum wrapper found among a number of German WWII artifacts. The wrapper is manufactured from color printed aluminium foil. *Courtesy Andreas Grote.*

How much bread can a soldier eat? *Bundesarchiv Bild 1011-574-1797-25, Foto: Schneiders, Toni 1943 Ende/ Licence CC-BY-SA 3.0.*

ENDNOTES

[1] The first Knäckebrot in Germany was manufactured in 1927 by the "Erste Deutsche Knäckebrotwerke" Dr. Wilhelm Kraft, Berlin-Lichterfelde. In 1931 the company moved to Burg bei Magdeburg as "Knäcke-Werke" and exists today as Burger Knäcke GmbH. There is no connection between Dr. Wilhelm Kraft and the Kraft's food empire, which had an office in Hamburg, Germany (**Kraft Cheese Company**). I haven't been able to determine the significance of the terms "Erste Deutsche Knäckebrotwerke" and "Knäcke-Werke", both of Burg bei Magdeburg. Both phrases seem to refer to the same factory, but it appears that products by Dr. Wilhelm Kraft were identified by the phrase "Erste Deutsche Knäckebrotwerke". Knäcke-Werke appears to have been used on non-branded Knäckebrot products or on Knäckebrot produced for companies other than Dr. Wilhelm Kraft.

This member of the Field Police doesn't seem too impressed with his meal. *Bundesarchiv Bild 1011-588-2185-06A, Foto: Zimmermann 1944/ Licence CC-BY-SA 3.0.*

Kraft's Knäckebrot manufactured at its first factory in Berlin-Lichterfelde.

Kraft's Knäckebrot advertisements from 1935 and 1939. In 1946 the Burger Company produced a carton that was almost identical to the 1939 version, except for the lack of printing on the side panels.

5

SPECIAL RATIONS FOR MOTORIZED TROOPS

Because of the nature of their operations, armored forces sometimes had to vary the way they utilized their regular rations. They were usually able to get a normal breakfast from the field kitchen. For lunch, two men shared an 850 gram can of meat and vegetables. Supper was usually supplied by the field kitchen. The crews usually got cold suppers four or five times a week. Two or three times a week, some type of hot food would be served. In the tanks the men carried one or two extra noon meal cans, plus three days of iron rations.

In the book *Der Feldkochunteroffizier* by Fritz Bein, dated 1943, the author states that units of Panzer Divisions, Motorized Divisions, Light Motorized Divisions, Reconnaissance Battalions, Tank Destroyer Battalions, and similar units could be issued up to three ration portions in addition to the standard iron ration. The author doesn't state under what conditions the allowance was provided. However, it's assumed the special allowance was given to units that would be operating independent of their field kitchens for an extended period. The determination of how many supplemental ration portions to issue was probably based on mission, as well as the tactical and logistical situation. The three types of supplemental portions are as follows:

The 1939 Special Allowance for Motorized Troops portion consisted of the following:

THE 1939 SPECIAL ALLOWANCE FOR MOTORIZED TROOPS
1 can of mixed meat and vegetables   *(Author's note: Probably 850 grams).*
600 grams of Dauerbrot or   500 grams of Knäckebrot
100 grams of Chocolate
5 grams of Lemon powder

By 1943, the following list of items was added and was considered a portion. The contents of the 1939 portion remained unchanged.

This is a recreation of 2 days' rations (minus meals from the field kitchen) issued to a Panzer crewman, including all supplemental rations.

A recreation of the 1939 Special Allowance for Motorized Troops. The ration consisted of the following items:
1. *Can of mixed meat and vegetables,*
2. *Lemon powder,* 3. *Knäckebrot (4 Packages total), and* 4. *Chocolate.*

THE 1943 SPECIAL ALLOWANCE FOR MOTORIZED TROOPS
200 grams Schmalzfleisch
25 grams of pressed coffee
15 grams of coffee beans
10 grams of sugar

Sometime in 1943 another supplement was authorized for tank crews. The goal was to increase the efficiency of the tank crews on days of increased operational deployment. Initially these items were issued to each man on a daily basis as authorized by the army or tank command, as long as supplies and stocks permitted. The menu for this supplement is shown below. I have elected to call this supplement the German Tank Crew Half Candy Ration, because its allowances are half of that identified for the German Tank Crew Candy Ration (U.S. Army nomenclature). It appears that this supplement was initially distributed as a daily ration and later distributed as a two day ration.

THE GERMAN TANK CREW HALF CANDY RATION
50 grams chocolate (Scho-ka- kola)
25 grams Dextro-Energen, or
30 grams fruit drops
80 grams fruit slices, or
50 grams sour grape sugar

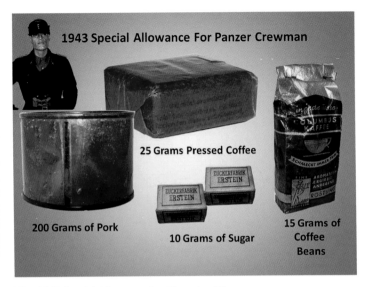

The 1943 Special Allowance for Motorized Troops.

The German Tank Crew Half Candy Ration.

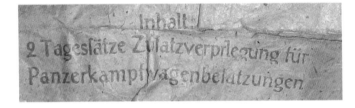

Original German Tank Crew Candy Ration bag. *Courtesy George Cone.*

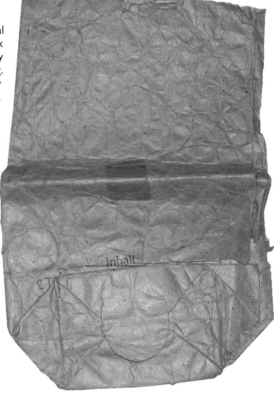

Contents of the Two Day German Tank Crew Candy Ration.

Sometime in 1943 or 1944 the German Tank Crew Half Candy Ration was packaged as a two day supplemental ration. The U.S. Army captured and evaluated the two day version, which is described as:

> The German Tank Crew Candy Ration was an attractive, acceptable ration consisting of two packages of tartaric acid confection, two fruit bars, and one round chocolate disc. The translation of the printed information on the package stated that it was 15.5 ounces and that it was a two day supplementary ration. It was packaged in a Kraft paper bag. One very noticeable fact with regard to the packaging was that no attempt had been made to camouflage the various wraps, but that rather a definite effort had been made to dress up the packages by the use of gay colors and white paperboard.
>
> This ration was packaged in a two wall (pasteboard) brown bag made of two sheets, 40 pound Kraft paper. On the lower section of one side of the package in which the ration was packaged was written "*Inhalt: 2 Tagessätze Zusatzverpflegung für Panzerkampfwagen Besatzungen.*" The translation is as follows: Contains: Two days supplementary ration for tank crew.

A complete discussion of each component of the German Tank Crew Candy Ration follows:

A. **Tartaric Acid Confection (Weinsäure Zucker)**. Two boxes, each containing 12 pieces of confections, totaling 55 grams were included in the ration. Each box was 1.875 x 0.625 x 4.437 inches. The box was mainly white, and was trimmed in gay colors of red, blue, and yellow. Each piece of candy was banded in a sheet of wax cellophane paper. The box was a reversed tuck and folding carton made of manila lined bending chip, having a thickness of approximately .014 inch. The proximate analyses of the German confection and U.S. Caramels were as follows:

Topic	German Confection	U.S. Caramel
Calories/100 g.	432.00	400.00
Moisture %	1.30	7.00
Protein %	0.00	2.00
Fat %	7.60	12.00
Ascorbic acid mg/100g.	0.00	0.00
Acidity %	1.70	0.00

Tartaric Acid Confection manufactured by the Wissoll firm.

B. **Fruit Bar (Suchard Fruchtschnitten)**. Two boxes, each containing 80 grams of fruit bars, were included in the ration (two bars in each box). The box was a tuck and folding carton made of bleached manila lined, solid sulfite paperboard, having a thickness of approximately .014 inch. The box was over wrapped with a sheet of moisture proof cellophane that was sealed with glue and appeared to be somewhat thicker than the 300 gauge cellophane produced in this country. The size of the package was 2.75 x 0.875 x 2.88 inches, and they were dated 16 and 17 March 1943. The proximate analyses of the German fruit bar and U.S. fruit bar were as follows:

Topic	German Fruit Bar	U.S. Fruit Bar
Calories/100 g.	415.00	320.00
Moisture %	8.80	18.00
Protein %	5.60	2.90
Fat %	10.60	0.80
Ash %	0.30	0.00
Carbohydrates %	75.00	74.00
Thiamin % mcg./g.	1.04	0.37
Riboflavin mcg./g.	1.18	0.56
Niacin mcg./g.	20.50	19.00
Carotene mcg./g.	1.70	1.33

Suchard produced the fruit bar.

C. **Chocolate (Scho-ka-kola)**. Two discs of chocolate were each individually wrapped tightly by machine in a sheet of brown non-moisture proof cellophane, and were packaged in a fiberboard can, size 3.5 inches in diameter by 0.875 inches tall. The following was printed on the label: "Scho-ka-kola, 43 percent content of cocoa, with addition of coffee and cola. Caffeine content is approximately two percent. Stimulating. Increases energy. Contains 100 grams. Stuttgart, Germany. Schoko-Buck, Inc". It was labeled 4-3/1942, indicating the date of packaging. The proximate analyses of the German chocolate and U.S. chocolate were as follows:

Scho-ka-kola produced by the Schoko Buck firm. *Courtesy Thomas Bock.*

Topic	German Scho-ka-kola	U.S. Chocolate
Calories/100 g.	520.00*	520.00
Protein g.	0.00*	10.00
Fat g.	30.00*	30.00
Carbohydrates g.	55.00*	55.00
Moisture %	0.00	1.50
Thiamin % mcg./g.	0.52	5.25
Riboflavin mcg./g.	0.73	3.28
Niacin mcg./g.	16.40	7.08
Vitamin A mcg./g.	1.50	0.00
*Estimated. Sample insufficient for testing.		

Armored crewman preparing some sandwiches. *Bundesarchiv Bild 1011-022-2948-30, Foto: Wolff, Paul Dr. / Licence CC-BY-SA 3.0.*

This soldier is distributing cigarettes and what looks like sweets of some sort.

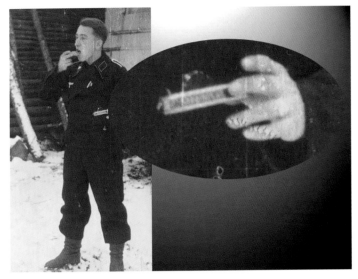

This soldier appears to be eating some type of chocolate or cookie.

Bicycle troops taking a break. *Bundesarchiv Bild 1011-213-0291-35, Foto: Gebauer Oktober1941 / Licence CC-BY-SA 3.0.*

Life inside an armored vehicle. *Bundesarchiv Bild 1011-158-0085-23, Foto: Koch 1941 / Licence CC-BY-SA 3.0.*

The crew of this Tiger I have just received a hot meal. *Bundesarchiv Bild 1011-277-0846-08, Foto: Jacob 1944 Januar-Februar / Licence CC-BY-SA 3.0.*

The turret substitutes as a dining table when needed.

Sonderverpflegung für Panzertruppen.

These soldiers appear to be eating the 1939 Special Allowance for Motorized Troops.

A nicely staged picture of ration items in North Africa.

This tank crew is peeling some potatoes for dinner. *Courtesy Todd Gylsen Collection.*

6

Special Rations for Fortress Personnel

Other than the Half Iron Ration, most emergency rations were developed for troops with specialized skills, special operational requirements, or who operated in conditions of extreme weather or terrain. Units serving in Atlantic fortifications, Norway, and in the Southeast, especially the Greek Islands, were permitted to maintain larger subsistence dumps than were permitted in other areas of operation. The difficulty of supplying troops in these areas and the fact that fortress personnel were expected to continue fighting even if isolated from their supply dumps was probably the reasoning behind that decision.

After the German defeat in Normandy in 1944, large numbers of German "Fortress Battalions" were mobilized to defend the West Wall. There were three basic types of Fortress Battalions: the Fortress Infantry Battalion, the Fortress Machine-gun Battalion, and the Super Heavy (Independent) Machine-gun Battalion. The following notes are taken from the February 1945 article in an Intelligence Bulletin entitled *Fortress Battalions...and how they are used*:

German Fortress Battalions are controlled by the Army High Command. As a rule, they are meant to be used only in the defense of fortified lines and other fortified positions. By assignment these Battalions operate under local commanders. If the field troops retire to new positions the Fortress Battalions are withdrawn to the nearest permanent fortifications.

The Germans may employ these battalions not only in a fortified line and in the outer defenses of forts, but in prepared rear defensive positions, entirely independent of the fortified line. The Battalions also may be committed as a screening force in threatened sectors or in sectors which may be tactically important for other reasons.

Normally, the Battalions will be assigned to existing fortified lines or positions, or to those under construction. To increase the effectiveness of their assigned sectors of defense, Battalions will make use of natural obstacles and will construct additional blocks. The units are told that they can greatly increase the defense potential of their positions by the skillful employment of all available automatic weapons and mortars; interlocking bands of fire, organization in depth, and flanking fire are stressed. However, only the local commander is allowed to alter the defense lines or to authorize changes in a fortification plan.

The Germans recognize that Fortress Battalions often will be on their own, especially in the early stages of an operation.

This is why the enemy believes in conducting tactical and terrain reconnaissance frequently, for a considerable distance, and in ample time to permit planning. The Germans believe that counterthrusts and other fighting outside the fortifications can be conducted successfully only by mobile elements. Such elements are selected at the earliest possible time (they may be drawn from the mobile forces of the Battalion), and are equipped with the necessary weapons and supplies.

Because of the independent nature of a Fortress Battalion, the *headquarters company takes care of the supply* of all companies in the Battalion. Thus the company commanders become free to devote their entire time to leading their units in training and in combat, and are not obliged to concern themselves with supply problems beyond maintaining a general supervision. (This type of organization is called *"freie Gliederung"*, or "freeing organization", since it frees the company commander for combat duties only. It represents a trend which is becoming noticeable in the organization of all German armored units and some Volksgrenadier units).

No mention was made of a "Fortress Ration" in the *U.S. Army Ration Report*; however, they did evaluate a containerized ration that could certainly fill that requirement. The particulars of that ration are discussed here:

During the war a request was received from the Research and Development Branch of the Quartermaster General's Office, to make a complete examination of a German Army Emergency Ration captured in North Africa, to determine whether it had any advantages which might be applicable to U.S. military ration plans. A sample ration was received from Captain LaRosa, consisting of one tin container, 5.75 x 7.5 x 14 inches and including 14 items. The results of that analysis are discussed below.

In general, the 14 components of the ration were found to be fairly acceptable. The canned meat was comparable to that found in the American ration. The dehydrated foods were found to contain weevils and were not very palatable. However, the age of these components was beyond the guarantee written on the package. Also, they had been kept here in America for some time before analysis was started. The outside container of the Emergency Ration was of heavy tin and was serviceable. It was not dented or banged up and could be carried or stacked quite easily. The weight and components of the ration seem to suggest it was a two or three day ration. A complete discussion of each component of the ration follows:

A. **Dried Sausage.** This component of the German ration consisted of two sausages, both 6.5 x 1.125 x 0.187 inches, and weighed 50 grams. This sample was hard and tough, but in good condition. There was no evidence of mold or other spoilage. However, the samplers were unanimous in pronouncing it unpalatable because of a bitter flavor. The proximate analysis of the sausage follows:

Moisture %	9.20
Fat %	43.50
Protein %	32.38
Ash %	6.80
Thiamin % mcg. /g.	0.40
Niacin mcg. /g.	60.20
Riboflavin mcg. /g.	3.00

B. **Canned Beef.** The sample weighed 304 grams net, in a 78 gram tin can. The can was of excellent construction, being much heavier and more carefully rolled than most American made cans. The sides were soldered and rolled. Tops and bottoms were rolled on over a rubber (or synthetic rubber) gasket. The can was heavily painted brown and there was no evidence of stain or corrosion. Evidently it was made in France, as it was stamped *"Boeuf Assaisonne"*. Translated from the French, this reads "Seasoned Beef". The contents, of excellent appearance and palatability, were packed solidly, so there was no waste of fat or juice. The quality was that of good American beef. The flavor would have been improved by the addition of salt. The proximate analysis follows:

Moisture %	63.40
Fat %	3.30
Protein %	31.75
Ash %	1.88
Thiamin % mcg. /g.	0.20
Niacin mcg. /g.	62.50
Riboflavin mcg. /g.	2.10

C. **Lentils, Beef, and Potatoes.** This sample weighed 850 grams, in a 150 gram enameled, bonderized can. Except for the finish, the construction of this can was similar to that used for the canned beef. It was of German make, as it was stamped *"Potsdam"*. The appearance of the contents was good in the freshly opened can, but the product discolored rapidly, turning from brown to dirty black. It was similar to our beef stew and of comparable quality and flavor. The proximate analysis follows:

Moisture %	76.90
Fat %	1.60
Protein %	7.50
Ash %	1.50
Thiamin % mcg. /g.	0.30
Niacin mcg. /g.	13.20
Riboflavin mcg. /g.	0.60

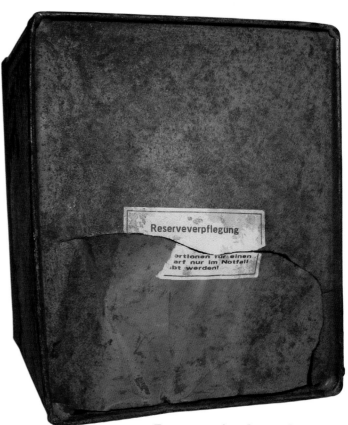

Tin container for a Reserve Ration. *Courtesy Thomas Bock.*

Two sausages with a wartime label wrapped around them. *Courtesy Thomas Bock.*

The 400 gram can was used to package a variety of products.

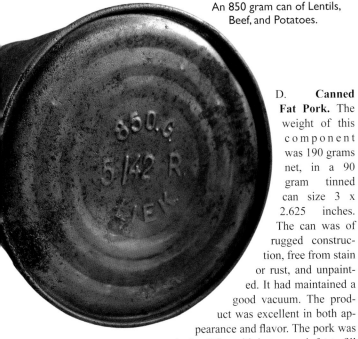

An 850 gram can of Lentils, Beef, and Potatoes.

D. **Canned Fat Pork.** The weight of this component was 190 grams net, in a 90 gram tinned can size 3 x 2.625 inches. The can was of rugged construction, free from stain or rust, and unpainted. It had maintained a good vacuum. The product was excellent in both appearance and flavor. The pork was packed solidly, with just enough fat to fill the spaces completely. The proximate analysis follows:

Moisture %	45.80
Fat %	40.10
Protein %	13.06
Ash %	1.25
Thiamin % mcg. /g.	0.20
Niacin mcg. /g.	18.80
Riboflavin mcg. /g.	1.10

A 200 gram can of pork. *Courtesy Thomas Bock.*

E. **German Bread Ration (Biscuit Type).** See Chapter 1.

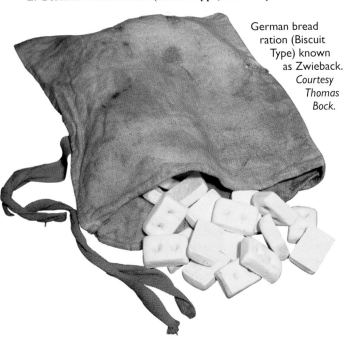

German bread ration (Biscuit Type) known as Zwieback. *Courtesy Thomas Bock.*

F. **Knäckebrot (German Brittle Bread).** See Chapter 1.

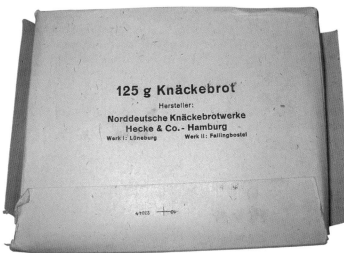

A 125 gram carton of Knäckebrot.

G. **Butter Type Spread.** This product was packed in a tin can and evidently came from France, as the can was stamped "*French*". It was extremely rancid and unpalatable, and had a disagreeable odor. Its color and consistency were like those of butter. The proximate analysis follows:

Moisture %	10.99
Fat %	85.20
Oil off melted completely	110 F.
Curd %	0.70
Salt	3.20

Life inside a bunker. *Bundesarchiv Bild 183-J16737, Foto: Schwarz, Februar 1944 / Licence CC-BY-SA 3.0.*

H. **Zucker (Sugar).** The sugar was in small cubes wrapped in transparent waxed sulfite and over-wrapped in unwaxed sulfite. The label read "*Wissoll Weinsäure Zucker*", or Tartaric Acid Confection. The product was not grainy, but rather caramel like in consistency. It had a slight acid taste and was not as palatable as an American caramel. The proximate analysis follows:

Protein %	0.24
Fat %	6.14
Ash %	0.21
Moisture %	9.03
Carbohydrate %	84.38
Calories/100 g.	394.00

Recreation of the Weinsäure Zucker carton. *Courtesy Thomas Bock.*

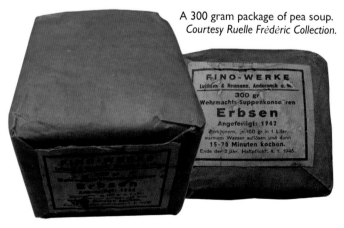

A 300 gram package of pea soup. *Courtesy Ruelle Frédéric Collection.*

I. **Soup Powder.** This product was in a package 2.5 x 2.125 x 1.125 inches of parchment over-wrap and glued transparent film inner wrap. It was sealed with tape. It contained 300 grams of compressed powdered pea soup, and the label stated it was intended for two portions. The product was packaged in 1940 and guaranteed for two years. Weevils were found in it upon examination. However, the guarantee had expired at that time. When reconstituted, the soup had a strong, pasty cereal taste and was not very palatable. The proximate analysis follows:

Protein %	20.88
Fat %	8.43
Fiber %	1.12
Ash %	11.23
Moisture %	8.23
Carbohydrate %	50.11
Calories/100 g.	360.00
Calcium %	0.09
Phosphorus %	0.51
Vitamin A ppm	1.20
Riboflavin ppm	1.70
Niacin ppm	12.50

J. **Schnittbohnen (Dehydrated Beans).** This product was a compressed cube of dried green beans, 4 x 4.5 x 1 inches, with an outer wrap of white parchment, adhesive sealed, and an inner wrap of bleached sulfite sealed with tape. The weight was 600 grams, and it was stated that the quantity was sufficient for ten servings. The sample was packed during the winter of 1937-1938, and when opened was found to be weevil infested. Complete instructions for reconstituting and cooking were given on the package. They stated that a period of two or three hours was required for cooking, and the addition of fresh beef or pork was recommended. Upon reconstitution it was found that the sample had no flavor of any sort and the texture was tough. Opinions of the testers were that the product was decidedly not palatable. The proximate analysis follows:

Protein %	18.77
Fat %	1.19
Fiber %	10.85
Ash %	5.68
Moisture %	9.44
Carbohydrate %	54.07
Calories/100 g.	302.00
Calcium %	0.60
Phosphorus %	0.48
Vitamin A ppm	2.70
Riboflavin ppm	2.30
Niacin ppm	33.40

A 600 gram package of dehydrated beans.

K. Iron Ration for Fortress Personnel: This ration was discovered on a German wartime 16mm film publicizing the contributions of the food service personnel. The ration contains chocolates, fish, canned good, spices, and most likely some sort of bread products. There are 22 cardstock containers which could be Soya/Smoked meat bread or the "bread baked in cartons" discussed in Annex 1. The pictures are courtesy of OSTFRONT Militaria.

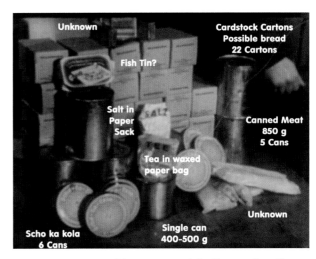

The contents of the Fortress Iron Ration.

A recreation of the emergency ration discussed in the *U.S. Army Ration Report*. Items 6 and 7 are reproductions. It consisted of: 1. *Knäckebrot*, 2. *Fish in oil*, 3. *Canned beans with potatoes and beef*, 4. *Dehydrated vegetables*, 5. *Canned pork*, 6. *Compressed pea soup* , 7. *Weinsäure Zucker*, 8. *Sausages*, 9. *Zwieback*, and 10. *Tilsiter cheese*. *Courtesy Thomas Bock.*

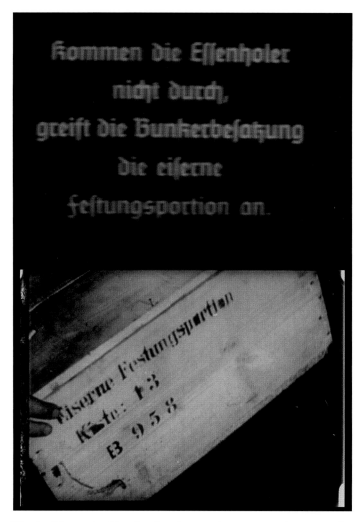

The lead in to the film showing the wooden crate used to store the ration.

The carton shown below was manufactured to hold a seven day Reserve Ration for one soldier. The term Kampfstände is interpreted to mean battle position. It's likely this ration was intended for soldiers manning pillboxes or other fortifications that might have to fight in isolation. Unfortunately the actual contents are unknown.

A carton for a 7 day Reserve Ration.

Fresh sausage was a common and popular addition to the menu. *Courtesy Todd Gylsen Collection.*

Laying a minefield will work up an appetite. *Courtesy Todd Gylsen Collection.*

Seven Day Reserve Ration

Bread

Vegetables

Miscellaneous

Meat Products

A recreation of the possible contents of the 7 day Reserve Ration.

Waiting for the enemy.

7

ASSAULT AND CONFECTION RATIONS FOR COMBAT ARMS PERSONNEL

The German military produced several confection and supplementary rations for the German soldier. At least four variations have been identified: the German Tank Crew Candy Ration for Armored Personnel (see Chapter 5), the German Front Line Assault Ration for Infantry Personnel, and the German Front Line Assault Ration for other personnel. Another series of Special Infantry Rations was discussed in *A Survey of German Wartime Food Processing, Packaging and Allocation*, Part II 27 September 1945. Some contemporary articles have categorized the German Front Line Assault Ration as the German equivalent to the prepackaged meals (K-Rations) available to the Allied troops. The evidence suggests otherwise:

A. The German Front Line Assault Ration appears to have been intended for personnel in forward positions. I wouldn't be surprised to learn that staff personnel and support troops in forward units also received the ration, whether it was authorized or not.

B. The issue of the ration was not tied to any operational requirement that the author is aware of. This ration appears to have been issued on a fairly routine schedule. According to interviews conducted with German Company Grade Officers, this ration was issued four to five times a month.

C. The majority of the items are colorfully packaged, like similar items available on the commercial market.

D. There are no food items that one would normally associate as being part of an actual meal. The majority of the ration consists of dessert items or other sweets. In wartime Germany, many of these items would probably be considered luxury goods by the German populace.

It is my opinion that this type of ration was developed solely to help boost the morale of the German soldier at the front. The rest of the chapter will describe these rations, their contents, packaging, and variations. Many of the descriptions are condensed versions taken from Volume I, the *U.S. Army Ration Report*, and other U.S. Army intelligence reports.

An undated (probably 1944) U.S. Army intelligence article titled "German Confection Rations" provides the following information about the confection ration:

German front-line infantry and tank troops are now receiving special emergency rations, composed largely of confections, which have not appeared before owing to the German policy of eliminating, as much as possible, emergency rations for common issue.

How frequently and under what circumstances the special rations are being issued is not yet known. The stress laid on the candy content of the ration indicates that it is considered a luxury item and therefore a morale booster for troops in active combat areas. It may also be intended as a supplementary issue, to stretch the canned meat components of emergency rations under conditions of extended operations, where it is impossible to live off the surrounding countryside or where unit messes cannot feed the front-line soldier.

Contents of the rations vary in quality. U.S. Quartermaster officers tasting the items judged the fruit bar in the infantry ration fair to good, the biscuits acceptable, the caramels poor, and the chocolate bar, which appears to be composed of cereal with finely ground fruit and nuts, bitter and rather unpleasant in taste. The fruit bars in the tank crew ration were judged poor and the chocolate excellent.

The U.S. Army conducted a detailed analysis of one version of the German Front Line Assault Ration during the war. The Großkampf variation is mentioned in the *Handbook on German Military Forces TM-E-30-451*, 1945, but not evaluated. The description of the Front Line Assault Ration as evaluated in the *U.S. Army Ration Report* is described below:

The German Front Line Assault Ration was an attractive, acceptable ration containing chocolate bar, fruit bar, cylinder of orange candy, and two cubes of chocolate caramels, six biscuits, and six cigarettes. One very noticeable feature in the pack was that no attempt was made to camouflage the over wraps, but rather a definite effort was made to dress up the package with gay colored labels and white pasteboard. Printed on the top front of the box in red letters was: '*Nur Für Frontkämpfer im Infanterieverband*', (Only for Front Line Infantry Troops). The carton was of a special one piece folded design with a lock assembly, which has not been used to any extent in this country. It was made of solid fiber board, with a fairly hard outside surface.

The top locking German Front Line Assault Ration carton weighs 10.5 ounces and measures 4.25 x 1.5" x 5.75". Lettering is red.

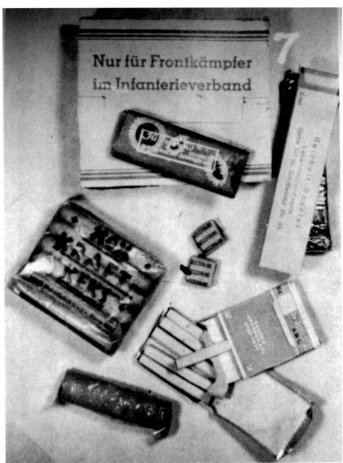

Another view of the German Front Line Infantry Assault Ration.

The German Front Line Infantry Assault Ration contains a 2.75 oz. fruit bar (top), a chocolate covered candy bar (left), six "strength biscuits" (right), a dozen discs of sticky hard candy, six Turkish cigarettes, and two chocolate caramels (below: one caramel missing).

A complete discussion of each component of the Front Line Assault Ration follows:

A. **Chocolate Candy Bar (Hildebrand Gefüllte Wehrmacht Schokolade)**. The chocolate bar weighed 1.5 ounces and was 3.75 x 1.375 x 1.5 inches. The bar was wrapped in a wax machine glazed, 25 pound sulfite paper in a folded closure. This was banded in a glued strip made of a printed bond paper of approximately 40 pound weight. The proximate analyses of the German candy bar and U.S. nougat bar were as follows:

Topic	German Candy Bar	U.S. Nougat Bar
Thiamin mcg. /g.	3.65	0.46
Riboflavin mcg. /g.	1.84	1.80
Niacin mcg. /g.	22.20	8.80

B. **Fruit Bar (Frucht Riegel)**. The fruit bar was 1.5 x 0.75 x 5.375 inches and weighed 2.75 ounces. It was wrapped in light weight moisture proof cellophane, and inserted in a straight tuck and folding carton made of double manila lined paperboard, approximately .018 inch thick, with cut scores. One print in red ink was used on the white boxed goods for labeling. The box was 1.5 x 0.75 x 5.375 inches in size and weighed 2.75 ounces. The proximate analyses of the German fruit bar and U.S. fruit bar were as follows:

The Hildebrand Gefüllte Wehrmacht Schokolade bar.

Fruit Bar by the Reichelt-Röseler firm.

Topic	German Fruit Bar	U.S. Fruit Bar
Calories/100 g.	390.00	320.00
Protein %	2.90	2.90
Fat %	0.80	0.80
Carbohydrates %	92.30	74.00
Moisture %	2.90	2.00
Vitamin A mg/100 g.	0.27	0.22
Thiamin mg. /100 g.	0.04	0.04
Riboflavin mg. /100 g.	0.09	0.06
Niacin mg. /100 g.	1.53	1.90
Ascorbic acid mg. /100 g.	unk	8.00

C. **Chocolate Caramels (Milupa B. C.).** Two cubes of candy were wrapped in paper reading *MILUPA B.C.* They were also over-wrapped with the same paper. The wrapping was of 30 pound waxed cellophane. The proximate analyses of the German caramels and U.S. chocolate drops were as follows:

Topic	German Caramels	U.S. Chocolate Drops
Thiamin mcg. / g.	0.64	3.87
Riboflavin mcg. / g.	0.76	1.79
Niacin mcg. / g.	19.20	9.20

D. **Orange Candy**. Twelve discs of the candy were stacked in an unlabeled cylinder that had a one inch diameter and was 3.5 inches long. There was an over-wrap with a twisted end closure in a sheet of moisture proof cellophane. The thickness of the cellophane was comparable to that of the 300 gauge cellophane made in the U.S. The proximate analyses of the German orange candy and U.S. commercial jelly beans were as follows:

Topic	German Orange Candy	U.S. Jelly Beans
Calories/100 g.	380.00	378.00
Moisture %	4.80	5.60
Fat %	0.30	0.00
Ash %	0.21	0.00
Carbohydrates %	94.70	94.40

E. **Biscuits (XOX Kraft Keks)**. The flavor of the energy biscuits is difficult to describe, since it was utterly unlike any American commercial biscuit or those types packed in United States Army rations. It can only be said that they resembled in texture the regular sweet dog biscuit. The indentation and impression on the biscuits indicated that they were baked on a wire mesh baking surface. Judging by the fact that some of them had one sealed and one open end, it appeared that the dough had been deposited in a long continuous piece and was cut to length after baking. The docker holes on the top surface were characteristic of this product and were employed to permit the release of gasses during manufacture.

A recreation of the Milupa-BC caramels. *Courtesy Thomas Bock.*

Several other variations of these supplementary rations were produced for the German soldier. The following is a brief description of the variations that have been identified to date. Since no complete factory packed assault rations have surfaced, the discussion centers mostly around the outer packaging. It's possible other styles of outer packaging were produced. As far as the contents go, we know from wartime pictures that there were variations in the products, packaging, and contents.

A. **Nur Für Frontkämpfer im Infanterieverband**. The carton for this ration differs in construction and materials to the ration discussed earlier. Printed on the top front of the box in red letters was "*Nur Für Frontkämpfer im Infanterieverband*" (Only for Front Line Infantry Troops). The carton was of a special one piece folded design with a standard lock assembly. It was made of lightweight card stock or fiber board.

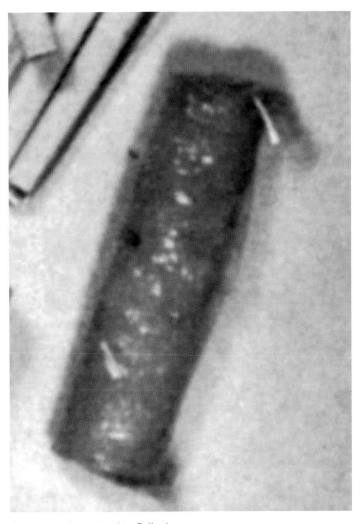

Orange candy wrapped in Cellophane.

The front locking German Front Line Assault Ration carton manufactured from light weight card stock.

B. **Zusatzverpflegung für Frontkämpfer im Infanterieverband**. This is a completely unknown variation of the Front Line Infantry Assault Ration. Unfortunately, the top and bottom of a carton are the only evidence of its existence. It is made of solid fiber board, with a fairly hard outside surface. Written on the top of the carton are the words "*Zusatzverpflegung für Frontkämpfer im Infanterieverband*", which translates as "Supplementary Ration for Infantry Units". The tank crew ration discussed earlier and the clear cellophane bags discussed below are similarly worded.

C. **Für Frontkämpfer im Großkampf.** This is another variant of the Front Line Infantry Assault Ration. Instead of saying "*Nur für Frontkämpfer im Infanterie verband*" it reads, "*Für Frontkämpfer im Großkampf*". This loosely translates into "For front line troops involved in the great battle". This version may have been manufactured for all front line personnel. This carton appears to be identical to the standard cartons already discussed.

XOX Kraft Keks.

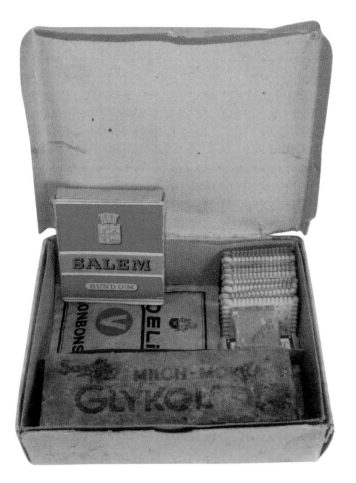

Possible contents of the front locking German Front Line Assault Ration carton.

Wartime picture of the Für Frontkämpfer im Großkampf carton.

Top of a Für Frontkämpfer im Großkampf carton.

Unassembled front locking German Front Line Assault Ration carton manufactured from solid fiber board.
Courtesy Clay W. Chambers.

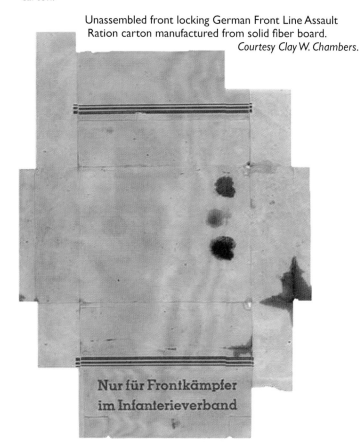

Recreation of the Zusatzverpflegung für Frontkämpfer im Infanterieverband carton. The top and bottom are original.

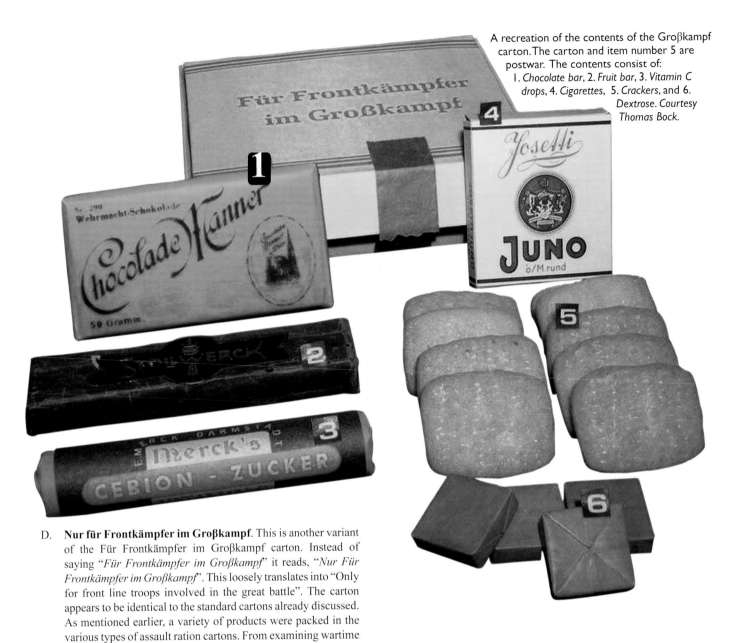

A recreation of the contents of the Großkampf carton. The carton and item number 5 are postwar. The contents consist of:
1. *Chocolate bar*, 2. *Fruit bar*, 3. *Vitamin C drops*, 4. *Cigarettes*, 5. *Crackers*, and 6. *Dextrose. Courtesy Thomas Bock.*

D. **Nur für Frontkämpfer im Großkampf**. This is another variant of the Für Frontkämpfer im Großkampf carton. Instead of saying "*Für Frontkämpfer im Großkampf*" it reads, "*Nur Für Frontkämpfer im Großkampf*". This loosely translates into "Only for front line troops involved in the great battle". The carton appears to be identical to the standard cartons already discussed. As mentioned earlier, a variety of products were packed in the various types of assault ration cartons. From examining wartime photographs it appears that the contents generally consisted of six basic items: cookie or biscuits (80 grams), chocolate bar (50 grams), fruit bar (80 grams), caramels or other individual candy pieces, a package of hard candy or drops, and a pack of cigarettes. There were a number of different manufacturers involved in producing the assault ration, which resulted in a variety of packaging and products.

E. **Clear Cellophane Bag**. Among the collecting community these bags are regarded as an alternative method of packaging for the Front Line Assault Ration. However, the construction of the bag suggests another use. The bag is long and narrow, has expanding side panels, has to be filled by laying it on its side, and is made of thin cellophane, which is totally unsuitable for even moderate handling without tearing. The authors handled a wartime packed example and were able to verify it was used to package two pieces of Knäckebrot. It's possible that bags of a similar type were used for other bread products. It reads "*Zusatzverpflegung für Frontkämpfer im Infanterieverband*", or "Supplementary Ration for Front Line Infantry".

Wartime picture of the Nur für Frontkämpfer im Großkampf carton.

SUPPLEMENTAL RATION FOR INFANTRY PERSONNEL: *STIMULATING*
50 grams Koffinos (Hilkola, Kola Bon-Bon, Mokka Candy, Mokka Bon-Bon) or **50 grams Glykolade or** **50 grams Scho-ka-kola**
80 grams Kraft Keks
6 Cigarettes

SUPPLEMENTAL RATION FOR INFANTRY PERSONNEL: *QUICKLY ACTIVE*
50 grams Dextrose (Dextro-Energen) or **50 grams Tartaric Acid Sugar or** **50 grams Nutritive Bars** *(Author's note: Could be Wehrmacht Chocolate).*
80 grams Kraft Keks
6 Cigarettes

SUPPLEMENTAL RATION FOR INFANTRY PERSONNEL: *SLOWLY ACTIVE*
80 grams Fruit Concentrates (Fruit Slices of fruit Bars) or **80 grams Wheat Drops** *(Author's note: Unknown Product).*
80 grams Kraft Keks
6 Cigarettes

F.   **Additional Rations for Infantry Personnel**. Another series of Supplementary Rations for Infantry personnel was identified in Part II of the report *A Survey of German Wartime Food Processing, Packaging and Allocation* dated 27 September 1945. It's likely that this ration was issued based on the tactical situation and expected physical exertion of the troops. It was compared to the supplementary ration for armored troops in the report. It was probably distributed at the end of 1943 or beginning of 1944. There were three distinct rations based on the amount of physical exertion anticipated by the troops:

Recreation of the Supplemental Ration for Infantry Personnel (*Quickly Active*).

Supplemental Ration for Infantry Personnel: Slowly Active

Recreation of the Supplemental Ration for Infantry Personnel (*Stimulating*).

Recreation of the Supplemental Ration for Infantry Personnel (*Slowly Active*).

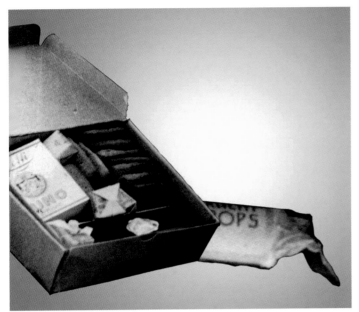

Keks were produced in a variety of shapes.

The contents of this carton are different from the ones evaluated by the U.S. Army.

This 50 gram bar of Wehrmacht-Schokolade was the perfect size to fit in the assault carton. *Courtesy Thomas Bock.*

Glykolade, along with Scho-ka-kola, were two of the most important Chocolate/Coffee products.

Stollwerck fruit bar. *Courtesy Thomas Bock.*

This Felsche fruit bar was found in an assault ration carton. *Courtesy Clay W. Chambers.*

A package of Deli V Bonbons.[1]

This roll of Deli V drops was found in an assault ration carton. *Courtesy Thomas Bock.*

A package of Achenwall V Bonbons. *Courtesy Zeugmeister.*

A package of Kanold "Four Fruit Drops".[2]

While not conclusive, this picture appears to show the cellophane bag for Knäckebrot discussed in Volume I. *Courtesy Chris Mason.*

A young German soldier enjoying his Front Line Assault ration. *Courtesy Kevin Barrett.*

A box of grape sugar, also called dextrose, which was a common component of many emergency rations.

Dextro Energen was an important component of numerous Emergency rations and widely available through the Kantine system, as well as the normal supply chain. *Courtesy Ruelle Frédéric Collection.*

ENDNOTES

1 In 1903 the company was founded as the k.k.priv. Schokolade- und Zuckerwarenfabriks AG in Lobositz. In 1926 it was renamed Schokoladewerke "Deli". After the German occupation in 1938 the Schokoladewerke Deli found itself in the Sudetenland, or Sudetengau. After the war this area was once again known as Czechoslovakia. No postwar history was found.

2 The Kanold firm was established in Berlin in 1914. By the mid-1930s there were factories in Berlin, Essen, Leipzig, and Nurnberg. The Kanold brand is still being produced. Here is the factory listing in the 1941 Berlin phone book.

Kanold AG. Zuckerw.-Fabr. O 17
Andreasstr 32   ✳ 59 14 91

8

MARCH RATIONS

The March Ration was a short term cold ration issued to units conducting movements by road, rail, air or sea, or a combination of transport. The March Ration was only intended to be utilized for a period of 3-5 days before hot food would be resumed. Of course, that was only for planning purposes, and the actual number of days March Rations were issued depended on many factors, including enemy action. *H.Dv. 86/1 Regulations for Rations of the Armed Forces, June 20, 1940* was essentially the bible on ration policy and procedures. When discussing the March Ration, *H.Dv. 86/1* does not appear to distinguish between administrative movements and movements conducted under enemy pressure. Administrative movements are conducted without fear of enemy ground contact, and under those conditions may have allowed for a combination of hot and cold rations. Whether the movements were carried out in an administrative environment or under enemy pressure, the parent unit assumed a large part of the responsibility for feeding their soldiers. However, long distance movements utilizing a variety of transport might entail coordinating the units feeding among several organizations (civil and military) along the route of march. *H.Dv. 86/1* does not provide the daily portion scale for the ration. The only guidance for unit feeding appears to be: bread will be supplied, no fresh meat, utilize canned or dehydrated vegetables, and issue one condiment and salt as available. It's likely that a modified standard daily portion rate was used. Further information on the portion rates is provided below.

H.Dv. 86/1 authorizes March Rations for the units of the Army and the Air Force in a staging area or deploying by train, motor vehicle, ship, or airplane transport. (*Author's note: The Waffen SS and Naval Ground Units were probably authorized the ration.*) The unit command provided ration in accordance with the following guidance:

A. When abandoning or leaving a position, or preparing for foot marches or road marches (also applies to mounted and motorized units).

    (1). One serving in the unit trains (in the field kitchen), including bread.

    (2). Three servings at the ration point (the composition of the meals may vary). Fresh meat is not provided. Vegetables are provided in dehydrated form. Rice, legumes, mill products, or pasta are also available. In addition, the unit will provide one condiment (usually vinegar, onion bulb, or food

seasoning) with a shelf life of one month and salt within the capacity of the salt storage box in the field kitchen.

B. The units of the Air Force carry five day provisions on their vehicles.

C. Immediately before each new deployment: As per paragraph A, but only stage two servings in the unit trains.

D. Movement by rail or other motor transport: One serving per individual per day to consume on the transport during movement. After the trip warm food should be served and the cold food stopped.

E. Transport on the ocean or inland water ways: The rations for each individual will be based on the Navy Department Schedule (K.M.D.) for each day of movement by ship.

U.S. Army intelligence reports describe the March Ration as a cold food ration issued for not more than three or four consecutive days to units in transit, either by carrier or by foot. The daily portion scale published in December 1943 showed that the ration consisted of 700 grams of bread and 180 to 200 grams of meat products (Lunch: 100 grams of fresh sausage, Pemmican, bacon, or cooked meat; Dinner: 100 grams of fresh sausage or 80 grams of canned meat, Pemmican, or other sausage products, 60 grams of bread spreads, 9 grams of coffee or 4 grams of tea, and 10 grams of sugar). By the end of the war it consisted of approximately 700 grams of bread, 200 grams of cold meat or cheese, 60 grams of bread spreads, 9 grams of coffee (or 4 grams of tea), 10 grams of sugar, and 6 cigarettes. It had a total weight of about 980 grams. This portion rate probably applies to both unit and individual movements. It's likely that the portion rate was routinely updated or modified during the war.

To support the individual movement of soldiers to and from the front required the establishment of ration stations along the route of travel. There are numerous circumstances that would require a soldier to travel on his own: leave, school, reassignment, etc. The parent unit probably provided the soldier with cold rations before he/she departed. Along the route of march Railway stations, Soldiers' Homes, Red Cross Stations, and Garrison Mess Halls probably all served as ration points for the soldier while in transit. The soldier's travel order or other documentation provided the authority to draw rations. A number of organizations, both

March Ration Issued from a Field Kitchen

Bread

Soup

Fatty Meat

Fish

Condiments

Tea

A recreation of a March Ration that might have been issued from a Field Kitchen.

March Ration 1943 Portion Rate

Bread: 700 Grams

Bread Spread: 60 Grams

Sausage: 200 Grams

Tea: 4 Grams

Sugar: 10 Grams

The 1943 daily March Ration portion rate.

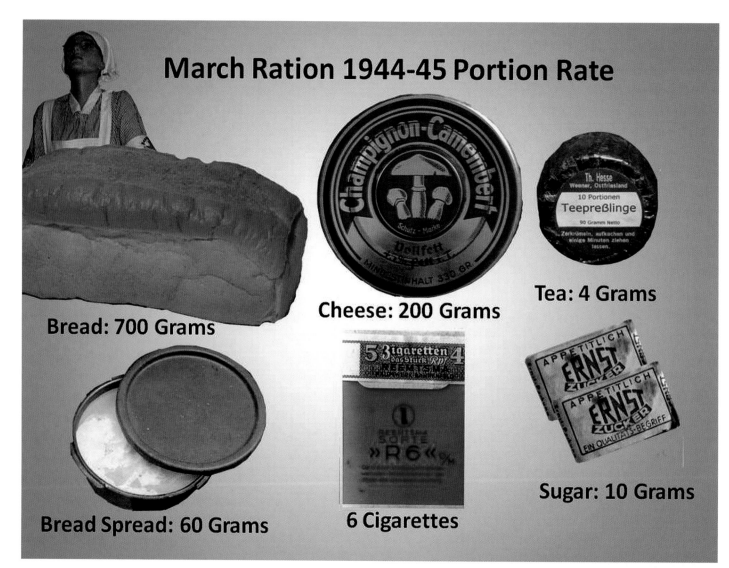

March Ration 1944-45 Portion Rate

Bread: 700 Grams

Cheese: 200 Grams

Tea: 4 Grams

Bread Spread: 60 Grams

6 Cigarettes

Sugar: 10 Grams

The 1944-45 daily March Ration portion rate.

military and civil, were required to keep this system operating. Female auxiliaries played a significant role in operating this system. What type of portion rates or meals the soldier was provided while travelling is not clear. However, from studying wartime pictures it appears that a combination of hot and cold rations were provided at designated transit points.

German soldiers in Northern France carrying bread. *Bundesarchiv Bild 1011-301-1953-08, Foto: Kurth, Summer 1944 / Licence CC-BY-SA 3.0.*

Soldiers waiting to get their evening meal. *Courtesy Todd Gylsen Collection.*

Bringing up the bread and fish. *Courtesy Todd Gylsen Collection.*

These troops being moved by rail are waiting to be fed. *Courtesy Paul Gromkowski.*

Nurses sorting through food items. *Courtesy OSTFRONT Militaria.*

Red Cross support and ration supply center. *Courtesy OSTFRONT Militaria.*

9

RATIONS AS GIFTS

I recently watched the 1958 classic movie "A Time to Love and a Time to Die" and got a pleasant surprise. Set in 1944, the movie is about a young German soldier, Hans Graeber, who we meet fighting as an infantryman on the Eastern Front. Early in the movie, his Company Commander informs him that his two week furlough to Germany has been approved. En route to Germany by train, a German officer distributes food packages at one of the stops. The officer explains that the package should be given to their families to show them how well things were going at the front. The package was simply a cardboard box over-wrapped in plain paper and tied off with string. Of course, this was one of the Führer Gifts which were initiated to recognize the sacrifices of the soldiers and citizens supporting the war effort. There were two distinct categories of Führer gifts: the Führergeschenk and Führer-Paket. Chronologically the Führer Paket was initiated first and was authorized from October 1942 to March 1943. The Führergeschenk was authorized beginning 15 October 1943 and rescinded on 1 September 1944. The gifts are explained in reverse order, since very little information is available on the Führer-Paket.

A. **Führergeschenk**: This gift was authorized by O.K.W., 22.9.43-6447/43-W Allg (IIb). It authorized the issuance of the Führergeschenk starting 15 October 1943. It was authorized for personnel on normal leave, wounded, ill, or recalled to Germany on emergency leave. The gift was rescinded on 1 September 1944 by O.K.W., 25.8.44-5150/44-AWA/W Allg (IIb).

Wehrmacht and Waffen SS personnel had to serve in the following areas to be eligible for the gift: the east front (eastward from the Reich, the General Government, and the Bialystok district), from Finland, Italy including Albania and the Italian Aegean Islands, Greece including Crete and the Aegean Islands, Serbia, Croatia, and Norway. Naval crews in the following areas were eligible: the Eastern Baltic, in Norwegian waters, in the Black Sea, and in the Mediterranean. Members of certain units of the Navy and Air Force serving in the West were also eligible. It is assumed that personnel in North Africa, Italy, and the Western Front (after June 6, 1944) were also eligible for the gift.

Members of the following organizations were eligible for the gift: Army, Air Force, Navy, Waffen-SS, Foreign Volunteers of the Army and Waffen-SS, Police, Customs, RAD, OT, NSKK Gruppe Todt, Railway (so called Blue Railroad men), civilian crews of warships, construction workers for the Air Force, NSKK Motorgruppe Air Force, Schutzmannschaft Battalions,

Wieder Führergeschenk für Fronturlauber

Berlin, 14. Oktober.

Als Dank des Führers für ihren Einsatz erhalten ab 15. 10. 1943 die Angehörigen aller Wehrmachtteile und der Waffen-SS sowie die Angehörigen der im Rahmen der Wehrmacht eingesetzten verschiedenen Organisationen der gesamten Ostfront, aus Italien, Griechenland, Serbien, Kroatien und Norwegen, sowie alle zum Kampf eingesetzten U-Boot-Besatzungen und das zum Kampf eingesetzte fliegende Personal der Luftwaffe, die als Verwundete, Kranke oder als Urlauber in die Heimat kommen und den Berechtigungsvermerk in ihren Papieren haben, wieder ein Führergeschenk in Gestalt eines Lebensmittelpaketes oder eine entsprechende Sonder-Lebensmittelkarte in Verbindung mit einem Geldbetrag von 10 Mark.

Das Führerpaket wird, ebenso wie das letzte Mal, nur einmal ausgehändigt und sein Empfang im Soldbuch oder Ausweis vermerkt. Die Sonderlebensmittelkarte, die dann ausgegeben wird, wenn der Empfangsberechtigte das Paket nicht erhalten hat, wird von der Kartenausgabestelle des Heimat- oder Urlaubsortes zusammen mit den Urlauberlebensmittelkarten oder von den Lazaretten ausgegeben und berechtigt zum Bezuge der gleichen Lebensmittel.

Newspaper announcement about the Führergeschenk.

Possible contents of the Führergeschenk: 1. *Two kg miscellaneous foods*, 2. *Half a kg of Honey*, 3. *One kg Jam*, 4. *Five kg Flour*, 5. *One kg Sugar*, and 6. *Half a kg of Butter* all packed into a cardboard box (item number 7).

and the Red Cross. Both men and women were eligible for the gift.

The gifts were a controlled item, and their abuse carried stiff penalties. When a person was entitled to receive the gift an entry was made in his Soldbuch, Einsatzbuch, or other identity document. This entry would generally match up with a leave date. Another entry was made in the identity document when the gift was received. Our research indicates that the gift could only be given out once. However, some references state that an order dated October 1943 allowed the gift to be given more than once.

The gift program was under the control of the Reichkommissars of the Ukraine Gauleiter Koch, via the various organizations of the Nationalsozialistische Volkswohlfahrt (NSV), or the National Socialist People's Welfare. Distribution points for the gifts were established at railroad stations in the following towns or cities: Zdolbunow, Gretschany, Przemysl, Kowel, Brest, Memel, Pogegen, Tilsit (moved to Pogegen), Eydtkau, Bialystok (moved to Wolkowysk), and Königsberg. Provisions were made for personnel who could not get to one of the authorized distribution centers.

The Führergeschenk consists of a Food Parcel (Lebensmittelpaket) containing: 5 kg Flour, 2 kg of other food stuffs, 1 kg Sugar, 1.5 kg Marmalade or 1 kg of Jam, and 0.5 kg Honey and 0.5 kg Butter or other Fats. In lieu of the Food Parcel a recipient could be given a Special Ration card (Sonderlebensmittelkarte) and funds in the amount of 10 RM necessary for the purchase of items.

B.   **Führer-Paket**: Very little is known about this gift. Heeresmitteilung 1942 p.582, Nr 1055, 30.11.42 authorized the gift after 30.9.42. A reference in one of the regulations on the Führergeschenk gives the dates for the Führer-Paket as

Possible contents of the Führerpaket: 1. *Two and a half kg Flour*, 2. *One kg Sugar*, 3. *One kg Meat and Fish*, 4. *One and a half kg Dry Cereal Products*, and 5. *One kg Butter* packed inside the paper bag (item number 6).

October 1942 to March 1943. It is assumed that the regulations governing the Führer-Paket were similar to those for the Führergeschenk. The special ration card was named the Führer-Paket für Osturlauber (Leader package for eastern vacationers), and consisted of the following items: 2.5 kg Flour, 1 kg Sugar, 1.5 kg Dry cereal products, starch or legumes, 1 kg Butter, and 1 kg Meat or meat products. Since the food products for the Führergeschenk and Führer-Paket were not provided by the military, it's likely that they were commercial off the shelf items.

Wer erhält das Führerpaket?

Nachlieferung kann beantragt werden

Zur Wiederaufnahme des Führergeschenks für die Fronturlauber gibt das OKW ergänzende Bestimmungen bekannt. Danach erhält nur derjenige das Führergeschenk, dessen Papiere mit einem ordnungsgemäßen Berechtigungsvermerk des Disziplinar- oder Dienstvorgesetzten versehen sind und der die Grenze zum Heimatkriegsgebiet nach dem 15. Oktober 1943, 00.00 Uhr, überschritten hat. Soweit Empfangsberechtigte das Führergeschenk nicht erhalten haben, sei es, weil sie ohne den vorgeschriebenen Berechtigungsvermerk in den Papieren in das Heimatkriegsgebiet kamen und eine nachträgliche Eintragung durch den zuständigen Standortältesten nicht erfolgte, sei es, weil andere Gründe vorliegen, können sie nach ihrer Rückkehr die Aushändigung der Sonderlebensmittelkarte und Geldvergütung von 10 Mark an ihre nächsten Angehörigen beantragen. Der Disziplinar- oder Dienstvorgesetzte übersendet dann der vom Antragsteller bestimmten Person eine Empfangsberechtigung. Gegen diese Empfangsberechtigung kann der Berechtigte von der zuständigen Kartenstelle bezw. Gemeindekasse die Lebensmittelkarte für Fronturlauber und die Geldvergütung von 10 Mark in bar in Empfang nehmen. Das Führergeschenk ist im übrigen nicht an den Erholungsurlaub gebunden, es kann auch allen anderen Arten von Urlaub zugebilligt werden. Jedoch steht es jedem Empfangsberechtigten auch bei mehrmaliger Beurlaubung nur einmal zu. Die Führerpaketaktion Oktober 1942 bis März 1943 bleibt hierbei unberücksichtigt. Soweit Verwundete oder Kranke nach dem Stichtag aus den in Betracht kommenden Gebieten in das Heimatkriegsgebiet verlegt werden, wird der Berechtigungsvermerk in den Papieren in Lazarette des Heimatkriegsgebietes verlegt werden, wird der Berechtigungsvermerk durch die Chefärzte nachgetragen. Zum einmaligen Empfang des Führergeschenks sind weiter berechtigt die in den in Betracht kommenden Frontgebieten eingesetzten männlichen und weiblichen Angehörigen des Deutschen Roten Kreuzes, die Personaleinheiten der Lazarettzüge des Feldheeres soweit sie ständig in Lazarettzügen zwischen dem Operationsgebiet und der Lazarettbasis Ost pendeln und die zivilen Gefolgschaftsmitglieder der zum Chef des Transportwesens abgeordneten Bauzüge, soweit sie Wehrmachtgefolge sind. Auch diejenigen Angehörigen der landeseigenen Verbände und Schutzmannschaften sowie diejenigen Hilfswilligen sind zum Empfang eines Führergeschenks berechtigt, die mit einem deutschen Wehrmachtangehörigen in das Heimatkriegsgebiet beurlaubt werden und ihren Urlaub in der Familie des deutschen Wehrmachtangehörigen verleben.

Newspaper announcement about the Führerpaket.

Lebensmittelpaket for wounded personnel, *With Greetings from the Führer.*

Variation cover for the Lebensmittelpaket for wounded personnel. *Courtesy OSTFRONT Militaria.*

The individual items were probably placed in a card stock box or paper sacks for ease of handling.

C. **Other Gifts**: There are several items in collections that are clearly identified as a gift from the Führer but are not large enough to be the Führergeschenk or Führer-Paket. They are not referenced in any of the pertinent regulations I have seen. I have elected to call them Lebensmittelpakets, because they are clearly made to hold food items. It's likely that these were special gifts given out for special occasions or circumstances, like Christmas or for being wounded. More than likely these gifts were distributed via the various organizations of the National Sozialistische Volkswohlfahrt (NSV) or by the German Red Cross. From surviving photographs and items in collections, it's evident that the German Red Cross was heavily involved in preparing gift packages for German soldiers. Of course individuals, companies, and towns also recognized the sacrifices of the military by preparing packages containing food, books, personal items, clothing, etc., for the soldiers. Some of these gifts will contain the word "Grüss" or "Greeting", usually in conjunction with the Führer, a town name, company name, or organization title. Greetings from towns, etc., are sometimes seen on postwar items. I have seen one postwar tin with the phrase "Christmas Greeting from the Home of the …Factory" embossed on it.

A Lebensmittelpaket given to soldiers with the thanks of the Führer. *Courtesy Zeugmeister.*

Special Christmas Lebensmittelpaket distributed by the NSV.

The Franz Dietl confectionery shop had special Feldpost cartons manufactured to send their products to the soldiers at the front.

Gift box from the Müller chocolate shop in Bad Nauheim.[1] *Courtesy Zeugmeister.*

The Türk and Pabst Delicatessen had these special "Nur Für Nahrungsmittel" jars manufactured to distribute their products to troops in the field. The firm specialized in fish paste, ketchup, salad dressing, and canned sausage.

WHW members sorting through food items that would eventually be distributed to the public. During the war the WHW also sent items to the soldiers in the field. *Bundesarchiv Bild 102-17313 Foto: o. Ang., 1 December 1935/ Licence CC-BY-SA 3.0.*

Food and drink were popular gifts to send soldiers during the holidays.
Courtesy Bill Petz.

Food was the second most important thing on the soldier's mind.

Wehrmacht Chocolate manufactured and packed
for the German Red Cross by the Hildebrand firm.
Courtesy Kevin Barrett.

This soldier has hit the jackpot at mail call.
Courtesy Bill Petz.

The German Red Cross prepared and distributed food packages to the soldiers, in this case German POWs in England.

Red Cross nurse distributing gifts to wounded soldiers.

Christmas bags.

Small paper trays containing food
and other small gifts.

This picture shows a Christmas bag that was sent to the troops. *Courtesy OSTFRONT Militaria.*

These soldiers are in the Christmas spirit. *Bundesarchiv Bild 201-MA34-370-91-13, Foto: o.Ang.Dezember 1939 / Licence CC-BY-SA 3.0.*

Christmas was a time to forget the horrors of war.

These two soldiers received a nice box of food. Notice the Nürnberger Lebkuchen tin. *Courtesy Todd Gylsen Collection.*

Identification tag and identity book for a volunteer Nurse.

Happy days are here again. *Courtesy Todd Gylsen Collection.*

Soldiers posing with their Christmas gifts. *Courtesy OSTFRONT Militaria.*

ENDNOTES

1 No history was found on Müller Schokolade in Bad Nauheim. Here is their listing in the 1929 Mosse Register of Firms.

> Müller, Heinrich Adam, Schokolade, ℋ 2282, Ps 68410 Fr.

10

MISCELLANEOUS RATIONS

This chapter will discuss miscellaneous rations and procedures not covered in the previous chapters.

A. **Pemmican**. Pemmican was described in an article originally published by the U.S. Army Infantry School, *The Modern Ration of the German Armed Forces (Translation)*, Infantry School Mailing List, Vol. XXI, Chapter 11 (February 1941):

"Concentrated foods play an important role in specialized rations, for example, rations for tank troops, fortress troops, mountain troops, and aviators. One of the best examples of highly concentrated food is Pemmican, originally used by the American Indian during long migrations. He prepared it from dried game and cranberries. Following our own experiments and those of Nansen, the German Army developed *Pemmikan-Landjaeger* which contains all the substances necessary for building up the body, such as carbohydrates, protein, fat, and mineral salts. *Pemmikan-Landjaeger* contains the following:

Meat, smoked, containing protein (beef and pork)
Bacon, containing fat
Soy bean flour, containing protein, fat, and carbohydrates
Dried fruits, containing carbohydrates
Whey, containing minerals
Tomato pulp, containing vitamins
Yeast, containing vitamins
Green pepper, containing vitamins
Cranberries, containing vitamins
Lecithin, containing lipoid.

The *U.S. Army Ration Report* provided the following details about Pemmican: "This ration was 0.5 x 4 x 4 inches in size and weighed approximately 12 ounces. It consisted of one block, resembling some of the experimental United States dehydrated meat or Pemmican type of ration, and was wrapped in a single tin foil wrapper of aluminum foil, .0005 inch in thickness, with no other protection. The German ration, although high in calories, was low in palatability, and would not be acceptable to U.S. troops."

A Survey of German Wartime Food Processing, Packaging and Allocation, Part I and II 27 September 1945 provided some additional information. Generally most dehydrated meat products were disliked by the German soldier. When eaten under emergency conditions it was monotonous and unpalatable because of its high fat content. It had a soapy and dough-like taste when eaten uncooked. There were exceptions, like a dehydrated smoked ground beef from an unnamed firm which was rated as excellent. The German researchers aware of these problems attempted to correct them by reducing the fat content, adding Knäckebrot crumbs, adding it to bread, and eliminating the use of bitter oats. The distribution of Pemmican was supposedly eliminated in late 1944, however, production continued into 1945, with two new products being added: spiced meat and meat goulash. As an Emergency Ration it was comparable to the U.S. "D" Ration as evaluated below:

Large shipping carton for Pemmican. *Courtesy Jens Kattner.*

German Pemmican.

Fig. 1. German Pemmican, similar to some of the experimental meat or Pemmican-type rations used by American troo[ps]

The menu for mobile troops in subzero temperatures.

Menu for Mobile Troops in Sub Zero Temperatures

Breakfast — Lunch — Between Meals — Supper

Knäckebrot: 250 Grams
Butter: 40 Grams
Tea and Sugar

Fatty Meat: 120 Grams
Knäckebrot: 250 Grams

Biscuits and Dried Fruits

250 Grams of Knäckebrot and Rest of Fatty Meat

Topic	German Pemmican	U.S. "D" Bar
Calories	2094.00	1766.00
Protein g.	168.00	35.00
Carbohydrate g.	0	195.00
Calcium g.	88.00	738.00
Iron mg.	23.00	15.60
Fat g.	158.00	94.00

B. Rations for Extreme Cold Weather. In extremely cold weather supplementary fat and sugar were authorized. Spirits, usually Schnapps, were authorized if approved by the Surgeon, most of whom realized that a momentary flush of heat was followed by a chilling effect, and so actually knew it was harmful. Company officers from nearly all types of units said that their men had received small quantities of spirits in the winter. An Army mountain troop officer who had served in Northern Finland said that it was important to supply non-freezing foods to combat troops in cold weather. Otherwise the difficulty of supplying enough fuel was great. He gave the following as a typical menu for mobile troops in sub zero temperatures: *Breakfast*: 40 grams butter, 250 grams rye crisp, tea with sugar; *Lunch*: 120 grams bacon, fat meat, or sausage (wurst); 250 grams rye crisp, corn meal or rice: or else canned stew, preferably with a low water content to prevent freezing; *Between meals*: dried fruit, fruit drops, biscuits, etc; *Supper*: 250 grams rye crisp and fat meat.

Front fresh bread wrapped in paper was provided to this soldier. *Bundesarchiv Bild 1011-081-3285-20, Foto: Müller-Schwanneke, Karl Hubert (Bert) 1942 Herbst / Licence CC-BY-SA 3.0.*

This picture appears to show V Drops being issued. *Courtesy OSTFRONT Militaria.*

C. **Supplement to Offset Vitamin Deficiencies**. Despite the best efforts to provide nutritionally balanced meals to the troops, mistakes were made and vitamin deficiencies, especially Vitamin C deficiencies, appeared. To offset scurvy, Vitamin A sugar candies and less often vitamin chocolate were issued. This, according to Colonel Neitzel, G-4 of the 1st German Army, removed the danger completely. A subsistence Depot officer said that three packages of candy were issued per week in his sector in Russia during the winter, when the danger was greater because of the lack of fresh vegetables and fruits. The men liked the candy and always ate it.

D. **Concentrated foods for military uses**. The following was reported in *Tactical and Technical Trends*, No. 20, March 11, 1943:

"The German technical press reports the large-scale preparation of a standard 30-pound (approximately) so-called dried vegetable 'bomb' containing an assortment of compressed dried beans, peas, carrots, cabbage, spinach, onions, and potatoes. These rations are designed to be dropped from airplanes to isolated German units. It also reports special balanced-meal units composed of dried vegetables, meat, fruit, and fats compressed into a single cube prepared particularly for use in long-distance submarines."

E. **Increasing the portion rates**. *H.Dv. 86/1. Regulations for the Rations of the Armed Forces with Specific Deployment* authorized commanders to increase the portion rate for individual components of the daily ration under certain conditions. The authority to permit changes rested with the "High Command."

Three packages of vitamin candy were issued a week to offset vitamin deficiencies.

but was probably delegated down. The bread serving could be increased when there was a reduction in the meat serving because of a supply shortage, etc. A second alcohol and beverage serving was authorized provided that extraordinary strain and climatic weather conditions justified it and as supplies allowed it. The distribution of .375 liters of wine or .05 liters of spirits for the first or second beverage serving is contingent upon the approval of the medical authorities. When particularly difficult conditions prevent or delay the bringing forward of warm rations to the soldiers and the only rations available are the cold components of the standard ration, the commander may approve supplementing the dinner meal by up to one half the portion rate, as well as 100 grams of chocolate or sweets. This additional allowance is only permitted as supplies and stocks permit.

F. **General Logistic Data.** *FM-E 101-10 Staff Officers' Field Manual Enemy Forces Organization, Technical and Logistic Data*, 1942, provided the following information on the amount and weights of rations carried within the division. The term "Field Ration" is the daily portion for each soldier in the unit.

Ration Supply		
Carried in the division	*Field ration*	*Iron ration*
With each man	NA	1 (reduced)
On each combat vehicle	NA	1
In the field kitchen	1	1
In the unit ration train	2	NA
In the division train	1	NA
Total	4	3
Total weight of ration carried in the division: 94.4 tons (approx.).		

Weight of 1 day's ration (field):			
Total weight (approx.)	Per man (lb.)	Per division (tons)	Per 300,000 men (tons)
	2.92	23. 6	420

G. **German Rations in Libya.** The following was reported in *Tactical and Technical Trends*, No. 18, Feb. 11, 1943:

"The following German food and water situation in Libya has been reported as a result of PW interrogations. The information showed that until July 1, 1942 no food or water difficulties had been experienced in the unit concerned, and after the fall of Tobruk canned fruit and vegetables had been added to the normal rations. The battalion rations officer was responsible for the collection of rations (requisitioned every 3 days by companies) from the supply dumps, and for the delivery to companies. For distribution to companies there were four 3-ton trucks, never loaded to more than half capacity. Thus for 3 days' supplies, a 6 ton truck capacity per battalion was necessary. Bread was collected separately from the field bakery. Apart from the regular 3 days' supply, companies carried 6 days' and each man 1 day' iron rations. Rations included one hot meal each day, always prepared in the field kitchen, which is brought as far forward as possible."

Rations per man per day actually issued were:		
Coffee	**Bread**	**Water***
1/2 Oz. Real Coffee	1/2 Lb. at Rest	About 5 Pints at Rest
1/4 Oz. Substitute	1/3 Lb. in Battle	About 3 Pints in Battle
*Drinking and cooking water, including water for coffee and tea.		

SECTION VI
SUPPLY DIAGRAMS

■ **45. RATIONS.—**

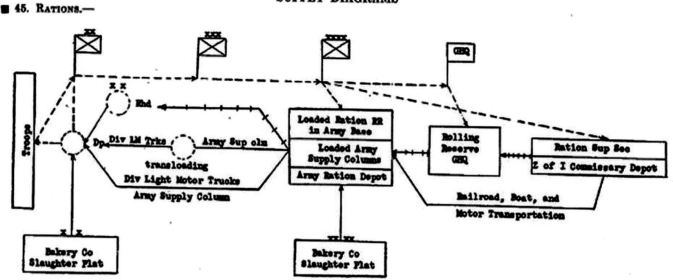

This diagram shows the system of distribution for rations. The division hauls from the Army distribution point. Battalions and regiments haul from the division distribution point. The companies haul from the battalion distribution point. (If units are motorized, unit ration trucks draw from the division.)

H. **Emergency Ration Air Droppable**. The German military established an individual portion rate which could be dropped by parachute to isolated or trapped personnel. The ration was identified in Part II of the report *A Survey of German Wartime Food Processing, Packaging and Allocation* dated 27 September 1945. It's likely this ration wasn't authorized until 1943 or 1944. The portion rate or composition could be modified depending on how much transport space was available. The composition of the ration and the instructions on using Notverpflegung Süß are shown below.

Emergency Ration Air Droppable
300 grams Pemmican or
300 grams Emergency Ration Sweets (*Author's note: I'm fairly certain this is Notverpflegung Süß)* **and**
300 gram s Fresh Bread or Dauerbrot

Emergency Ration Sweet
Daily portion per man 300 grams
Composition: Contains the essential foodstuffs and active substances, fats, powdered eggs, whole soya, rolled oats, sugar, fruits, and sweet spices.
Detailed instructions:
1. Cold Meal: Eat raw.
2. Soup: Break cubes into 2 liters of boiling water, stir frequently and cook for 5 minutes. Salt to taste.
3. Pudding: Cut up cubes and add to 1 liter of boiling water, stir frequently and cook for 5 minutes, rinse with cold water and let stand until firm.

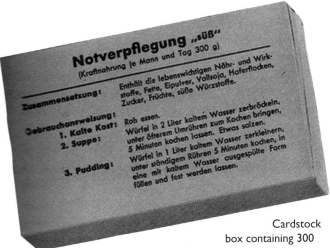

Cardstock box containing 300 grams of Notverpflegung "Süß", a dessert like product packed in cubes. It could be eaten raw or mixed with water to form a soup or pudding. This could be the "belated" 300 gram emergency ration mentioned in the foreword. *Courtesy Bahlsen GmbH & Co. KG.*

This shelf is packed with a number of ration and personal items. *Courtesy Bill Petz.*

Good to the last drop. *Bundesarchiv Bild 169-0151, Foto: o. Ang, Summer 1941 / Licence CC-BY-SA 3.0.*

For some unknown reason this soldier is opening up a large number of canned food products. *Courtesy Bill Petz.*

Soldiers taking a snack break somewhere in Italy. *Bundesarchiv Bild 1011-310-0864-11, Foto: Engel February 1944/ Licence CC-BY-SA 3.0.*

These troops are picking up supplies to restock their unit Kantine. *Bundesarchiv Bild / Licence CC-BY-SA 3.0.*

Insulated containers were used to deliver hot meals to troops in forward positions.

Gathering around the Field Kitchen. *Bundesarchiv Bild 1011-725-0194-29, Foto: Götz, Winter 1943/1944/ Licence CC-BY-SA 3.0.*

Is it red wine or white wine that goes with chicken?

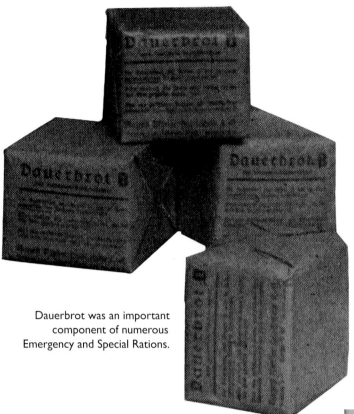

Dauerbrot was an important component of numerous Emergency and Special Rations.

These workers appear to be packing something similar to donuts. *Courtesy Todd Gylsen Collection.*

Loading up survival equipment into a Stuka. *Bundesarchiv Bild 1011-433-0859-13, Foto: Billhardt, September 1941 / Licence CC-BY-SA 3.0.*

I. **Air Force Rations**. In Volume I, the authors covered the various Air Force flight Rations as best we could with the limited references available. A more complete listing was detailed in Part II of *A Survey of German Wartime Food Processing, Packaging and Allocation* dated 27 September 1945. No specifics about the packaging were provided. I think the following is probably the most accurate list of flight rations available. Please refer to Mick Prodger's excellent book *Luftwaffe vs. RAF: Flying Equipment of the Air War, 1939-45* to see pictures of the cloth Winter emergency container and rescue supply buoys, as well as other interesting ration items.

Starting Provisions: Additional food issued prior to flying.
0.5 Liter Whole Milk or   **0.33 Liter Can of Condensed or Evaporated Milk**
1 Egg
25 grams Butter
200 grams White Bread
65 grams Rösta Cookies

Plane Provisions: Additional food to guard against fatigue and exertion during flight.
50 grams Bitter Kola Chocolate or   **50 grams Glykolade**
25 grams Dextro-Energen or   **80 grams Fruit Slices or**
80 grams "Student food" (candied mixed nuts)

30 grams Spear mint or sour drops or lemon or mixed Bon-Bons
50-100 grams Keks or 80 grams Soya Keks

Plane Provisions: Additional food to guard against fatigue and exertion for flights over six hours. Sandwiches could be issued in lieu of the following.

50 grams Bitter Kola Chocolate or 50 grams Glykolade
25 grams Dextro-Energen or 80 grams Fruit Slices or 80 grams "Student food" (candied mixed nuts)
30 grams Spear mint or Sour Drops or Lemon or Mixed Bon-Bons
50-100 grams Keks or 80 grams Soya Keks

Plane Provisions: Additional food to guard against fatigue and exertion for flights over 10 hours.

120 grams Fresh meat with bones or 100 grams Preserved or smoked sausage
50 grams Cheese
20 grams Cocoa or 20 grams Coffee
500 grams Fresh fruit or 280 grams Canned Fruit

A Winter Emergency Ration Container. The components differ from those listed in the Allied report. It added 100 grams of pressed coffee, a can of salt, 5 portions of tea, 300 grams of sugar cubes, and 2 cans of cigarettes. The 500 grams of soup cubes were eliminated.
Courtesy Militaria-Versand Emig.

Plane Provisions in case of Emergency Landing over water or isolated areas.

100 grams Scho-ka-kola
20 grams Chewing Gum

Emergency Ration Container Desert

250 gram Can of Mutton and Rice
500 gram of Mutton and Green Beans (Two 250 gram Cans)
4 Packages of Sliced Fruit (80 gram Each) or 250 gram Can of Fruit
6 Packages of Kössen bread (Knäckebrot)
2 packages of Scho-ka-kola 100 gram each
1 can Vitamin Drops (50 gram bag) or (22 gram roll)
4 packages of Dextro-Energen

Emergency Ration Container Winter

1 Portion of Knäckebrot (375 grams), 3 Cartons
500 grams Zwieback in two linen bags
4 cans of Pork 200 grams each
2 cans of Schmaltz 200 grams each
8 portions of Maggi soup cubes (50 grams each)
3 packages of Scho-ka-kola 100 grams each
10 packages of Dextro-Energen
500 grams of Soup Cubes

Emergency Ration Container Life Raft

4 packages of Zwieback, 100 grams each *(Author's note: Wartime photographs show one 250 gram bag of Zwieback).*
2 packages of Scho-ka-kola 100 grams each
1 package of Dextro-Energen 50 grams

Winter Emergency Ration Accessory for Seat Parachutes

250 grams Zwieback in linen bag
1 can of Pork 200 grams
1 package of Scho-ka-kola 100 grams

Sea Emergency Provision Buoy

Small container
1 package of Scho-ka-kola 100 grams
1 package of Dehydrated Fruit 150 grams
1 bag of Chewing Gum 20 grams
Large container
450 grams of Kössen bread (Knäckebrot) loose

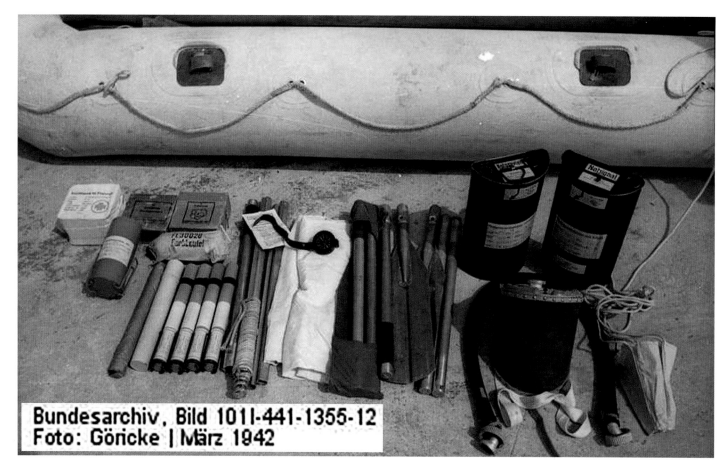

Air Force NCO inspecting the contents of the Emergency Supply Container Life Raft. *Bundesarchiv Bild 1011-441-1355-(02), (03), (04), and (12)/ Foto: Göricke/ Licence CC-BY-SA 3.0.*

J. **Naval Supplement to H.Dv. 86/1.** *Regulations for the Rations of the Armed Forces with Specific Deployment.* During the research for this volume Thomas Salazar provided me with the naval supplement to *H.Dv. 86/1*. The Naval equivalent to *H.Dv. 86/1* is named *M.Dv.Nr. 595*, and only applied to naval shore based units to include air assets. With minor exceptions the regulations governing the Army were also followed by shore based naval units. The majority of the naval supplement highlighted the ration responsibilities of the Naval Chain of Command and the associated administrative functions required to feed ground based naval personnel.

The Air Force Scho-ka-kola containers were issued in 90 and 100 gram sizes. *Courtesy OSTFRONT Militaria.*

Color picture of the Air Force Emergency Scho-ka-kola container. The Scho-ka-kola was wrapped in paper before it was placed in the can.

A sailor looking over some rations.

11

RATIONS DURING OFFENSIVE OPERATIONS AND SPECIAL FEEDING CHALLENGES

A. *Rations During Offensive Operations*

Over the years a lot of misinformation and myths about German rations have been circulated among the collecting and reenacting community. Some of this misinformation has managed to find its way into otherwise reputable books, like *Deutsche Soldaten* by Agustín Sáiz. In his book the author writes:

> Lack of food, or worse still, hunger, was one of the nightmare scenarios of a soldiers' existence. The Blitzkrieg, in spite of all its advantages in terms of warfare, meant an ongoing serious problem for the supply corps. Supplies had to be transported across un-surfaced roads and along trails, often under enemy fire and in all kinds of weather. Of course, ammunition that was essential for the development of the campaign and maintaining what could be a fluid front was given priority. In consequence, and *more often than not*, the troops suffered alarming ration shortages until positions were stabilized and supplies delivered regularly. *Until that time, the men had to survive on combat rations, more popularly as "iron rations" that-whenever possible-were swapped for fresh products with the local population.*

This idea that the German soldier in the attack had to sustain himself solely on a Half Iron Ration and by foraging is of course false. The German military, like most successful armies throughout history, conducted in-depth staff work before conducting any type of operation. Courses of action were developed along with the pros and cons associated with each option. Logistic planning was just as thorough as the tactical planning. Rations were given equal priority in the planning process, along with ammunition, fuel and lubricants, medical, postal, etc. More often than not, in the actual execution of operations fuel and ammunition were given priority over rations in the allocation of transport.

Once a course of action was decided upon the preparations began. For a large scale offensive that meant filling unit ration requirements and stocking depots. By the end of the war the German military kept 20 days of rations in the field. The troop units stocked three days of normal supplies and two days iron rations (1 half and 1 full). Corps and Division dumps stocked five days' rations. The Army Depots stocked 10 days' rations and the Army Group five days'. Once operations began, rations were requisitioned as needed to keep the depots and units stocked. Local stores obtained by purchase or confiscation were not considered when conducting combat operations. Localized offensive actions to stabilize a sector, disrupt enemy plans, gain intelligence, etc., probably didn't require additional logistic planning or stockage.

The rest of this chapter is written from the perspective of the ordinary German infantryman. The infantry made up the great majority of the German military and were the most difficult to supply. Unlike their mechanized comrades, the infantryman had to carry everything with him. There are numerous types of offensive operations, each having their own logistic challenges. For the purpose of this exercise I have chosen a breakthrough scenario, pursuing an enemy against light to moderate resistance in an air power neutral environment. The unit commander would assess his situation and determine the best options to keep his troops fed. The fact that the field kitchen could move and cook simultaneously was certainly a capability the unit commander was cognizant of. It's likely the smart commander would try to feed his troops before an operation began and issue the Half-Iron Ration, as well as cold components of the next day's normal rations. As mentioned, at the troop level there were three days of normal rations and two days of iron rations on hand. The cold components of the normal ration were meant to sustain the soldiers until the field kitchen could get forward and established. The question is just how much of the normal ration should be issued? Remember, the infantryman had to carry everything with him: food, ammunition, extra clothing, personal kit, field gear, weapon, etc. At some point weight becomes an issue, because it impacts the soldier's ability to function. This paragraph in *Merkblatt 18a/17 Taschenbuch für den Winterkreig*, dated 1942, shows a deep understanding of the common infantryman's plight:

> If it is anticipated that serving from field kitchens will not be possible, powdered coffee, tea and other rations should be issued in advance, to enable the soldiers to prepare their own hot drinks and hot food. To prevent overloading the men, however, only essential rations should be issued. Otherwise they will throw away whatever seems unnecessary at the moment.

The daily food allowance for the German infantryman till the end of 1944 is shown below. Unlike the U.S. Army, there were no standardized or prepackaged meals like the C-Ration or K-Ration for the German commander to distribute. I have not encountered a menu of suggested cold components to issue to the troops during offensive operations. Special Patrol ration menus and Confection Rations discussed in Chapters 7 and 10 could serve as guides when determining exactly what cold components to issue. *H.Dv. 86/1* also contains portion rates for selected cold food items and meals. So there was sufficient guidance available to assist the commander in determining what to issue.

700 grams of bread: Fresh bread in loaves seems to have been popular. However, other bread products in cans, cartons, wrapped in paper, etc., were also options.
173 grams of meats, soy bean flour, cheese, fish or eggs: Fresh sausage or salami seemed to be popular. However tube cheese, canned meat/fish, and pemmican were also options.
650 grams of vegetables: Dehydrated soups, mixed canned meat/vegetables, fresh products, and fruits/vegetables in jars were potential candidates.
45 grams of pudding powder or skim milk: Pudding powder required some preparation. The small aluminum cans of milk were perfect candidates.
19 grams of spices, salt, and other seasoning.
9 grams of coffee or tea.
60 grams of fat and bread spreads: Butter, lard, fats, and bread spreads were probably put into the butter dish. Marmalades and jams were usually issued in jars or cans.
40 grams of sugar. Units were amply supplied with a wide variety of chocolates and other sweets. These would have been perfect for troops in the attack.

Ideally, the commander would want the field kitchen to get in position to provide a hot meal within 24 hours after the start of operations, or supply the cold components of the normal ration to sustain the troops until that occurred. If the soldier was lucky, someone in his squad had an Esbit or other stove to cook hot food. Each soldier also carried a Half Iron Ration for emergency use, in the event food could not be provided within the 24 hour window. Only the commander, platoon leader, or in special circumstances the squad leader could authorize the Half Iron Ration to be eaten.

At the unit level mess personnel would requisition, receive, stock, cook, and distribute rations as required. Rations would be delivered to or picked up by the unit using available transportation. During combat operations, the front line units would generally send troops back to a predetermined location to pick up rations (hot or cold) for their units and take them forward. In extreme cases the Air Force would fly rations to forward airfields or utilize drop canisters to get rations to forward units. (At the strategic level, the German military maintained pre-packed 10 day ration packs to support 500,000 troops for 30 days. These food packs were packed in chests equipped with parachutes and stored in four ration warehouses. Light weight, space saving, and readily prepared foods were selected for this purpose. This policy was initiated after the Stalingrad debacle.)

Sorting out and inventorying rations at a Regimental or Battalion distribution point. *Courtesy Mike Hamady.*

Taking cold rations to the forward positions. It consists of bread, sardines, canned meat, and probably some type of bread spread in the mess kit lid. *Courtesy Todd Gylsen Collection.*

Distributing hot and cold rations.

Sorting out and inventorying rations at the Company or Platoon level. *Courtesy Mike Hamady.*

Laying out cold rations for a squad. Bread, sardines, and cigarettes are clearly shown. *Courtesy Thomas Bock.*

Time to eat! *Courtesy Bill Petz.*

H.Dv. 86 *Feldkochbuch*, 16.8.1941, English translation by John Baum, provides a hypothetical sequence of events for field kitchen personnel to follow in support of offensive operations against light resistance. I have summarized that sequence below:

After 24 hours without food the commander could authorize his troops to eat their Half Iron Ration.

The company is ordered to attack at 0600 hours 25 July. At 2300 hours, 24 July the company is served the evening meal, bread, and bread spreads. The field kitchen is already stocked with the ingredients for the warm meal for July 25th (beans, no potatoes). The supply column carrying food for July 26th is expected on July 25th.

At **0700 on July 25th** the Field Cook Sergeant is told to be prepared to move around noon to support the advance. The hot meal will be served as the situation allows.

By 0900 hours the field kitchen has been cleaned, water stocked, fuel gathered, and beans cleaned.

By 1100 hours heat up the field kitchen, meat prepared, and put into the kettle, cut eyes from 100 pounds of potatoes, and gather spices and onions.

By 1300 hours wash, peel, and store potatoes. Wash and cut up onions. Supply column carrying provisions for July 26th arrive and are transferred to the field kitchen.

In the afternoon the bread, bread spread, and evening portions for July 26th are divided up. The order is given to move forward to a new assembly area, which is accomplished by 1700 hours.

By 1900 hours seasoning is prepared and the meat removed from the kettle. The kettle is emptied and cleaned.

At approximately 1900 hours the order is given to move forward and serve the evening meal upon arrival at the company location. A two hour road march is anticipated. Before departing, the beans, meat, and water are placed into a kettle and cooked.

At 2100 hours potatoes and onions are added to the kettle while still on the march.

The field kitchen arrives at the company area at 2115 hours. Meat is placed into insulated containers to keep warm. The rest of the food is cooked and seasoned. Coffee is prepared.

Special drop canisters were available to distribute rations when other means of transportation were not feasible. *Courtesy Todd Gylsen Collection.*

Meal is served at 2145 hours.

The field kitchen moves to the rear, which is accomplished by 0100 hours, 26 July.

In the final analysis there was nothing unique about the German method of feeding their troops during offensive operations. It was almost identical to that employed by most of the major combatants it fought against. Simply put, the German infantryman in the attack carried enough rations on his person to sustain him until normal feeding operations could resume.

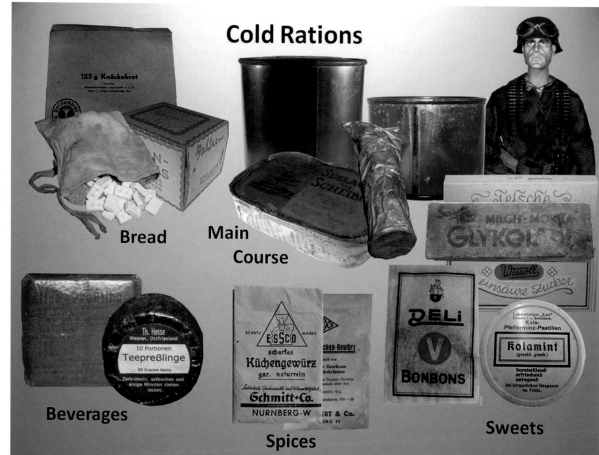

Cold Rations

Bread

Main Course

Beverages

Spices

Sweets

Some of the many cold components the German Commander could issue to his soldiers during offensive operations.

Some cold rations consisting of salami, butter, and powdered cheese.

Artificial Honey was a popular cold ration.

While fresh bread was the preferred component of the cold ration, canned bread could have been substituted. *Courtesy Thomas Bock.*

Dehydrated products, while lightweight, required long preparation times, which limited their usefulness as a cold ration for the individual soldier.

This soldier has tied his bread ration with a string and attached it to his uniform.

Honey and jam were commonly mentioned as a component of the cold ration. Glass jars were certainly not the most practical form of packaging for troops in the attack.

Two styles of March Drink containers issued to the German soldier. The cardstock tube held enough lemon flavored tablets for 2.5 liters of water.

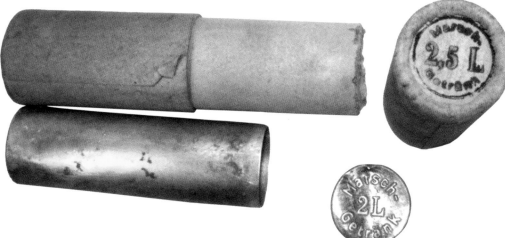

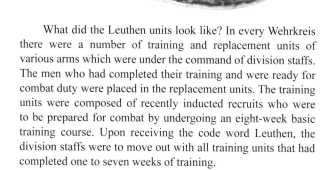

A can of Portuguese "Marca Nacional" sardines as described in the *U.S. Army Ration Report.*

B. *Special Feeding Challenges*

After the disastrous summer of 1944, with crushing defeats on both the Eastern and Western fronts, Germany turned to its last untapped reserves of manpower; the very young and very old. Until now the ration discussion has centered on standard German military formations with organic logistic assets. But these last ditch formations were anything but standard. The formation of the Volkssturm, the transition of organizations like the Hitler Youth into combat status, and calling up the Replacement Army all placed a tremendous strain on the already fragile logistic system.

The Volkssturm, or People's Army, was announced by Führer Decree on September 25, 1944. It's important to remember that Volkssturm formations reported to the National Socialist Party until committed to combat. In combat the military assumed tactical control over Volkssturm units. The Replacement Army provided logistical support for Volkssturm units until they came under military control. Volkssturm formations never exceeded battalion strength, and initially the Volkssturm was only to be employed in the immediate defense of their homes. However, it became standard practice to deploy Volkssturm units away from home. It's not my goal to provide an in depth look at the Volkssturm. Suffice it to say that the Volkssturm lacked proper clothing, weapons, training, and logistic capability. Volkssturm formations had no organic messing capability.

David Yelton's book *Hitler's Home Guard: Volkssturmmann* provides an excellent overview of ration supply for the Volkssturm. If fortunate, a Volkssturm unit would find itself attached to a standard military formation for ration support. But more often than not Volkssturm units had to improvise ration support. Some examples of how these Volkssturm units were fed are cited in Yelton's book:

(A). Eat at garrison mess halls.
(B). Utilize Party entities like the Red Cross or Peoples Welfare.
(C). Go to the citizens or local businesses in the area.
(D). Improvise a Field Kitchen.
(E). Obtain food using ration stamps.

Numerous small combat units organized from political or civil organizations like the Hitler Youth, Landwacht, Landesschützen, Reinforced Border Control Service, etc., were encountered in combat by the end of the war. Like the Volkssturm, most of these formations lacked any organic messing capability and were attached to standard military formations for support, if possible. Independent formations probably had to resort to the same procedures as the Volkssturm in order to feed themselves.

These last ditch political or civil formations were not the only units forced to improvise in order to feed themselves. By the end of the war Military Schools and Demonstration units, as well as the Training and Replacement units of the regular military were thrown into the fray in a futile attempt to stem the tide of defeat. Department of the Army Pamphlet NO. 20-201, *Military Improvisations during the Russian Campaign,* August 1951, provides the following information on the "Leuthen Project", which was the activation of Training and Replacement units to combat status:

What did the Leuthen units look like? In every Wehrkreis there were a number of training and replacement units of various arms which were under the command of division staffs. The men who had completed their training and were ready for combat duty were placed in the replacement units. The training units were composed of recently inducted recruits who were to be prepared for combat by undergoing an eight-week basic training course. Upon receiving the code word Leuthen, the division staffs were to move out with all training units that had completed one to seven weeks of training.

The Training and Replacement units, as well as the Schools, were essentially administrative formations tied to garrison locations for support. As such they lacked organic transport, weapons, and equipment, including field kitchens. These units were supported by fixed dining facilities. Given the appropriate time, the unit cadres could have transitioned these Training and Replacement units into combat effective formations. It's likely that some of these formations were able to acquire some mess equipment through the supply system or were attached to other units for support. If the unit conducted operations near its home station it could have utilized its garrison mess hall. In the end, operation Leuthen was an example of too little too late. Some units, like the SS NCO School in Metz, the armor training center at Paderborn, and Training and Replacement Brigade Grossdeutschland fought well, but for the most part Leuthen units simply disintegrated upon contact.

I think that the following paragraph in Alex Buchner's book *The German Infantry Handbook 1939-1945* captures the essence of the German ration system during the war:

Naturally, there were times of hunger and deprivation often enough, when supply problems or critical situations brought rations to a stop. But no soldier starved as long as he was with his troops (with the exception of the Sixth army's defeat in the Stalingrad basin). And it probably would have been impossible for half-starved German soldiers to have marched forward and back for thousands of kilometers through all of Europe in campaigns that went on for years.

By February 1945 commercial products were becoming scarce. *Bundesarchiv Bild 146-1996-030-12A, Foto: o. Ang. / Februar 1945, Licence CC-BY-SA 3.0.*

The spoils of war. These troops are sorting through captured Russian rations.

Feeding Volkssturm members from an insulated container. *Bundesarchiv Bild 146-1979-106-03, Foto: Michels / Dezember 1944, Licence CC-BY-SA 3.0.*

Christmas at a Volkssturm Headquarters. *Bundesarchiv Bild, Licence CC-BY-SA 3.0.*

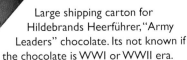

Large shipping carton for Hildebrands Heerführer, "Army Leaders" chocolate. Its not known if the chocolate is WWI or WWII era.

The ever popular Scho-ka-kola. *Courtesy Marcin Jonczyk Collection.*

Are you sure it's done?

A quick meal before heading out.
Courtesy Todd Gylsen Collection.

Cooking on the move. *Bundesarchiv Bild 1011-258-1319-36, Foto: Langhaus /1942, Licence CC-BY-SA 3.0.*

A chicken in every pot.

Stoves like this ARARA 37
allowed soldiers to heat up their
cold rations and prepare hot beverages.
Courtesy Militaria-Versand Emig.

12

GARRISON MESS HALLS AND PROVIDING MEALS IN THE FIELD

Anyone who has lived in, visited, or served in Germany is probably familiar with the military Kaserne (barracks). A Kaserne is much more than just a simple collection of barracks. A typical Kaserne consisted of Troop Barracks and Headquarters buildings surrounding a parade field. There were also aid stations, motor parks or stables, and a mess hall. Generally, a Kaserne was home to a Battalion or Regimental sized unit. When Hitler came to power a major effort was made to renovate older Kasernes and build new ones for the expansion of the military. The German Army that went to war in 1939 was one of the best trained, best cared for, and best fed in the world. The troop Mess Halls were equipped with the most modern appliances and served a variety of nutritionally balanced meals to the troops. It was operated by a combination of military and civil servant personnel. The Kaserne Mess Hall was only meant to feed troops in a garrison environment, but by the end of the war they were serving food to troops fighting in the immediate area. Here are some pictures of the modern German Mess Hall.

According to TM-E-30-451 *Handbook on German Military Forces*, German units that were deployed away from their garrisons were fed using mobile field kitchens, field ranges, fireless cookers, or Cooking Outfit 15.

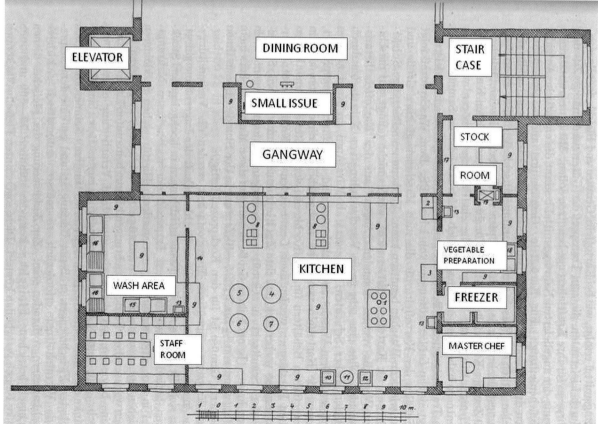

Floor plan of a
large kitchen:
1. Stove
2. Fish Oven
3. Baking and
Roasting Oven
4. Meat Vat 200 L.
5. Potato Vat 300 L.
6. Vegetable and
Coffee Vat 300 L.
7. Tilting Frying Pan
8. Warm Side
Board
9. Table
10. Sink
11. Chopping Block
12. Sink
13. Sinks
14. Cup Boards
15. Kitchen Sink
16. Dish Rinse
17. Shelves
18. Vegetable Sink
19. Elevator.

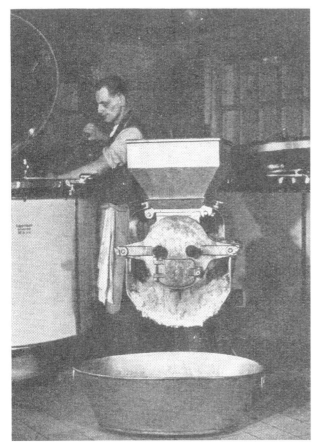

Strainer.

Bread slicer.

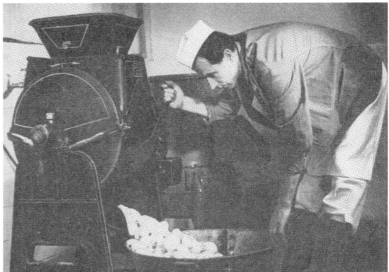

Potato and beet peeler.

Filling machine.

Food processor with attachments.

97

Machine to clean beets and potatoes.

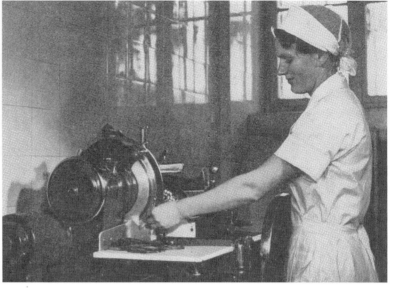

Slicer.

High performance food processor.

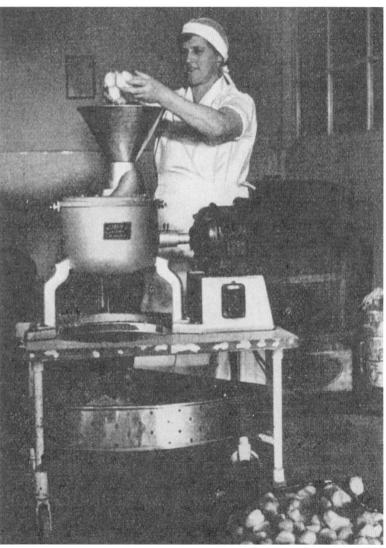

Food processor for cutting and shredding vegetable products.

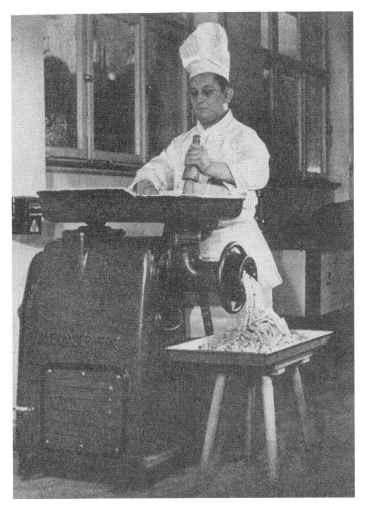

Cleaning dinner ware.

Processor for raw and cooked meat.

Serving steamed vegetables to the troops.

Dish washer.

This sequence of pictures shows a food storage area at a Field Hospital. Note the standard 1/1 canned food, sauerkraut, powdered cheese, fish cans, and alcohol.

A variety of German and foreign rolling field kitchens were employed by the German military. *Courtesy Todd Gylsen Collection.*

Small field range mounted on a truck. *Courtesy Todd Gylsen Collection.*

Horse drawn, truck drawn, or truck mounted field kitchens were issued to units with 50 or more personnel. The large kitchen would feed 125-225 personnel, the small kitchen 50-125 personnel. Smaller units that were not authorized a field kitchen were issued fireless cookers or Cooking Outfit 15.

The rolling field kitchen consisted of a detachable limber and trailer, on which the kitchen was mounted. It was drawn by horses. The limber was used to carry most of the supplies, including the iron rations. After the kitchen was set up the limber was used to get additional supplies. Sometimes motorized units were issued just the field kitchen and used a light truck to transport the kitchen and function as the limber.

The range mounted on the trailer can burn coal, coke, briquettes, or wood. The range was used as a fireless cooker, especially on the move. Fires were built in fire boxes, and as soon as the steam started to escape from the safety valve, the fire was banked and allowed to go out. This saved fuel and prevented smoke from revealing the unit's position. This also allowed meals to be prepared while on the move.

A. The main part of the range was a large stew kettle. The cooking capacity of the kettle of the large range was 46 gallons. The small range could cook 29 gallons of soup, stew, boiled meat, or vegetables at one time.

B. The coffee kettle on the large range could prepare 24 gallons of coffee and 16 gallons in the small one. There was a faucet to draw off the coffee. Some ranges are equipped with a broiler. All had a separate fire box, but used the same chimney.

Large field range mounted on a truck.

Troops lining up to eat at a truck drawn field range. *Bundesarchiv Bild 1011-755-0164-12, Foto: Bieling /1940, Licence CC-BY-SA 3.0.*

Field ranges were also provided for motorized units. Essentially it was identical to the rolling field kitchen, except for being mounted on the back of a truck.

Large or small fireless cookers were provided for units of less than 60 men. The large fireless cooker outfit, which weighed 77 pounds, had an insert kettle of 25 liters capacity. The small fireless cooker outfit weighed 53 pounds and had an insert kettle of 15 liters capacity. A cooking fork, butcher's knife, ladle, and coffee sieve completed the outfit.

The Cooking Outfit 15 was issued to groups smaller than those using the fireless cooker. It consisted of three nesting pots of 9, 10, and 12 liters capacity with a ladle, 10 plates, and 10 combination fork-spoons.

This may be an example of a fireless cooker. *Courtesy Todd Gylsen Collection.*

Die Goulaschkanone, a monthly newspaper published for the Field Cooks.

A humorous view of cooking in the field.

This appears to be the Cooking Outfit 15. *Courtesy Todd Gylsen Collection.*

The author was informed that this type of stove came with a pot which is inserted into the stove and used for cooking. *Courtesy Todd Gylsen Collection.*

13

THE GERMAN AND AMERICAN RATION ORGANIZATIONS: A COMPARISON

In the light of history, just how well did the German Ration system fare when compared to that of its Western enemies, like the United States? If asked most historians, collectors, and reenactors would probably give the U.S. system very high marks. By comparison how would the German system fare? From some of the comments I've read in books, on forums, etc., I would guess not so well. Was the U.S. system as good as many believe it to be? Conversely, was the German system as antiquated as many believe it to be? This chapter will take a closer look at both organizations and sort out fact from fiction. I would like to express my gratitude to the staff of the U.S. Army Quartermaster Museum, Ft. Lee, VA, who assisted in the preparation of this chapter. It's probably appropriate to add a short explanation of U.S. ration terminology at this point.

A Ration-The term used in the United States Army for a meal provided to troops which is prepared using fresh, refrigerated, or frozen foods. "A" ration meals may be served in dining facilities or prepared by field kitchens.

B Ration-Term used in the United States military for a meal provided to troops prepared using canned or preserved ingredients.

C Ration-The term used in the United States Army for the individual canned, pre-cooked, or prepared wet ration. It was issued to U.S. military land forces when the "A" Ration and "B" Ration were impractical or not available.

D Ration-The term used in the United States military for an emergency ration consisting of bars of concentrated chocolate combined with other ingredients to provide high calorie content.

K Ration-Term used in the United States military for the individual assault ration for paratroopers and other specialized light infantry forces.

In September 1945, the U.S. Army issued a report titled *German Clothing, Equipment, and Rations*. The report summarizes the major differences between the U.S. and German ration organizations. While not particularly damning of the German organization, it does manage to avoid pointing out any shortcomings in the U.S. organization. Here are the comments from the report.

The U. S. Quartermaster Corps supplies troops in the field with the 'B' rations whenever possible, even under combat conditions where supply problems are not too difficult. This consists primarily of normal civilian diet made up of nonperishable items. Sometimes it is possible to supply "A" rations instead. The "A" ration is practically the same as the "B" ration, but some fresh foods are substituted in place of the nonperishable items.

The Germans used the "A" and "B" types of rations much more extensively than the U.S. troops. These Rations I, II, III, and IV did not always contain all the nutritive qualities needed by the individual and some scurvy and other deficiency diseases did occur. The chief reasons for this were local procurement and the lack of a master menu. All the rations were not shipped from Germany to the area where they were needed, but were locally procured whenever possible. Thus, German troops often got an excess of some types of food and were deficient in others. This led to an unbalanced diet, even though definite amounts of each type of food (such as meat, bread, coffee, etc.) were carefully specified.

The Germans, too, were sometimes deficient in calories. There was no easily distributed universal combat ration and so when the supply situation got difficult; it often happened that food could not be brought forward. In fact it was policy to stop advancing rations if it might slow down the supply of ammunition, fuels, and lubricants. The German "iron ration" could not take care of this situation adequately. Like the U.S. "D" ration, it was intended only for emergencies. It could not be eaten except on orders of the company commander or platoon leader and thus was not comparable to the U. S. combat rations. The portion carried by the individual soldiers consisted only of canned meat and biscuits and so can hardly be considered a balanced diet.

Until 1944, the typical German Infantry Company had a Supply Train, Commissary Unit I, and Commissary Unit II tasked with the mission of feeding the troops. The Supply Train consisted of 14 personnel, two bicycles, three two-horse wagons (or three single-horse infantry carts), one four-horse supply wagon, and one four-horse field kitchen. Commissary Unit I had three personnel, one bicycle, and one two-horse mess wagon. Commissary Unit II consisted of four personnel, one motorcycle, and one three-ton truck. During offensive operations the Battalion Staff directed the efforts of the Company Supply Train and Commissary Unit I. The Regimental Staff directed the efforts of the Commissary Unit II. In positional warfare the trains generally set up 3-5 Kilometers behind the Company sector.

In 1944, the trend in the German military was toward centralizing logistic functions. Volksgrenadier Divisions formed in 1944 were organized with the infantry battalions having supply platoons instead of battalion and company trains, and divisional services were combined into a divisional supply regiment. The goal was to reduce manpower and free company commanders of logistic responsibilities.

The German soldier was normally fed three times a day: breakfast, lunch, and dinner, with the possibility of supplements in between. It was the goal to get at least one hot meal a day to the troops, usually lunch. The hot meals were usually served from the field kitchen or pushed to the forward positions in thermos-like containers. Cold rations were provided for two meals a day or longer when it was anticipated that a hot meal could not be provided, i.e. during the attack. The actual composition and palatability of the hot meals depended on many factors: training of cooks, time available, and availability and variety of rations supplied through the system, as well as the availability of fresh produce, livestock, and other food stuffs on the local economy. As noted in *German Clothing, Equipment, and Rations*, the Germans were more focused on getting hot meals (A or B Ration) to the troops than the U.S. military was. Because of its reliance on the Field Kitchen no serious attempt was made to develop prepackaged meals for the troops. In situations where serving hot meals wasn't practical, a selection of cold components drawn from unit stocks was issued instead.

Doctrinally, the U.S. Army conducted mess operations in a manner similar to the German Army. Each Company was equipped with a field kitchen: either a mobile version mounted on 2 1/2-ton trucks or a static version which consisted of a mess tent, tables, burner units, trays, trash cans, etc., all packed into the back of a truck. Obviously it took the U.S.

mess section a lot longer to get in a position to feed using the static version. In most other respects the U.S. and German militaries were remarkably similar when it came to feeding their troops. Both armies had schools for cooks, research laboratories, procurement agencies, mobile bakeries, butcher units, and utilized dehydrated and refrigerated food products, etc. While the U.S. military didn't operate unit level kantines, they were well served by the Post Exchange system. The following information was extracted from TM 10-205, *Mess Management and Training*, October 3, 1944, which is a detailed look at U.S. Army field mess operations in the combat zone.

"**Menu**: When operating in the field, the messing unit is faced with a different situation from that of a unit in the garrison. When supplies arrive, the mess sergeant can inventory them to see what is on hand, and break them up into as practical a menu as circumstances permit. The menu must be designed to suit the mess kit and the conditions under which the troops will be fed.

Plan for feeding: The regimental supply officer determines the best plan for feeding his regiment. He must consider the method of distribution prescribed by the division or higher authority, the ration cycle, the tactical situation, the terrain, the weather, the availability of trucks and routes, and the traffic conditions in general. When his plan has been approved by the regimental commander, it is made known to the battalion supply officers and the commanders of companies and other attachments not parts of battalions. The details of the plan are sent to the company commanders as early as practicable so that they can give the necessary instructions to the mess personnel of the different companies in time. In the absence of other instructions each company will be responsible for drawing its rations at the regimental supply point and for solving its own problems as to where the meal will be prepared and how the

Troops lining up for food at a static field kitchen. *U.S. Army Signal Corp.*

company troops will be fed. The feeding plan includes any of the following instructions that might be appropriate:

The location of the kitchen bivouac(s) (usually in the regimental-train bivouac).

The place where each meal will be prepared (in the regimental-train bivouac, in the advanced regimental or battalion kitchen areas, or in company mess location).

The number of kitchen and baggage vehicles per battalion to be used to deliver food to troops (usually one truck per company - two per battalion when necessary to conserve transportation or keep down traffic).

Any additional items of supply to be sent forward to troops.

The time kitchen trucks will leave the bivouac to deliver meals to troops.

Any restrictions upon movement.

Preparation: The Mess sergeant should be notified when the supplies are ready for distribution. Company supplies are turned over at the regimental distribution point to details from company mess groups, who carry them to their kitchens. If the kitchen locations are beyond hand-carrying distance from the distribution point, one or more kitchen trucks of a battalion are used for delivery. When the rations are received at the company kitchens, they are divided into three meals, and the menu and recipes to be used are worked out. Each company's mess detail prepares the meals on its field ranges:

At the kitchen locations in the regimental-train bivouac,

At battalion kitchen bivouacs located nearer the troops than the regimental-train bivouac,

At some forward location near the company, or

In the kitchen truck either while in movement or at a halt.

It will seldom be feasible to advance the kitchens to the locations of units which are dispersed for combat. During combat, meals are usually prepared at a rear kitchen location. This is usually in the regimental-train bivouac, but sometimes

A field kitchen mounted on the back of a Deuce and a Half truck. *U.S. Army Signal Corp.*

in the battalion kitchen bivouac. When possible, cooked food should be sent forward under cover of darkness. Plans should provide for timing the preparations of supper so that the trucks carrying it to the troops leave the field-train bivouacs just after dark and for timing breakfast so that trucks can return before daylight.

The fundamentals of cooking are the same in field as in garrison. The chief difference is in the equipment used. Since Field Range M-1937, a gasoline burning range can be operated with wood if necessary; the cook should be trained in the handling of both types of fuel. Dishes that require long preparation should be avoided when cooking time is limited."

So at least on paper the goal of the U.S. Army was to provide hot meals to the G.I. as long as combat conditions allowed. However, despite all the good intentions it appears that the U.S. military relied heavily on packaged meals for the troops in lieu of preparing hot meals. The two most common packaged meals issued to the G.I. were the C-Ration and K-Ration. The majority of the information about the C- and K-Ration was obtained from the following two web articles (no authors): *K-ration*, http://en.wikipedia.org/wiki/K-ration and *C-ration*, http: //en.wikipedia. org/wiki/C-ration.

The C-Ration was the preeminent individual canned, pre-cooked, or prepared wet ration issued to the G.I. in lieu of prepared meals from the Field Kitchen. Each individual meal consisted of one M-Unit (canned meat) and one B-Unit (bread and dessert can). Each daily ration for a soldier consisted of six 12 ounce (340 grams) cans (three M-Units and three B-Units).

The cans were 3.5 inches high and 3 inches in diameter with an opening strip and soldered key. The finish on the cans changed from an aluminum finish to a gold lacquer, and ended the war painted in drab green. The can products were initially identified by paper labels which frequently fell off. This practice was replaced by stenciling the product information on the can. The daily caloric value was in the 3,500 range. The C-Ration had a very limited menu:

The M-Unit (Meat): Meat Hash, Meat Stew with Vegetables, Meat Stew with Beans, Meat and Spaghetti in Tomato Sauce (1943), Chopped Ham, Egg, and Potato (1944), Meat and Noodles (1944), Pork and Rice (1944), Frankfurters and Beans (1944), Pork and Beans (1944), Ham and Lima Beans (1944), Chicken and Vegetables (1944) and Beef Stew with Vegetables (1945).

The B-Unit (Bread and Dessert): Five Hardtack crackers (1944 reduced to 4), 3 sugar tablets, 3 Dextrose Energy tablets (in 1941replaced with loose candy) (in 1944 loose candy replaced with a candy disk or cookie sandwich), and a beverage mix (instant coffee, powdered lemon drink, bouillon soup powder) (orange drink powder, sweetened cocoa powder, and grape drink powder added in 1944).

The B-Unit (Breakfast): Introduced in 1944 this unit consisted of pre-mixed oatmeal cereal and was usually paired with the Chopped Ham, Egg, and Potato M-Unit.

Accessory Pack: The brown paper accessory pack contained sugar tablets, water purification tablets (in 1945 replaced with salt tablets), wooden spoon, chewing gum, cigarettes, matches, P-38 can opener, and toilet paper.

The C-Ration was never intended to be issued for more than 3-5 days without supplementation with other rations. Unfortunately, the G.I. was often forced to subsist on C-Rations for weeks on end. Given the limited

The 1943 C-Ration. *U.S. Army Signal Corp.*

The 1945 C-Ration. *U.S. Army Signal Corp.*

menu and the fact that "A" and "B" rations prepared by the Field Kitchen were often identical to the C-Ration menu, it's little wonder that the G.I. quickly grew tired of C-Rations. The monotonous menu, the unpalatable nature of several of the meals, and the fact that the cans were bulky and cumbersome all added to the unpopularity of the C-Ration among the G.I.s. The C-Ration would undergo several revisions, and continued to be the military's major individual ration until officially phased out in 1958. The C-Ration was replaced in 1958 with the Meal Combat Individual (MCI), which was derived from and very similar to the original C-Ration, and in fact continued to be called "C-Rations" by American troops throughout its service life (1958-1980).

On the other side of the hill, the Germans issued cold components of the standard rations when the Field Kitchen could not support the soldier with hot meals. Theoretically, the German soldier could end up with a meal very similar to the U.S. C-Ration. In both armies the daily ration was assembled by taking available components and packaging them into some type of balanced meal for the soldier. For the U.S. Commander, it was simply a matter of pulling three "B" and three "M" units, plus an Accessory Pack per soldier. For the German Commander the approach was identical, except that the German rations were not conveniently segregated into nutritionally balanced groupings. This probably meant additional time to plan and issue the daily ration to the German soldier, though I doubt if it was significant. If it became necessary to feed using C type rations for an extended period of time, the German system offered some advantages, the most obvious being the potential variety of meals

This 850 gram can of bread, 850 gram can of meat/vegetables, Sho-ka-kola, and lemonade powder was equivalent to the daily C-Ration issued to a G.I. This combination provided roughly 3,500 calories, in line with the caloric value of the C-Ration.

it could offer. The C-Ration only offered 12 different meat entrees, compared to over 50 canned meat entrees in the German system. The Germans also stocked a wide selection of cheese and fish products that could be substituted for the meat entrees, thus offering an even wider selection for the soldier. For soldiers of both armies, and especially the common infantryman, this type of ration proved to be bulky and cumbersome.

The U.S. Army conducted evaluations on some of the components found in the C-Ration against similar German products. The results were published in *German Rations and Subsistence Items*, Quartermaster Food and Container Institute for the Armed Forces, May 1947. The German examples compared favorably with their U.S. equivalents:

Topic	Lentils/Beef/ Potatoes	U.S. Meat/Vegetable Stew
Calories/100 g.	106.00	127.00
Moisture %	76.60	72.70
Protein %	7.00	11.90
Fat %	3.80	5.40
Ash %	1.30	unk
Carbohydrate % By Diff	11.30	7.90
Thiamin mcg/g.	0.29	0.47
Riboflavin mcg/g.	0.59	1.41
Niacin mcg/g.	17.06	26.20

Topic	Potatoes,Peas,Pork	U.S. Meat/ Vegetable Stew
Calories/100 g.	116.00	128.00
Moisture %	79.00	72.90
Protein %	3.40	11.90
Fat %	7.20	5.40
Ash %	1.00	unk
Carbohydrate % By Diff	9.40	7.90
Thiamin mcg/g.	0.57	0.47
Riboflavin mcg/g.	0.49	1.41
Niacin mcg/g.	9.51	17.06

Topic	Blood Sausage	U.S. Pork Sausage Meat
Calories/100 g.	284.00	295.00
Moisture %	57.20	55.40
Protein %	12.60	15.30
Fat %	24.00	25.90
Ash %	1.80	unk
Carbohydrate % By Diff	4.40	0
Thiamin mcg/g.	0.14	2.07
Riboflavin mcg/g.	0.70	2.41
Niacin mcg/g.	9.51	3.00

Topic	Pork, Cured, Ground	U.S. Pork Luncheon Meat
Moisture %	32.60	55.90
Protein %	10.10	15.10
Fat %	56.00	24.90

The other packaged meal issued to the G.I. was the K-Ration. The K-Ration was originally manufactured as an emergency daily ration for Paratroopers, Tankers, etc., but was adopted as a lightweight, short term (3-5 days), complete field ration for all front line troops. A single K-Ration consisted of three components: Breakfast meal, Dinner meal, and Supper meal. The daily allowance was strictly enforced as one K-Ration per man per day. The caloric value of the K-Ration (all three meals) was in the 2,800-3,000 range.

The K-Ration packaging consisted of a cardboard outer carton and a waterproof wax cardboard inner carton. Several styles were produced. The entrees and meat came packed in a small, round metal can. The menus were:

Breakfast Unit: Entrée (chopped ham and eggs or veal loaf), biscuits, fruit or cereal bar, water purification tablets, cigarettes, chewing gum, instant coffee and sugar.

Dinner Unit: Entrée (processed cheese, ham, or ham and cheese), biscuits, 15 malted milk tablets (early) or 5 caramels (late), sugar, salt, cigarettes, matches, chewing gum, and a powdered beverage package.

Supper Unit: Canned Meat (chicken pate, pork luncheon meat with carrot and apple, beef and pork loaf, or sausages), biscuits,

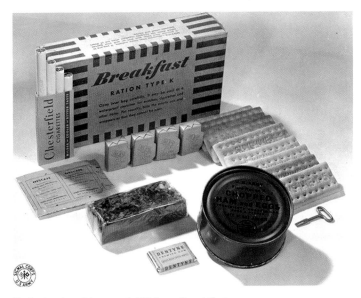

K- Ration breakfast meal. *U.S. Army Signal Corp.*

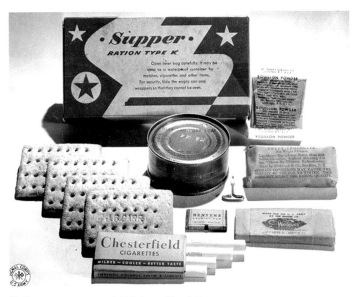

K- Ration supper meal. *U.S. Army Signal Corp.*

K- Ration dinner meal. *U.S. Army Signal Corp.*

2 oz. D Ration chocolate bar, chocolate bar, toilet paper, cigarettes, matches, chewing gum, and a powdered or bouillon soup.

The K-Ration, like the C-Ration, found itself the target of much criticism. A major criticism was its inadequate caloric and vitamin content. During field trials the portion rate for the K-Ration was determined based on a soldier marching over cleared roads in good weather. It appeared that the military planners didn't factor in the effects of weather, terrain, combat, etc., when they established the one man, one meal a day rule. Despite evidence that G.I.s suffered weight loss and vitamin deficiencies when fed K-Rations for an extended period, the policy was never modified. Unlike the German system, which allowed the unit commander to adjust portion rates based on weather, physical activity, etc., no such policy was in place for the U.S. commander. In 1948 the K-Ration was declared obsolete. The Germans did not field a ration comparable to the K-Ration, but were generally complimentary about the concept.

In 1939 the U.S. Field Ration-D was adopted as a reserve and emergency ration. It was designed as a small, high calorie ration sufficient for daily use. From the beginning its purpose as a standalone Emergency ration was misunderstood, and by 1944 it was utilized as a supplement for other rations. By the end of the war it was replaced as a combat food by the C-Ration and K-Ration. Through misuse and the lack of a coherent policy on its purpose, the D-Ration proved to be a failure. In the *U.S. Army Ration Report* the D-Ration is compared to German Pemmican. While the German High Command praised Pemmican as an emergency ration, its actual acceptance by the German soldier was less than praiseworthy. The most widely distributed German Emergency ration was of course the Half Iron Ration, which was issued to all front line troops.

One major criticism leveled at the German ration system by U.S. logisticians during the war was that it lacked a "Master Menu". So what is the "Master Menu" and why is it so special? In the small prewar U.S. Army, soldiers were fed based on a so called garrison ration. Each unit mess was provided so much money based on unit strength, food prices, etc. Mess personnel would work out the monthly menu and purchase the food at local markets. The major issue with this system was it wasn't based on the nutritional needs of the soldier, but on the mess officer's ability to manage funds. When the United States mobilized for war the concept of the garrison ration was mostly eliminated. The "Master Menu" took its place. Under this concept the Pentagon or one of the nine Army Service Commands (ASC) would publish the monthly menu for that particular command. Under this concept, when steak was served at Base "A" of ASC One, steak would also be served at Base "B" of the same ASC. The individual ASCs each had different menus to prevent overtaxing the supply system.

One of the most significant changes under the Master Menu concept was that the makeup of the meals was driven by the nutritional needs of

The U.S. Army D- Ration. *U.S. Army Signal Corp.*

the soldier and not by finances. The usual daily allowance was determined to be 3,000-4,000 calories a day. The monthly menu reflected food stuffs from all the major food groups based on calories, vitamins, fats, starch, proteins, ethnic and regional tastes, area of operation, and availability of stocked items, as well as locally available products. Another major change was that feeding the troops could no longer be accomplished by going to the local market. The issue of ration supply could only be addressed through a centralized global logistics system. The fact that unit mess personnel no longer had to concern themselves with what to feed the soldiers on a daily basis was also seen as an advantage.

The Germans did, in fact, utilize a Master Menu system of sorts. Starting at the highest levels, the planning division of the OKH submitted their requirements to the Ministry of Food on the 1ˢᵗ of September for the coming year. The common food materials were obtained from various manufacturers who submitted samples for examination and testing by the OKH. The conditions upon which purchases and delivery would be made were set up by the OKH. The purchase and procurement of raw materials by the manufacturers was also controlled by the OKH and various committees of the Ministry for Food.

Monthly the OKH would send out menus in an effort to direct the use of available foods, so as to make the most of the varieties and to provide tasty, nutritious, and satisfactory meals. Monthly inventories of foodstuffs in the warehouses were sent to the OKH. These reports were used as the basis in making out the Menus. However, in some cases theory could not be put into practice, as foods had to be used, at times, before they spoiled, and in other cases to await the new harvest. The bread, meat, cheese, fat, and sugar portions were generally stable. The vegetable portions were driven by availability and controlled by monthly directives (Feldkostzusammenstellungen for the Field Army and Speisenzusammenstellungen for the Replacement Army) issued by the OKH. The vegetable portion was based on available supplies, military strategy, climate, and number of personnel.

It appears that menus were formatted in a variety of ways. The 30 day menu would identify the specific food item, the portion size, and how many times in the 30 day period it could be served. Additional menus were published that identified what meal was served on specific days, etc. Whether these menus were published specifically for each theater of operation or command is unknown. Examples of an OKH 14 day eating plan and 21 Day Magazinverpflegung plan are shown below. The term Magazinverpflegung refers to the concept of supplying all ration requirements through a depot system without having to rely on local resources. In the case of the OKH plan, backup documentation accompanied it which provided detailed information, including recipes. The planning process involved in publishing a master menu was essentially the same in both armies.

In *A Survey of German Wartime Food Processing, Packaging and Allocation*, the authors made the following assessment of the German planning process: "By means of procurement laws and regulations

the quality, kinds, and amounts of foodstuffs required were assured. Speiseplänen issued every month made it possible for the OKH to direct the use of potatoes and vegetables in the Army rations and to make sure that foods were used to best advantage, in so far as possible."

So in the final assessment, how did the German Ration organization stack up against the U.S. organization? Doctrinally and operationally there weren't many significant differences between the two armies. When it comes to the availability of food stuffs, quality of packaging, the quality of the food stuffs, and the standardization of products, the edge goes to the United States. This is understandable, since we are talking about a U.S. industrial base that was largely unaffected by the war, versus one that from 1943 on was subjected to ever increasing assaults from the air, and in the end from the ground. However, from the samples of food items evaluated in the *U.S. Army Ration Report*, the quality of the German products wasn't all bad, and in some instances better than their U.S. equivalents.

In the actual execution of mess operations I would probably give the edge to the Germans. The priority in both armies was to get hot food to the troops as often as possible. Based on numerous assessments conducted on the effectiveness of C-Rations and K-Rations, it's evident that, for whatever reason, far too many U.S. units relied on them (C-Rations and K-Rations) as the primary means of feeding the G.I. This had a detrimental effect on morale and health for the units involved. As an emergency ration for short term use the C-Ration, D-Ration, and K-Ration were certainly excellent products. However, the Germans proved much better at routinely providing hot food to their troops, and the act of issuing cold components outside the standard feeding plan was only viewed as a temporary measure. Even though the Germans admired the concept and packaging of the K-Ration, as a short term emergency ration they never produced an equivalent ration. This might be due to a lack of production capabilities, or simply because they didn't see a necessity. However, as a long term ration, a role it was not designed for, the K- Ration lacked the calories and vitamins required without supplements. If American commanders had the authority to make adjustments to ration portion rates, like their German counterparts, the negative health impacts associated with extended use of the K-Ration could have been mitigated.

On balance neither system was perfect, but both were certainly worthy of praise. The U.S. logisticians have to be commended for the professional and decisive manner in which they transitioned from a peacetime ration operation, totally unsuited for global warfare, to one envied by both enemies and allies alike. The German logisticians performed admirably under conditions few armies in history have had to endure. By mid-1944, with pressure coming from all sides, there certainly wasn't much for the German Landser to smile about. Yet it's hard to find a picture of German soldiers gathered around their beloved Goulaschkanone where they aren't sporting a smile.

Aus den Speisenplänen für die Sommerzeit.		
	Mittagskost	Abendkost
Sonntag	Einlaufsuppe Schweinebraten Gurkensalat Kartoffeln Rhabarbergrieß	Tee Schinken 100 g Butter 50 g
Montag Eintopf- und Feldküchen- gericht	Saures Graupengericht aus Rindfleisch Graupen Kartoffeln Sauren oder Gewürzgurken	Kaffee Geräucherter Seefisch 150 g Margarine 50 g
Dienstag	Frikandellen Braune Tunke Schotengemüse Kartoffeln	Tee Dauerwurst 125 g Schmalz 50 g

A portion of an Oberkommando des Heeres (OKH) 14 day menu for the summer.

Speisenplan für 21 Tage Magazinverpflegung.			
1. Woche.			
Fleisch	**Gemüse**	**Gewürz**	**Edelsoja**
1. Tag fr. Schweine- fleisch	+ Erbsen	+ getr. Majoran	
2. Tag fr. Rindfleisch	+ Reis	+ Hefeextrakt	+ Edelsoja
3. „ fr. Schweine- fleisch	+ getr. Kartoffeln Sauerkraut	+ Wacholderbeeren	
4. „ fr. Rindfleisch	+ Graupen	+ getr. Suppengrün	+ Edelsoja
5. „ Konserven- fleisch	+ getr. Gemüse und getr. Kartoffeln	+ Hefeextrakt	+ Edelsoja
6. „ fr. Schweine- fleisch	+ saure Linsen	+ Essig und Suppengrün	
7. „ fr. Rindfleisch	+ Teigwaren	+ Tomatenmark	
1. Woche =			
3 × fr. Schweinefleisch	2 × Hülsenfrüchte	1 × getr. Majoran	3 × Edelsoja
3 × fr. Rindfleisch	1 × Teigwaren	2 × Hefeextrakt	
1 × Konservenfleisch	1 × Graupen	1 × Wacholderb.	
	1 × Reis	1½ × getr. Suppen- grün	
	½ × Sauerkraut	½ × Essig	
	½ × getr. Gemüse	1 × Tomatenmark	
	1 × getr. Kartoffeln		

The 21 day Magazinverpflegung.

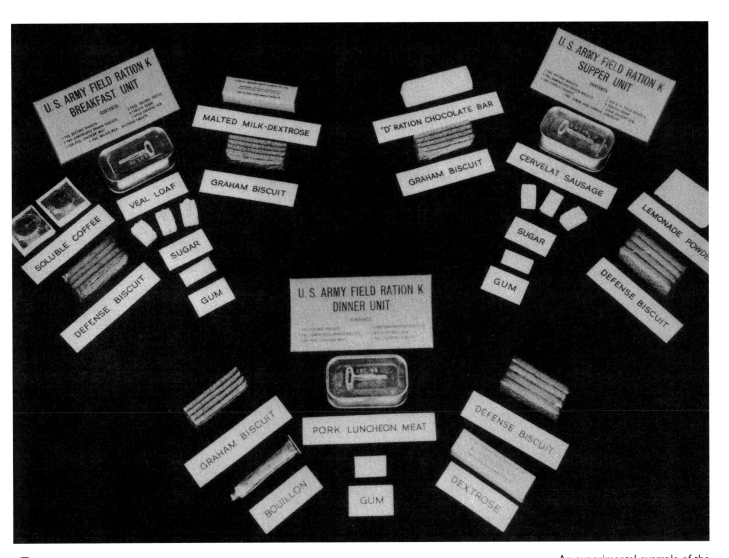

Labels visible in image:

U.S. ARMY FIELD RATION K
BREAKFAST UNIT

U.S. ARMY FIELD RATION K
SUPPER UNIT

MALTED MILK-DEXTROSE

"D" RATION CHOCOLATE BAR

GRAHAM BISCUIT

CERVELAT SAUSAGE

GRAHAM BISCUIT

VEAL LOAF

LEMONADE POWDER

SOLUBLE COFFEE

SUGAR

GUM

SUGAR

DEFENSE BISCUIT

GUM

DEFENSE BISCUIT

U.S. ARMY FIELD RATION K
DINNER UNIT

GRAHAM BISCUIT

PORK LUNCHEON MEAT

DEFENSE BISCUIT

BOUILLON

GUM

DEXTROSE

An experimental example of the K-Ration. The flat style cans were preferable to round cans; unfortunately, U.S. industry could not fulfill the requirement. *U.S. Army Signal Corp.*

German POWs being issued C-Rations. *U.S. Army Signal Corp.*

The Germans prided themselves on their ability to get hot food to the troops. *Courtesy Todd Gylsen Collection.*

This picture shows the 500 gram can of ADA cheese, fresh bread, and a can of fish. *Courtesy Todd Gylsen Collection.*

Man! What the hell is this? *Courtesy Kevin Barrett.*

Rations being received and sorted in the field. *Courtesy OSTFRONT Militaria.*

I

CEREAL AND BAKED PRODUCTS

Since the publication of *Rations of the German Wehrmacht in World War II* in 2010, a variety of new and interesting ration items have surfaced, as well as new information from British wartime sources. In Volume I the major food groups were the focus of the chapters, while annexes were used to cover special subjects. In this volume the food groups are covered as special subjects in the annexes. The most important new references used in writing the Annexes were *A Survey of German Wartime Food Processing, Packaging and Allocation*, Part I and II, 27 September 1945 and *A Survey of the Practices of the German Can Industry during the Second World War*. The following additional report was also used in the preparation of this annex: *Production of Flour and Bread in Germany* and *Manufacture of Pulp Paper and Related Products from Wood in Western Germany*. Owners of grocery stores and delicatessens were served by a number of trade publications to include the *Dekofei*, a trade paper which was published till the end of the war. This particular trade paper discussed the state of commodities, rationing, pricing, and availability of food stuffs, etc. Several copies were used as references in writing this book.

Bread was a major component of the individual daily diet in Germany. In 1938 there were 116,282 bakeries and 800 bread factories in Germany. Most of the bakeries were small operations employing 1-5 workers, but these small firms accounted for 82% of all bread production in Germany. The average pure rye bread was the most popular bread in Germany, followed by a type of bread containing 70% rye flour and 30% wheat flour. The intelligence reports were quick to point out that Germans enjoyed rye bread, a sympathy not shared in the United States.

Bulk delivered flour, farina, and feed were packed in 100 kg jute sacks. Later in the war ersatz materials and paper were mixed with the jute, which reduced the strength of the bags by as much as 75%. Flour was generally sold to the consumer packed in paper bags composed of two layers of paper. Prior to the war three layers of paper were used. The most common bags were of 0.5, 1.5, 1, 2, and 2.5 kg capacity. A paper strip about 0.25 inches wide and 9 inches long with two metal fastenings were stamped on the opposite ends of the paper strip; this strip was then placed at the top of the flour sack and three or four folds of the sack made over the strip. Closure of the metal seals was then completed. The whole packing process was done manually. Metal cans of various sizes were also used to package flour.

Here is a summary of flour types used by the Germans from 1934-1945:

Rye: 610, 700, 815, 997, 1150, 1370, 1600, 1790, and 1800.
Barley: 2000
Wheat: 405, 450, 502, 550, 563, 630, 790, 812, 1050, 1100, 1350, 1470, 1600, 1700, 1950, and 2800.

From *Production of Flour and Bread in Germany*:

"As a matter of policy the German government appears to have preferred storage of grain rather than flour, because of the greater stability of the former. During the war there seems to have been no production of flour over current requirements and in consequence storage problems were not encountered, even with very high extraction flours. Army flour was however specified to be of not more than 14% moisture content and some flour for use in Africa was stated to have been dried to 12%."

The formulas or recipes for the German military breads were in general representative of the average commercial practice. There were two general types of bread produced for the Wehrmacht and Waffen SS: front fresh bread (packaged or unpackaged) and canned bread for naval units and troops in isolated regions. Bread produced for the military by field bakeries had to weigh 1.8 kg and from commercial bakeries 1.5 kg after baking and cooling. Packaged front fresh bread is standard Army bread packed in a sterile protecting wrap to prevent mold. When packed, the bags had to be in accordance with High Command specifications, which state that the inside wrap consists of a single layer of cellophane AST or Natron double seal (waxed paper) and an outside wrap of brown wood paper, both of which were heat sealed in the shape of a bag, with unsealed ends. The bread was carefully inserted into the bag using a putting device made from plate or paperboard, being careful not to damage the bread. Gummed strips were then used to seal the wraps. If the materials designated by the High Command were unavailable, front fresh bread would be packed in the following manner:

Pack the bread in cellophane paper. The bottom of the bread is put on the cellophane sheet; the two ends (longitudinal) are rolled together, on the front sides the cellophane is folded, and the closures are turned down to the bottom of the bread.

Over this wrap there is laid a protective envelope of brown wood paper. The bread packed in the cellophane is placed bottom side down on the brown wood paper, the two ends (longitudinal) are rolled together, the ends are folded, turned upwards to the front side of the bread, and sealed by a gummed strip (4-5 cm in breadth).

After the front fresh bread was packed, it was sterilized by baking it until the inside of the loaf attained a temperature of 85 degrees Celsius without damaging the packaging or opening the seals.

In order to identify the day of baking for front fresh bread, the shaped dough was inscribed with a date stamp like normal army bread. The date and month are marked in the following manner (Aug. 15 = 158). If possible add a period to separate the day and month. If the day of manufacture can be marked on the bag (gum stamp) in the same manner of notation, this is preferred. The bags must be marked before filling.

The finished packaged front fresh bread is loosely loaded into wagons for transport in the same manner as usual fresh bread. Special care must be taken to avoid damaging the packaging.

The following specifications from a contract between the Wuelfeler Brotfabrik and an Army depot dated Oct. 17, 1944, provides some insight into the standards established by the military for commercial firms to adhere to:

Bread units weighing 1.8 kg must be obtained from 1.287 kg of flour (715 grams of flour per 1 kg bread).
The dough going into the oven must weigh 2050 grams.
The bread coming out of the oven must weigh 1840 grams.
After cooling 24 hours the bread must weigh 1.8 kg.
On the second day the bread shall not lose more than 20 grams.
On the third day after baking, the bread shall not lose more than 34 grams.
It shall not lose more than 45 grams thereafter.
Bread shall be stamped as to date of manufacture by marking the shaped dough. In the case of front line breads the dates are marked on the outside of the packaging.
The prices paid were 8 pfennig for unwrapped bread and an additional 6 pfennig for packing and sterilization should front line bread be required.

During the Polish campaign the German Army produced bread that had been baked in cartons having two aluminum foil layers between three paper layers (ECO Package). The cartons were formed and one end left open. These cartons were placed in metal containers, and enough dough to yield a 500 gram loaf was placed inside the carton. Complete sealing of the carton was to take place during the baking process, and as added insurance the bread and carton were dipped in a wax resin mixture to seal it. Unfortunately the efforts to seal the bread were often unsuccessful, resulting in moldy bread. Despite efforts to improve the process it never proved as successful as the cellophane/brown wood paper wrap method. *(Author's note: I don't have a picture of this style of package, and it's unclear if this type of bread was manufactured after the Polish campaign.)*

The British Intelligence Objectives Sub-Committee published a report *Production of Flour and Bread in Germany* based on investigations conducted immediately after the war. Some of the more interesting observations are summarized below:

A. During the course of their investigations the Allies noticed the use of sawdust as a final dusting material for rye dough to prevent sticking to the baking tins. No grease was used and the process seemed quite effective. With wheat doughs, a finely ground material from the outer skins of buck wheat was used for a similar purpose. The practice of using sawdust and buck wheat bran instead of fat to prevent sticking began before the war. This may well account for the unofficial rumors that the Germans were using sawdust as a raw material for the manufacture of bread.

B. An interesting component of several Emergency Rations is a product called Soya meat bread. Soya meat breads were produced under a single frame formula which unfortunately was not included in the report. This was one of several methods used to improve the acceptability of Pemmican. Smoked meat baked in bread was a tasty and agreeable heavy food which was covered with rye or mixed flour dough and baked. Soya was commonly used as an extender in many food products. Smoked meat bread was approved for fielding, and is probably the same thing as Soya meat bread. They were packaged in 100 gram portions.

C. Three bakeries involved in wrapped and canned bread production were visited after the war was over. Dosenbrot, or canned bread, was made exactly like other bread products, except for the shape. Almost any bakery was capable of producing canned rye bread. The rye bread was of a heavy, extremely close structure, with a strong flavor. It was usually a sourdough rye. The crust is so thin that crust staling is unimportant, and because of the closeness of the structure, crumbliness does not develop. Canning was the perfect means of preservation, since it prevents moisture loss and maintains sterility. The bread was baked in the cans for 40 minutes at 250 degrees before sealing, or baked in long insulated cylinders for 20 hours, cooled, sliced, placed in the cans, and sealed. Pumpernickel bread, a heavy and slightly sweet rye bread, was also canned. Wheat bread was not canned for the Wehrmacht because staling was pronounced, and because the military didn't have a requirement for it. The few surviving canned bread products are coded with a "G". In Volume I the authors put forth the theory that the "G" stood for getreide, or grain. Another possibility is the "G" stood for Gerstenbrot, or barley bread made from barley flour, rye flour, potato flour, salt, Arcady (yeast), water, and final sour. *(Author's note: I have no evidence to confirm Gerstenbrot was produced for the military.)*

D. Dauerbrot, or long lasting rye bread, was wrapped in pergament, then in cellophane, and finally in ordinary paper and sterilized for 1 hour at 100 degrees Celsius. Pergament consists of two ply wax paper sealed together with wax, and the cellophane was a special grade of glaspapier. Dauerbrot had a storage life of six months, but bread stored for two years was still edible. See Volume I for other methods of packaging Dauerbrot. Dauerbrot was manufactured as Dauerbrot A, Dauerbrot B, or Dauerbrot C. I believe that the rate of evaporation and weight loss determined how Dauerbrot was categorized. The daily portion rate for Dauerbrot was set at 600 grams. The 1/1, or 850 gram can, was the only standard can which could have held a daily portion of Dauerbrot. I'm guessing that Dauerbrot packed in paper, cellophane, or aluminum foil, etc., weighed 300 grams.

E. Field Zwieback was considered an Iron Ration which provided a useful and palatable substitute for normal bread. Any bakery was capable of producing it. The Wuelfeler Brotfabrik was one commercial factory that produced Zwieback for the military. After they baked the Zwieback it was packed into paper bags (250 grams of Zwieback) and sealed with adhesive, after which it was delivered to the military.

Type of Bread	Weight Loss in grams per day/kg Bread	Water Evaporation in grams per day/kg Bread
Dauerbrot A	0.25	0.32
Dauerbrot B	0.19	0.26
Dauerbrot C	0.37	0.37

This chart shows the allowable weight and water loss for the three types of Dauerbrot.

The Bahlsen firm was said to have had the most up to date biscuit making machinery in Germany, and to have produced the highest quality products. The owner stated that he knew of no special stabilization techniques for biscuits, and the only method for producing long keeping biscuits was to bake the product to reduce the moisture content below 2%. In the early days of the war, when proper wrappings and packaging were available, no storage difficulties were encountered. But without the proper wrappings and packages it was found that the biscuits deteriorated in all but the driest climates, like that of Russia. A limited amount of canning was carried out especially for submarine rations, but normal good quality biscuits were used for this purpose. Prewar quality was maintained for as long as possible, but in the later war years shortages of fat and sugar caused the formulas to be modified. They had a base formula for "Army Hard

Keks" which was similar to other standard commercial Keks products. At the beginning of the war the Wehrmacht accounted for 10% of Bahlsen's customer base. By the end of the war the Wehrmacht accounted for 25% of its production.

According to the reports, the Bahlsen firm only produced three special rations for the Wehrmacht. The first was a thin, slightly sweetened biscuit intended to replace bread in airmen's rations. While not mentioned by name, they were referring to Rösta. Rösta was packed in 65 gram cartons. See Volume I for additional information. The other product mentioned was a sweet fruit bar. There is a picture of a large shipping label from Bahlsen in Volume I which ends in the letters "…schnitten", or slice. The Bahlsen Fruchtschnitten was packed in cartons weighing 80 grams. The owner stated that the Fruchtschnitten was developed specifically for aircrews. It's likely this product was identical to the Suchard Fruchtschnitten discussed in Chapter 5. The Sarotti firm developed the Fruchtschnitten base formula used by Suchard and Bahlsen. Notverpflegung "Süß" was the final emergency ration that Bahlsen produced for the military.

The production of pulp and paper was a critical aspect of Germany's wartime industry. Paper and pulp containers were a viable substitute to replace metal and glass packaging for all types of rations. The Allies conducted an in depth investigation into the pulp and paper industry, but were generally unimpressed with what they found. The German industry was described as "backward" when compared to the United States and British technology of the period. To quote one of the reports: "It was only

Product Name	Ingredients	Packaging	Weight	Notes
Pumpernickel	Rye, water, malt, salt, basic sour, potato flour and moldex	Can	850 g	Would have used standard 1/1 can
Rye	Rye, water, salt, syrup and yeast	Can	850 g	Would have used standard 1/1 can
Kössenbrot or Knäckebrot	Hard Rye Bread	Paper or Cardstock Carton	125 g	
Feldzwieback or Zwieback	Wheat, rye or potato flour, sugar, yeast, salt, seasoning and water	Zwiebackbeutal, paper sack, cellophane bags	250 g	
Dauerbrot or Wittlerbrot	Corn flour, sour dough, water and salt	Various paper and cellophane wraps	300 g ?	
Dauerbrot or Wittlerbrot	Corn flour, sour dough, water and salt	Cans	600-700 g	Would have used standard 1/1 can
Kraft Keks in Assault Ration Carton	Similar to Army Hard Keks Recipe	Cellophane	80 g	Made by XOX
Hard Keks in Assault Ration Carton	Similar to Army Hard Keks Recipe	6 square biscuits wrapped in wax paper and placed in paper carton	80 g ?	Carton measures 2-1/16" x 2-9/16" x 1- 7/16"
Army Hard Keks	Flour, fat, sugar, water, salt, ammonium bicarbonate, sodium bicarbonate	Wrapped in paper with large eagle on front	250 g	Recipe is from H. Bahlsen
Hard Keks	Similar to Army Hard Keks Recipe	Cardstock cartons or paper wrapping	110 g to 125 g	
Soya Meat Bread	Rye or mixed flour dough, Pemmican and other ingredients to make bread	Cardstock cartons	100 g	The square cartons pictured as part of the Fortress Iron Ration could be an example
Front fresh bread	Rye, sour dough, water and yeast	Cellophane and paper wrapping	1.8 kg	Individual portion is 500-650 g
Special bread baked in carton	Rye, sour dough, water and yeast	2 aluminum foil layers, between 3 paper layers	500 g	Not known if it was manufactured after 1939
Rösta-F	Wheat grist cookie	Blue cardstock carton	65 g	For LW Aircrew Rations
Rösta-F	Wheat grist cookie	Plain paper or cardstock carton	65 g	12 Pieces for Frontline Troops

A summary of the most important bread products issued to the German soldier.

in the development of technologies for certain normally sub marginal fields to meet war time expedients or in the use of pulp and paper products as substitutes for critical materials that the German industry had shown any recent developments". Every decision and action undertaken by German industry during the war was driven by a lack of raw materials. That's not necessarily to say that all German products were inferior when compared to Allied products. It might be fairer to say that German industry had to look at unconventional measures in order to overcome their lack of critical

raw materials. Paper and pulp products used in the food industry were generally of fair to good quality, and achieved their goals of protecting food products during transport and storage. Certain paper products like Greaseproof and Glassine papers continued to be produced at a very high quality level due to the skills of the workers in the paper industry.

Large shipping carton from the Chemnitzer Teigwaren factory. *Courtesy Zeugmeister.*

There is no manufacturers' information on this carton of oatmeal.

Edlich brand kommissbrot label.[1] *Courtesy Zeugmeister.*

Knorr brand Macaroni.

117

Sugared oatmeal from the Niedersedlitz Malt factory.[2] *Courtesy OSTFRONT Militaria.*

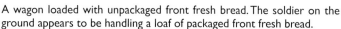

A wagon loaded with unpackaged front fresh bread. The soldier on the ground appears to be handling a loaf of packaged front fresh bread.

Knorr brand oatmeal.

Carton from the Batscheider Knäckebrot-Fabrik.[3]

Large shipping carton for Knorr macaroni. *Courtesy Zeugmeister.*

Wartime advertisements explaining the health benefits of whole grain bread.

Lebkuchen manufactured by the Homa Lebkuchenfabrik, formally known as the E. Otto Schmidt firm.[4] *Courtesy Kevin Barrett.*

A better photograph of the side locking Knäckebrot carton shown in Volume I. *Courtesy Marcin Jonczyk Collection.*

Storing rations in a footlocker. Notice the paper sacks. *Bundesarchiv Bild 1011-394-1497-09/ Foto:Wanderer. W. / License CC-BY-SA 3.0.*

These troops have picked up various rations including a 10 kg carton of Lebküchen. *Courtesy Jens Kattner.*

Numerous subjects were covered by the trade paper *Dekofei*. This 1944 edition discussed how flour was mixed in Switzerland.

A carton of Knäckebrot from the Hammerbrotwerke, Wien. The evidence suggests it's of wartime manufacture.[5] *Courtesy Chris Mason.*

Large grain sack. *Courtesy Zeugmeister.*

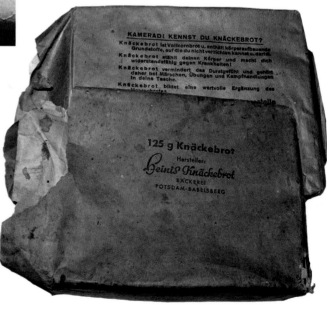

A variant package of Heinis Knäckebrot. *Courtesy Marcin Jonczyk Collection.*

ENDNOTES

[1] No history was found on the Edlich Bakery. Here is their listing in the 1929 Mosse Register of Firms.

> **Bäcker.** Bauch, O. – Baumann, Br., ℜ 2192 – Bellmann, A. – Clau-nitzer, B. – Donath, B. – Dubiel, Doris – Edel, R. O. – Edlich, E. (elektr.), ℜ 2685 – Endert, E., ℜ

[2] The Niedersedlitz Malt factory was founded in 1889. The company was still in operation until at least 1990.

> **Malzfabriken.** *Malzfabrik Nieder-sedlitz, A-G, ℜ 600–602, Ⓖ, Ps 31146 Dr.

[3] The fact that the carton is stamped as being manufactured by Knäcke-Werke as well as the Batscheider Knäckebrot-Fabrik is interesting. I'm not sure why it's stamped in this manner. Is the carton a fantasy? Did the Batscheider Knäckebrot-Fabrik subcontract their product to Knäcke-Werke, or were the cartons recycled? I don't have any answers, but I do believe the carton is original. As mentioned in Chapter 4, the phrase Knäcke-Werke is generally associated with non-Dr. Wilhelm Kraft products.

[4] The firm of E. Otto Schmidt was founded in 1927. Sometime prior to or during the Third Reich the company name was changed to "Homa". Today it is known as Lebkuchen Schmidt. Here is the company listing in the 1938 Nürnberg phone book.

> **– E. Otto, Lebkuchenfabrik G. m. b. H.,** Nbg.-S, Gyulaer-straße 9   **4 32 18**

Bakery unit of the Totenkopf Division.

[5] The Hammerbrotwerke of Vienna, Austria, was a people's cooperative started in 1909. They didn't make a profit until WWI, when they started producing bread for the military. In 1919 they opened a second plant in Floridsdorf, and shortly afterwords a plant in Leopold. In 1937 the Hammerbrotwerke purchased one of their competitors, the Wiener Kronenbrotwerke, which was shut down. In the 1970s, the United Food Industry Ltd. was founded by merging Ankerbrot AG and the Hammerbrotwerke. The Ankerbrot Company is still in operation. Here is the Hammerbrotwerke listing in the 1943 Wien phone book.

> **Hammerbrotwerke-A.-G.** Zen-tralbüro II/27 Obere Donau-str 15 a   **✶ A 4 15 40**
> F a b r i k e n :
> II/27 Obere Donaustr 15 a
>   **✶ A 4 95 20**
> X/75 Hardtmuthg 53/55
>   **R 1 33 45**
> Floridsdorf XXI/141 Schwai-gerg 19   **✶ A 6 05 10**

121

II

DAIRY PRODUCTS

In addition to the references cited in Annex I, the following reports and books were consulted in writing this Annex: *Deutsche A.G. fur Nestle Erzeugniss Kiel Milchwerke Angeln, Nestlé 125 Years 1866-1991*and *Paper Pulp Moulding Industry in Germany.*

According to the British reports, relatively little evaporated or condensed milk was manufactured for anyone other than the Kriegsmarine or infants after 1940. The use of extruded two piece aluminum cans of 170 gram capacity (2 5/16" diameter x 2 15/16" high) for milk products was worthy of mention in the Allied intelligence reports. Similar products are pictured in Volume I. Both sanitary style and hole-in-cap cans were also used for milk products. The large number of extruded aluminum cans, as well as the sanitary style, and hole-in-cap cans found in German positions throughout Europe seems to indicate a much wider distribution of evaporated and condensed milk products than the intelligence reports suggest.

Many milk packers manufactured their own solder-tipped, vent-hole style, snap-end seam cans, and did not want or could not get the machinery to manufacture the black steel cans. Some drawn and extruded aluminum cans were used by the evaporated milk canners to reduce the need for hot dipped tinplate cans.

Because Nestlé products are so prominently featured in this Volume, I decided to provide a more detailed look into the company's operations in wartime Germany. As I soon discovered, this proved to be easier said than done. Even armed with the company's own official history by Jean Heer, titled *Nestlé 125 Years 1866-1991*, I was unable to put all the pieces together. However, I think I've managed to put together a good starting point.

In order to understand the wartime Nestlés operation we need to go back to the very beginning of the Nestlé story. The Nestlé story is actually the story of two major Swiss companies and several other players which would later form the core of the wartime Nestlé operation. In 1867 Henri Nestlé developed a milk-based baby food (**Farine Lactée/ Kindermehl**) in Vevey, Switzerland. In the same year the Page brothers from Illinois established the Anglo-Swiss Condensed Milk Company in Cham, Switzerland. In 1872 the Anglo-Swiss Condensed Milk Company acquired a milk factory in Rickenbach, Germany, near Lindau. In 1874 **Milchmädchen** (Milk Maid) brand sweetened condensed milk began production at the Rickenbach plant. By 1877 the Anglo-Swiss Condensed Milk Company, already the leading manufacturer of condensed milk in Europe, entered into cheese and baby food production. Nestlé responded by launching a condensed milk product of its own. Until 1898 Nestlé kept all manufacturing within Switzerland and exported its products around the world. That year Nestlé ventured outside Switzerland by purchasing a Norwegian condensed milk company. In 1902 Nestlé established a subsidiary in Berlin called the Nestlé Kindermehl Gmbh., Berlin. In 1903 Nestlé built its first factory outside Switzerland, in Germany at Hegge.

In 1905 Nestlé and the Anglo-Swiss Condensed Milk Company merged to create the Nestlé and Anglo-Swiss Milk Company. It was an equal partnership and run out of two registered offices, one in Vevey and one in Cham. The company now included nineteen factories worldwide, including one in Germany (Hegge). When World War I broke out Nestlé's operations, particularly in Britain and Germany, were seriously affected. To deal with these problems Nestlé expanded into countries less affected by the war and began purchasing existing factories. By 1917 Nestlé had 40 factories. By 1921 the firm had 80 factories and 12 subsidiaries and affiliates. It also introduced a new product that year: **Lactogen**. In 1905 Nestlé reached an agreement with the Swiss chocolate firm of Peter, Cailler, and Kohler to sell their products along with Nestlé products.

By consolidating certain operations and expanding others to include those in Germany, Nestlé was also able to widen its traditional range of products. The late 1920s were a profitable time for the company. In addition to adding some new products of its own, including **Milo**, **Nestogen**, and **Eledon**, the company also bought interests in several manufacturing firms.

In 1927 the Deutsche Aktiengesellschaft für Nestle Erzeugnisse, in cooperation with Peter, Cailler, and Kohler, was created. This company was responsible for the manufacturing and sales division of the Linda-Gesellschaft and Otto Quantz Schokoladenwerk AG, which marketed products bearing the Nestlé and Peter, Cailler, and Kohler trademarks. In 1928 Nestlé acquired an interest in the Berlin based chocolate business Sarotti A.G., which began manufacturing Nestlé, Peter, Cailler, and Kohler chocolates, along with its own Sarotti brand. In 1928, Nestlé officially merged with Peter, Cailler, and Kohler, Chocolats Suisses S.A., adding 13 chocolate plants in Europe, South America, and Australia to the growing firm. The merger between Nestlé and Peter, Cailler, and Kohler resulted in perfecting the milk chocolate manufacturing process. The Linda-Gesellschaft leased the factory at Kappeln, Germany, from Milchwerke Angeln in 1928.

Nestlé was so established that the Great Depression had little effect on it. In the 1930s Nestlé created new subsidiaries in Argentina and Cuba and added more production centers around the world, including Denmark, Czechoslovakia, Chile, and Mexico. **Nescao**,

Nestogen, **Perlargon**, and **Nestrovit** were added to its growing list of products. Still the company couldn't totally avoid the effects of the worldwide depression. The company closed several factories, including its two oldest in Cham and Vevey. In 1935 the Nestlé factory at Lindau, Germany, was closed.

By 1936 the Nestlé and Anglo-Swiss Condensed Milk Company, Limited was established to handle production and marketing on the Swiss market, while the parent company officially became a holding firm, called the Nestlé and Anglo-Swiss Holding Company, Ltd.

Nestlé's next endeavor, coffee, was a far cry from its traditional milk based products. Debuting in 1938, **Nescafé** was the world's first commercially viable instant coffee. Although Nestlé wanted to manufacture Nescafé in Brazil, the hurdles were too great, so it was decided to produce Nescafé by local factories in the country it was to be consumed in. Nescafé was first manufactured in Switzerland at the Orbe factory and introduced to the market on 1 April 1938. In 1939 Nescafé was being manufactured in Britain, the United States, and France. **Nestea**, a soluble powdered tea, debuted in the early 1940s. (*Author's note: The Nestlé website gives 1947 as the year Nestea was introduced.*)

The history of Nescafé and its relation to wartime Germany is somewhat muddy. The few available references state that Nescafé was first manufactured in 1943 at the Kappeln, Germany, factory. The "Cremilk Kappeln" website states it was only produced for the members of the Wehrmacht. According to the Nestlés official history by Jean Heer, raw materials and especially coffee beans were difficult to come by, except for the 12 European countries supplied by the Société de Produits Nestlé SA, which managed to overcome some of the import barriers. The fact that the factory at Kappeln was able to get coffee beans to produce Nescafé as late as 1943 is amazing in itself, even if they were or were not the first to produce Nescafé. The following paragraph on page 200 of *Nestlé 125 Years 1866-1991* leaves open the possibility that Nescafé was actually available in Germany prior to 1943:

In 1944, Nestlés chairmen, Edouard Muller, and his associates found themselves at the head of a global coffee concern. However, much of the technical know-how related

to the production of Nescafé had all but passed into the public domain. And the company immediately gave considerable thought to its future position in Europe and elsewhere in the face of the fierce challenge from its American competitors. As early as this period, Nestlé already planned to extend the local manufacture of Nescafé-which had been produced *for several* years in Switzerland, Great Britain, France, Germany, South Africa, Argentina, and Mexico-to coffee producing countries such as Peru, Brazil, Cuba, and Colombia as well as to Asia, Europe, Oceania, and Latin America. (*Author's note: The fact that the United States also manufactured Nescafé is implied*).

Notice that the countries are not listed alphabetically, but by what I think is the year that Nescafé was actually introduced to that country. We have Switzerland (1938), Great Britain, and France (1939), followed by Germany, etc. I confirmed that Nescafé was available in Argentina in 1941. So if my premise is correct it's likely that Nescafé was produced, or at least available, in Germany sometime between 1939 and 1941. See Annex 6 for an additional discussion on Nescafé.

So how many factories did Nestlés operate in Germany? I believe the answer is two, however, there were several other factories belonging to subsidiaries that also produced Nestlés' products. In order to explain which factories Nestlés operated in Germany I used the manufacturing information taken from pre-May 8, 1945, Nestlés products. (*Authors note: Some of these same statements were also used on postwar products!*)

A. **Deutsche A.G. Für Nestle Erzeugnisse Verkaufszentrale Berlin, Berlin-Tempelhof Teilestraβe 16**: This was a sales office, and was colocated with the Sarotti Chocolate Factory. The Sarotti firm produced their own line of products, but its possible they manufactured some Nestlés branded products.

B. **Deutsche A.G. Für Nestle Erzeugnisse Lindau-Bodensee, Deutsche Nestle Aktiengesellschaft Lindau-Bodensee and Deutsche Aktiengesellschaft für Nestle Erzeugnisse Lindau-Bodensee**: These phrases probably referred to the factory at

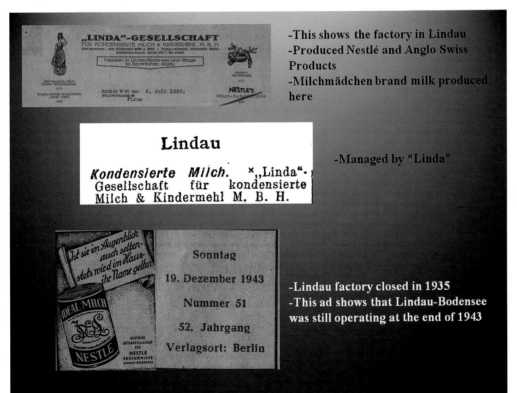

-This shows the factory in Lindau
-Produced Nestlé and Anglo Swiss Products
-Milchmädchen brand milk produced here

-Managed by "Linda"

-Lindau factory closed in 1935
-This ad shows that Lindau-Bodensee was still operating at the end of 1943

This chart highlights the relationship between Nestlé and Lindau.

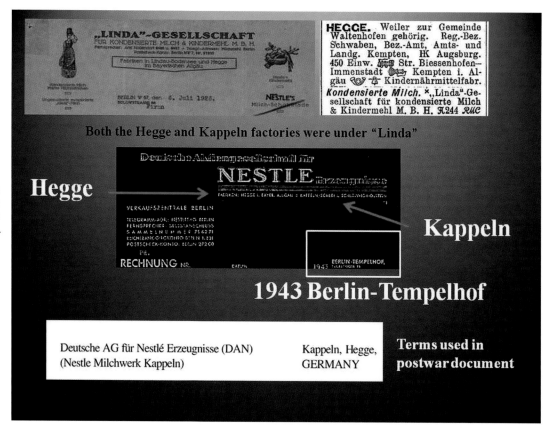

Both the Hegge and Kappeln factories were under "Linda"

This chart highlights the relationship between Nestlé and the factories at Hegge and Kappeln.

Hegge

Kappeln

1943 Berlin-Tempelhof

| Deutsche AG für Nestlé Erzeugnisse (DAN) (Nestle Milchwerk Kappeln) | Kappeln, Hegge, GERMANY | **Terms used in postwar document** |

Rickenbach, Germany. In the 1929 Mosse Register of Firms Rickenbach is considered a part of Lindau, Germany. Lindau was strategically situated on the border between Germany, Austria, and Switzerland. The Anglo-Swiss Condensed Milk Company acquired the Rickenbach milk factory in 1872. By the early 1930s the Rickenbach factory was referred to as the Nestlé factory. According to *Nestlé 125 Years 1866-1991*, the Nestlé factory at Lindau, Germany, was closed in 1935. I believe this was the Rickenbach factory. If there was no factory after 1935, why was Lindau-Bodensee referenced until at least the end of 1943? I couldn't find an answer. Maybe products manufactured at the Hegge factory used this phrase, as well the phrase in paragraph C.

C. **Deutsche A.G. Für Nestle Erzeugnisse Berlin-Tempelhof**: I believe this phrase was used for products produced at the Kappeln and Hegge factories. The first Nestlé factory was built in 1903 at Hegge, Germany. Hegge is only 30 miles from Lindau, Germany, near the Swiss border. Linda-Gesellschaft leased the factory at Kappeln, Germany, from Milchwerke Angeln in 1928, and Nestlé purchased the plant in 1942. The Kappeln factory produced **Ideal** brand milk and cheese. When Nestlé acquired the plant in 1942 they started producing milk powder and infant formula. According to the Kappeln website, it was the "Linda" that produced the first Nescafé in Germany during 1943. The same source states that Nescafé was only produced for the Wehrmacht. Other sources state that after 1943 all production capacity at Kappeln was devoted to supporting the military.

As part of their investigation Allied personnel visited the Nestlé factory at Kappeln, Germany. Herr T. Thalmann, a Swiss national, was put in charge of the factory in 1943. According to the comments in *Deutsche A.G. fur Nestle Erzeugniss Kiel Milchwerke Angeln*, he was not able to discuss specifics about the plant operation, possibly to protect patent information belonging to the parent company. The plant was still operating in July 1945 when Allied personnel visited it. The focus of the Allied visit was to review the process used to make powdered milk. The productions of other products, like coffee or chocolate, were not evaluated or even mentioned. Evaporated (unsweetened) milk and spray dried whole milk powder appeared to be the companies' primary products. Sweetened condensed milk, spray dried skim milk powder, and modified milk spray dried for infants were also being manufactured. The overall quality of the products was judged as good. The final products were packed in aluminum and tin plated cans. The aluminum cans were deemed superior to the tin plated cans.

There is one final phrase that I haven't exactly figured out, which is **Deutschen A.G. Für Nestle Erzeugnisse Lindau-Bodensee**. This phrase was frequently used on postwar Nestlé publications, and possibly on some postwar products. However, I have a Milchmädchen can which I'm certain is wartime that uses the phrase. The can is shown below, and it states on the label that the product is made in Switzerland in cooperation with the Deutschen A.G. Für Nestle Erzeugnisse Lindau-Bodensee. I have never seen another can of Milchmädchen with a label that almost appears to be camouflaged. The can appears to be of German origin with the body manufactured from tin, with one lid in camouflaged green paint and the other in black plate steel. Another mystery!

Germany made the maximum use of containers made from convolute-wound paper bodies with metal foil, cellophane, parchment, synthetic resin, and nitro cellulose lacquered paper and other similar lining materials, in combination with lacquered black plate ends and closures, for the packing of dry and non-processed oily food and industrial non-food products.

One of the all-paper rigid containers shown below was of special interest to Allied intelligence. It was an ordinary convolute-wound paper body, but the top is reformed from its cylindrical form to a small opening-neck type, similar to a milk bottle. The interior is coated with wax or resin to obtain suitable resistance against penetration by the products being packed inside. These containers were used for oil and a number of other products, but were *not ordinarily* used for milk.

Some details of the Milchmädchen can.

This paper container was of special interest to Allied investigators.

Standard drawn or extruded Aluminum cans used for milk and other products.

Various styles of convolute wound paper body containers were used as packaging for a variety of products, to include food.

Can of Nestlé powdered milk for children.[1] *Courtesy Zeugmeister.*

Pulp molded containers were manufactured as substitutes for metal containers. In simple terms, a pulp mixture is manufactured from cellulose, wood pulp, or waste paper with the addition of binders. The pulp is forced into molds, dried, trimmed, impregnated, supplied with covers, and packed. Pulp-molded containers were used as packages for foodstuffs, dry and powdery chemicals, ointments, and as protective packages for bottles. The pulp-molded process is capable of making round, square, and oblong containers, bottles, and containers with holes.

Pulp paper Kraft's Velveta cheese carton.[2] *Courtesy www.raskantik.com*

A pulp paper carton for Enzian brand cheese.[4] *Courtesy OSTFRONT Militaria.*

A DRP marked jar of Bulgarian yogurt. *Courtesy Andreas Grote.*

Aluminum cans were widely used for milk products. *Courtesy Andreas Grote.*

A small can of evaporated milk.[3] *Courtesy OSTFRONT Militaria.*

Ground dug lid for
a 875 gram can of
Bona cheese.

Bundesarchiv, Bild 101I-090-3912-23A
Foto: Etzhold | 1944 Frühling

German Mountain trooper spreading lard or butter on his bread.
Note the butter dish in his mouth. *Bundesarchiv Bild 101I-090-3912-
23A/ Foto: Etzhold/ License CC-BY-SA 3.0.*

A can of Nestlé
brand Ideal Milk.[6]

IDEAL MILCH

Evaporierte ungezuckerte Vollmilch.

IDEAL MILCH eignet sich vorzüglich für jeden Zweck in Küche und Haushalt. Wird sie an stelle von Rahm zur Zubereitung von Mehl- und Süßspeisen sowie anderer Gerichte oder als Beigabe zu Kaffee, Tee und Eingemachtem verwendet, so soll sie unverdünnt genommen werden.

Sie hält sich in der geschlossenen Dose sehr lange. Zum Oeffnen ist der Deckel in Randnähe an zwei einander gegenüberliegenden Stellen zu durchstechen. Nach Oeffnen der Dose soll Ideal Milch wie frische Milch behandelt werden.

DEUTSCHE AKTIENGESELLSCHAFT
NESTLÉ

Large
shipping carton
for Ideal milk.
Courtesy Zeugmeister.

A can of Libby's
evaporated milk.[5]
*Courtesy OSTFRONT
Militaria.*

A can of Nestlé brand Eledon powdered buttermilk.

This wartime advertisement shows a variety of milk products.

Loading some rations onto a ship. Notice the case of Milch-Wunder.

Wartime advertisement for Glücksklee evaporated milk.

128

Endnotes

[1] A 1941 dated advertisement for the same product.

[2] Kraft Foods was founded in Chicago in the early 1900s. In 1927 Kraft Germany set up operations in Hamburg under the direction of Edwin Kenworthy-Koolhaas. They initially focused on the import of English-Chester cheese. In 1937 "Velveta" was introduced to the German market and proved to be popular. Early postwar containers are almost identical to wartime containers. Here are some 1941/42 advertisements for Kraft Velveta.

[3] No history was found on Heida Werk. However, it's believed they are still in business. Here is their listing in the 1929 Mosse Register of Firms.

Malzkaffeefabr. ×Heida Werk Müller & Co., Kom.-Ges., ℋ 153, Ps 22545 Ka.

[4] No history was found on the Enzian Cheese Company. It's believed they are still in business under another name. Here is their listing in the 1929 Mosse Register of Firms.

[5] Libby's is an American based company best known for its canned foods. It was founded in Chicago, Illinois, in 1869. In 1927 Deutsche Libby Gesellschaft M.B.H. established a factory in Leer-Ostfriesland, Hannover. Libby's is still in operation today. Here is a Libby's advertisement from the 1930s courtesy OSTFRONT Militaria.

[6] An Ideal Milk advertisement from a 1943 copy of the *Dekofei*.

III

FISH, FATS, AND POULTRY PRODUCTS

In addition to the references cited in Annex I, the following reports were consulted in writing this Annex: *German Light Metal Industry (Fancy Goods)*; *Light Alloys: Notes on German Technique On, Summary of Field Investigations, Fats, Oils, and Oilseeds*; *The German Herring Curing and Herring Canning Industries*; *Certain Aspects of the German Herring Canning Industry*; and *Certain Aspects of the German Fishing Industry*.

Edible fats and oils were another important part of the German soldier's diet. It was a well-recognized fact that the shortage of fats and oils contributed greatly to Germany's defeat in WWI. In prewar Germany fats made up 25% of the population's total caloric intake, without taking into account "invisible fats" contained in cheese, meats, nuts, etc. The most important product was butter, followed by lard/raw pork fat, margarine, and then all other fats. During the war alternative forms of fats and oils, including synthetic products, were pursued in order to offset shortages of standard products.

Before the war Germany depended on the import of oilseeds to supply its requirements for both edible and technical fats. The processing of oilseeds, fats, and oils was a major industry in Germany, and much of the worldwide oilseed technology originated in Germany. The greatest concentration of oilseed industry was in the Hamburg-Harburg region. Large mills that processed soybeans, copra (dried coconut meat), palm kernel, cottonseed, sunflower seed, linseed, and practically every other oilseed known in commerce were found in this region. Germany possessed almost 600,000 metric tons of fats and oils when the war began. Large amounts of oils and fats were imported from occupied countries during the war. Over 100,000 tons of whale oil was captured from Allied tankers. Before Germany invaded Russia they were able to import 100,000 tons of soybeans and 20,000 tons of peanuts and copra. By 1941 rapeseed (canola) was the predominant oilseed being processed in German mills. Germany subsidized the production of rapeseed, which reached 250,000 tons a year by the end of the war, in order to offset shortages of other fats or oils.

The "Reichstelle für Fette und Eier" administered the wartime German oilseed industry. Fachgruppes, or a type of trade union, were organized by the manufacturers to deal with the government. Much of the German fat and oil industry was controlled by large companies like the Lever Brothers and Unilever, Ltd. In 1929 the Margarine Union, which was a union of smaller firms, merged with the Lever Brothers and Unilever, Ltd.

German butter and margarine production methods, as well as the overall quality of the products, were praised by Allied intelligence personnel. The Germans produced two types of butter, the standard sweet cream butter and what is called "Alpha Butter", a sweeter and more cream like (in flavor) butter. The German Army consumed normal commercial butter to a large extent, but efforts to improve quality led to experimentation with dehydrated butter, Schmalz butter, etc. Palm oil fats (Palmin) were used by the German Navy, and to a lesser degree by the other services. When cold, this type of fat was hard and brittle. It was used primarily for frying or general cooking. It was wrapped in parchment paper and packed in wooden boxes. A synthetic butter known by the "Prima" brand name was manufactured by the Märkische Seifenindustrie at Witten/Ruhr. It was manufactured from coal byproducts with added vitamins and butter flavoring. By 1944 the firm was producing 440,000 lbs a month.

The Allied analysts were quick to point out that German margarine was not manufactured or used the same way it was in the United States. The Germans used it as an all purpose fat, employed for frying, baking, as a spread on bread, and for many other uses. Before the war it was manufactured using ripened skim milk, hard and soft fats, and several minor ingredients. During the war the milk was replaced with water and rapeseed replaced most of the other fats.

Lecithin, a synthetic product from soya oil, also played a significant role in the German food industry. It was chiefly used in making margarine, but was also used in the manufacture of chocolate and other food products.

Fish was a very important part of Germany's food chain. The most important suppliers of fish other than German fishermen were Norway, Denmark, and Portugal. Holland, France, and Italy, as well as other countries also supplied fish to Germany on a smaller scale. The three major methods of supplying fish were fresh, frozen, or canned. As far as canned products are concerned, the Germans differentiate between the terms conserves and preserves. The term conserve is applied to products which in the process of canning have been rendered sterile, whereas preserves are products which have not been rendered sterile and must be consumed within a comparatively short time after preparation.

The Germans were found to have a greater variety of recipes and preservation methods for fish than in England. For example, Herring was prepared bücklinge (smoked), marinated, fried, or canned. Canned Herring was both boiled and packed in tomato, mustard, wine sauces, etc., or hot smoked and dried as kippers and canned in oil. Herring, sardines, and other fishes were also used to make fish paste and packed in cans, jars, or aluminum tubes.

Sardines are small oily fish related to Herring, and are found throughout the world but vary by region. Sardines are made from any of 11 different species of fish, including herring, sild, pilchard, and sprats or brisling. Some are smaller, some are larger. All are subject to various standards around the globe. Cooler waters tend to yield sardines, while warmer waters tend to have sprats and brisling (basically small Herrings).

Canned seelachs, or "Sea Salmon", was another popular fish in Germany, and despite its name is actually a whitefish known as Coalfish or Pollock. Prepared using a soluble red dye of coal origin and then cold smoked or immersed in "Smoke Essence", the meat takes on a color which looks like salmon. The product is packed in cans with soya, sunflower, or brassica oil, and then sealed without sterilization.

The relationship between Germany and the Norwegian fishing industry was explored in some depth by the Allies. The Norwegian fisherman landed his catch at one of the many Norwegian packers along the coast, negotiated a price, and offloaded his catch. The packer cleaned, packed, and iced the catch. 50% of the catch was sold to the Norwegian population and 50% was set aside for the German market. The FEG-Fischeinkaufsgemeinschaft purchased the German quota until 1944, when Fiskinkjøp A/S assumed that responsibility. 90% of the German quota went straight to German freezing factories, bypassing Norwegian fishermen and packers. The following German firms operated freezing operations in Norway: Nordsee, Andersen and Co. (Reemtsa), and Lohmann and Co. K.G. The fish were processed and packed into cardboard boxes before freezing. The majority of the frozen fish was shipped to Germany in refrigerated ships; however, at least one factory used rail to transport the fish. In Germany the fish was purchased by wholesalers and distributed throughout Germany and Austria. Some portion of the fish caught in Norway was also canned and transported to Germany.

Due to the Wehrmacht's interest in tin-free cans, German can makers had more opportunity to work with aluminum or aluminum clad steel as a manufacturing material than American can manufacturers. There were numerous discussions within Germany's food industry to determine the most economical and efficient styles of packaging to use, e.g. tin cans, black steel cans, aluminum cans, or glass. The OKH showed special interest in the following types of aluminum containers: collapsible tubes, 200 gram cans, 400 gram cans, and fish cans (the most urgent priority). While aluminum certainly had its advantages, most cans manufactured from aluminum were of small to medium size. One reason was cost, but there was the technical issue of how to solder or weld aluminum to achieve stability without using heavier and more costly aluminum sheets. It cost RM 0.35 for 1 kg of tin plate and RM 2.17 for 1 kg of aluminum. Black sheet steel with a coating of lacquer on both sides cost about 13% more than tin plate, but was cheaper than aluminum. The Germans did conduct storage tests (25 October 1943 to 30 January 1944) on standard open top 400 gram and 850 gram aluminum cans using a variety of coatings and food products. While the findings of the tests were positive, no further attempts were made to replace 400 gram and 850 gram tin and black plate cans with open top aluminum cans.

Originating in Norway, the oblong aluminum cans for fish products gained international renown and were commonly referred to as Dingley cans (oblong cans approximately 20 mm high). Oblong is generally interpreted as an elongated square or circular form. In this case it refers to the elongated square aluminum can. Aluminum cans were not held in high regard by the German fish canning industry because of the high loss rate due to can damage, as compared to regular tin cans. Even though aluminum took on greater importance within the German fish packing industry, it couldn't completely replace the need for tin plate. It appears that tin plate was still being distributed to the German fish canning industry as late as 1944.

The huge demands for aluminum by the aero industry and other more essential war industries discouraged all but a limited use of aluminum cans for packing non-acid products (such as fish and meat products in oil), rather than acid tomato and mustard sauces and evaporated and condensed milk products. Aluminum cans were not used for fruits or acid products due to high costs and low service life. A very limited quantity of Aluminum coated steel was used to produce shallow drawn cans for packing oily fish and meat products. Only the highest purity of virgin aluminum, having a purity of 99.9% aluminum or better, was necessary for the successful manufacture of extruded, thin-walled cans and collapsible tubes.

Some, but certainly not all sizes of Aluminum containers utilized by the Germans are described below:

A. Round drawn or extruded Aluminum cans, Diameter x height:

        99 mm x 33 mm or 200 gram can.
        135 mm x 33 mm or 500 gram can.
        160 mm x 46 mm or 1000 gram can.
        73 mm x 56 mm or 1000 gram Wehrmacht ration can.
        87 mm x 76 mm or 2000 gram Wehrmacht ration can.

B. Non Round drawn or extruded Aluminum cans, Length x width x height:

        105 x 73 x 16 mm or 125 gram can.
        105 x 73 x 22 mm or 166 gram can.
        123 x 76 x 30 mm or 250 gram can.
        148 x 81 x 34 mm or the popular 500 gram oval can.

The manufacture of collapsible tubes for cheese was one of the most important products manufactured from aluminum. These tubes consist of a drawn aluminum bag, the open end of which is folded several times after filling the tube. These tubes are in most cases spray lacquered on the inside. These tubes were easy and convenient to open and useful for packing single portions. See Volume I for pictures. Attempts to use aluminum tubes/bags for meat products, like sausages, were not successful, as the closures could not be considered safe. However, meat products in aluminum bags were specified for some emergency rations, and there is evidence that limited quantities were actually produced.

As of the date of publication, I have not encountered any drawn oval or oblong aluminum or aluminum coated can that was definitely manufactured to hold a meat product. The 1942 *Taschenbuch für den Verpflegungs-lagerbeamten* specifically states that aluminum cans were only used to pack fish in oil. However, these new Allied intelligence reports leave no doubt that some meat in oil products were packed in aluminum cans. This likely began in late 1942 or 1943. Given the higher relative cost to produce aluminum cans and the high incidence of damage compared to other types of cans, I suspect that meat products were only packed in aluminum cans on a limited basis. The question remains, though, how these aluminum cans were stamped or marked to differentiate between a meat or fish product? Because of the guidance in *Taschenbuch für den Verpflegungs-lagerbeamten* I believe that any drawn oval or oblong aluminum can without a product code contained some type of fish product. I believe that meat products packed in aluminum cans would have used the same product codes found on standard open top sanitary

Drawn aluminum cans were used to pack fish and meat in oil.

cans. Of course, until an example actually surfaces this is still just speculation. Aluminum cans with Norway or Denmark stamped into them contained fish products.

The frozen food industry played a definite role in feeding the Wehrmacht. It was estimated that in 1944 frozen food production reached 40-45 million kilos, for both the civilian and military market. Fish was the most important frozen food supplied to the Wehrmacht. Frozen meats, fruits, and vegetables also saw limited distribution. The Germans developed a special system of storage and transportation named the "cold chain" to supply frozen foods to the military. The term "cold chain" was coined to apply to the complete storage and transportation system from the time a product was first frozen until they were delivered to the consumer. The "cold chain" was set up to support the African campaign, however, by the time it was established shipping losses were so severe that very little if any refrigerated foods were shipped to Africa. In general frozen foods were mainly used in early spring when other foods were more difficult to obtain. Likewise, it appears that frozen foods distributed to the Wehrmacht went primarily to Norway and Russia. The use of the "cold chain" was curtailed later in the war because of transportation difficulties and shortages of the actual products. Two styles of containers were generally used to pack frozen foods (see Volume I for pictures):

A.   The fiber containers used for commercial frozen foods vary from a small size holding 250 grams to the large institutional size carton holding from 10 to 12 kilograms. The 0.5 and 1.5 kg sized containers appeared to be the most popular. The Nicolaus Co., Kempten, was one of the largest suppliers of fiber cartons. The fiber cartons were made in the lap side seam style, conventional folding type from sulphite pulp paper board. Early in the war these cartons were coated both inside and out with paraffin. It was customary to pack frozen fruits/vegetables with an inside cellophane liner and outside cellophane wrapper. As shortages of materials occurred only the inside of the carton was paraffined and only a narrow outside band of cellophane was retained to keep the carton closed, and to protect the manufacturer's label. As further shortages occurred a large square pergament or parchment paper bag was developed. This bag held about 50 to 100 of the small cartons and was lapped sealed after filling with the smaller frozen cartons.

B.   The ECO package is a rectangular, aluminum foil-laminated fiber carton with lap side seam and countersunk ends. The package came in several sizes, and the ends are sealed on by a heat setting adhesive. The package was a joint development of the Nicolaus Co. and the Jagenberg-Werke, Düsseldorf. The ECO package was manufactured in two standard sizes designated as the 450 ccm and 800 ccm package. The Nicolaus Co. manufactured 135 million packages in 1943 and 1944. The ECO package was widely used for sugared fruit, fruit juices, and fruit juice concentrates. ECO package was a term generally given to any laminated paper package.

Egg substitutes were developed to counter the shortage of eggs in Germany. These materials were widely used by the Wehrmacht. Substitutes were divided into four distinct classes:

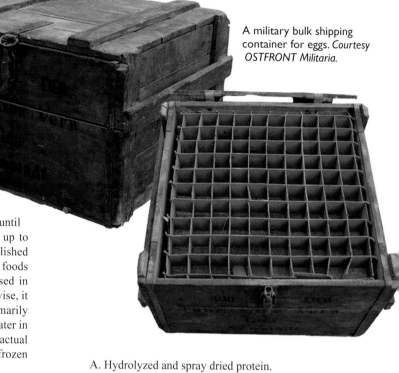

A military bulk shipping container for eggs. *Courtesy OSTFRONT Militaria.*

A. Hydrolyzed and spray dried protein.

B. Spray dried plasma from beef blood.

C. Spray dried milk albumin and whey mixtures.

D. Blends of numbers 2 and 3.

A very important egg substitute manufactured from fish was "Wiking Eiweiss", hailed as a wonder raw material. It was a substitute for egg protein with such extraordinary properties that it allowed the baking industry to continue making pastries during the war. Wiking Eiweiss is mixable with fat and flour, absorbs sugar, can stand great heat, can be boiled, and after boiling can rise again and cannot be over-beaten.

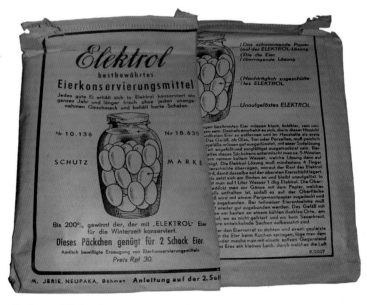

Package of Elektrol egg preservative.[1] *Courtesy Ruelle Frédéric.*

All of the above substitutes had excellent whipping properties and could be used for nougats, meringues, etc. These substitutes could not be used as an egg replacement in custards and in certain types of cakes, because they could not replicate the coagulative properties of real eggs. Nevertheless, egg substitutes were used in large volume in both civilian and military kitchens.

A tin of Smoked Sea Salmon from Wulst, Müller, and Company.[3] *Courtesy OSTFRONT Militaria.*

100 gram jar of Sardine Paste. The cap appears to be a urea-formaldehyde plastic.

A can of fish from the Gottfried Friedrichs firm.[2] *Courtesy Kevin Barrett.*

The popular 500 gram oval can measuring 148 x 81 x 34 mm. Notice that it is gold lacquered on the outside as well as the inside.

Black plate steel can from the Fischindustrie Hinze and Company.[4] *Courtesy OSTFRONT Militaria.*

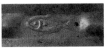

Drawn Aluminum tin of fish from Norway.

Large cans being weighed. *Courtesy OSTFRONT Militaria.*

Wrapping paper for Rahma Margarine. *Courtesy Zeugmeister.*

Another style of Aluminum can, with plain top, dated 1941. *Courtesy Demyansk Battlefield Militaria and Collectibles.*

A can of imitation salmon from the Seeadler firm.[5] *Courtesy OSTFRONT Militaria.*

These soldiers are using a margarine carton as a bed. *Courtesy OSTFRONT Militaria.*

NORDSEE was one of three German freezing plants operating in Norway.

ENDNOTES

[1] The firm that manufactured ELEKTROL egg preservative was founded in 1924. No postwar history was found. Here is an advertisement from the 27 February 1944 edition of *Dekofei*.

[2] The Gottfried Friedrichs company started production in Hamburg-Altona in 1908. In 1926 the "fish in the ring" logo with the founder's initials GF was adopted. The logo would not change until 1978. The firm was the market leader for smoked fish products. "FRIEDRICHS eel" and "FRIEDRICHS salmon" were trademarked products. During the war the Friedrichs firm worked closely with the Dutch government to help it build up its fishing industry. The company is still in business. Here is a 1937 receipt from the company courtesy OSTFRONT Militaria.

[3] No history was located on the company, however, a patent filed in the 1950s confirms they existed after the war. The picture of the Ocean Liner *Europa* and the construction of the can are the major clues which lead me to believe the can is wartime. The *Europa* was launched in 1928, remained largely inactive during the war, and was renamed the USS *Europa* after her capture by U.S. troops in 1945. She was turned over to the French in 1946/7 and renamed the *Liberté*. She was scrapped in 1962.

[4] No history was located on the company. Here are some listings from the 1929 Mosse Register of Firms.

> ×Nordische Herings-Einfuhr-Gesellschaft Hinze & Co.
>
> **Fischindustrie Hinze & Co.**
> Cuxhaven *3681

[5] No history was located on the company, but they did show up on a list of companies accused of using forced labor shown below. I also ran across a reference that indicates the firm was still operating in 1962.

Liste der Unternehmen, die im Nationalsozialismus von der Zwangsarbeit profitiert haben.	
Seeadler, Lager, Deutsche Fischindustrie GmbH	Cuxhaven

IV

MEAT PRODUCTS

In addition to the references cited in Annex I, the following reports were consulted in writing this Annex: *The German Ham Canning Industry* and *Cellophane and Sausage Casings Made at Kalle and Co., Wiesbaden*.

By 1938, canned foods had gained some degree of acceptance and popularity in Germany. In that year approximately 400-500 million 1/1 equivalent cans were produced for fruits and vegetables, fish, meat, and milk products. The German canning industry was composed of both large and small operations. It was common for the small operations to not only conduct canning operations, but to also carry out other operations, notably dehydration, freezing, and production of food or specialty or saccharine products, such as marmalades, etc. This practice ensured year long operations by these firms. While canning operations were distributed throughout Germany, there were concentrations of certain products. The major fruit and vegetable packing occurred in the provinces of Hannover, Brunswick, Magdeburg, Baden, and Saxony. Fish canning was conducted in Hamburg, Cuxhaven, Luebeck, and Wesermunde. Evaporated milk canning was located in Schleswig-Holstein and Bavaria. Important meat packing localities were in Bavaria, Bremen, Hamburg, Kulmbach, Frankfurt, Hessen, Westphalia, Thueringen, and in the Berlin area. Certain canning firms also operated plants in occupied countries, like the firm of Gunther Wagner, which operated plants in Vienna, Warsaw, and Holland, as well as in Germany. Here is a partial list of some of the more important canners and packing factories during the war. It should be noted that there were approximately 300 meat canning firms in Germany, of which 46 were considered significant by the Wehrmacht.

Location	Name of Plant	Product
Bad Schwertau	Schwartauer Werke	Fruit and vegetables
Berlin	Efha Fleisch Kons.Fabrik	Meat
Bockenem	Ambergau A.G.	Fruit and vegetables
Braunschweig	Struck & Witte	Meat
Braunschweig	C. Th. Lampe	Fruit and vegetables
Braunschweig	W. L. Ahrens	Fruit and vegetables
Braunschweig	H. Backmann	Fruit and vegetables
Braunschweig	Braunschweig Cons. Beenke	Fruit and vegetables
Braunschweig	A. Daubert	Fruit and vegetables
Braunschweig	Cons. Fabrik Braunschweig	Fruit and vegetables
Braunschweig	F.W. Freimann	Fruit and vegetables

Braunschweig	Br. Cons. W. Freimann Co.	Fruit and vegetables
Braunschweig	Albert Froboesse	Fruit and vegetables
Braunschweig	Gebr. A. G. Grabe	Fruit and vegetables
Braunschweig	E.K.G. Herrling	Fruit and vegetables
Braunschweig	Hine & Co.	Fruit and vegetables
Braunschweig	Jakobi-Scherbening	Fruit and vegetables
Braunschweig	Jentsch & Sohn	Fruit and vegetables
Braunschweig	Paul Kasper	Fruit and vegetables
Braunschweig	A. Knigge	Fruit and vegetables
Braunschweig	Max Koch	Fruit and vegetables
Braunschweig	Kons. Fabrik Braunschweig	Fruit and vegetables
Braunschweig	H. L. Krone	Fruit and vegetables
Braunschweig	F. Langeheine	Fruit and vegetables
Braunschweig	P. Linder	Fruit and vegetables
Braunschweig	F.L. Loesnich	Fruit and vegetables
Braunschweig	W. Maseberg	Fruit and vegetables
Braunschweig	H. Meinecke	Fruit and vegetables
Braunschweig	Nährmittel Fabrik Columbia	Fruit and vegetables
Braunschweig	Karl Manjoke	Fruit and vegetables
Braunschweig	M. Oertel	Fruit and vegetables
Braunschweig	J.H. Pillman	Fruit and vegetables
Braunschweig	H. Pinkemann	Fruit and vegetables
Braunschweig	A.W. Querner	Fruit and vegetables
Braunschweig	Reichert & Heinemayer	Fruit and vegetables
Braunschweig	Roever A.G.	Fruit and vegetables
Braunschweig-Alper	H.Lanenroth	Fruit and vegetables
Braunsch.-Querum	Gustav Dommes	Fruit and vegetables
Bremen	R. Max Kohl	Meat
Buehl (Baden)	Konserven Badenia	Fruit and vegetables
Bünde	Dorfler	Meat
Calvoerde	W. Bowling	Fruit and vegetables

Calvoerde	C. Herms & Sohn	Fruit and vegetables
Calvoerde	F. Springer	Fruit and vegetables
Cuxhaven	Fischindustrie Elbe	Fish
Cuxhaven	Heinrich Gunkel Gmbh	Fish
Dachau	Wülfert	Meat
Dresden (Saxony)	Sachsische Konservenfabrik	Fruit and vegetables
Dresden (Saxony)	C.H. Schmieder	Fruit and vegetables
Dresden (Saxony)	Wachs and Floessner	Fruit and vegetables
Esslingen A.N.	R. Hengstenberg	Fruit and vegetables
Euskirchen	Rheinische Obst & Gemüse	Fruit and vegetables
Frankfurt/M	Cons. Fabrik Lacroix	Meat
Frankfurt/M	Tuerk & Pabst	Meat
Frankfurt/M	Philip Abt AG	Meat
Frankfurt/M	Heinrich Bauer AG	Meat
Frankfurt/M	Friedr. Emmerich	Meat
Frankfurt/M	Cons. Fabrik Eugen	Meat
Frankfurt/M	Ludwig Mullerleide	Meat
Gebhardshagen	Wittnebe & Co.	Fruit and vegetables
Gera	Carl Oertel Gmbh	Meat
Gütersloh	Vogt & Wolf AG	Meat
Halberstadt	Halberstadt Wurst Cons. Fabrik	Meat
Hannover	Fritz Ahrberg AG	Meat
Hannover	Heines Wurst Fabrik	Meat
Hamburg	Steinike & Weinig	Fruit and vegetables
Hamburg	H.W. Appel AG	Fish
Hamburg	Bruno Bruesso AG	Fish
Hamburg	Deutsche Lysell Fisch Cons.	Fish
Hamburg	Johann von Eitzen	Fish
Hamburg	Brix Hansen	Fish
Hamburg	Trognitz & Co.	Fish
Hamburg	O. Borchers	Meat
Heilbronn	C.H. Knorr	Fruit and vegetables
Heilbronn	Loewenwerke A.G.	Fruit and vegetables
Helmstedt	Cons. Fabrik Helmstadt	Fruit and vegetables
Herten (West)	Schweisfurth	Meat
Hessen	Georg Duchart	Meat
Hessen	Hans Wirth Conserven	Meat
Kaiserslautern	Phalizische Fleischwaren Fabrik	Meat
Karlsruhe	Fritz Brenner A.G.	Fruit and vegetables
Königslutter	H. Kreuzburg	Fruit and vegetables
Kulmbach	Sauermann	Meat
Lage (West)	Siekmann	Meat
Leer	Libby McNeill & Libby	Milk
Lemgo	W. Thospan & Siedman	Fruit and vegetables
Lommatsch	Lommatsch Gemüse	Fruit and vegetables
Lommatsch	Gebrüder Those	Fruit and vegetables
Luebeck	H. Bade & Co.	Fish
Luebeck	Gustav Herbst	Fish
Luebeck	Heinrich Ihde	Fish
Luebeck	Nikolai Jaeger	Fish
Magdeburg	Carl Meusel	Meat
Mecklenburg	General Milk Co.	Milk
Meindorf	Amberga & Bockemann	Fruit and vegetables
Meindorf	J. Plog	Fruit and vegetables
Munich	Bernese Alps Milk Co.	Milk
Munich	A. Sieber	Meat
Münsterberg	Carl Schneider & Co.	Fruit and vegetables
Neuss	Gebrüder Derendorf	Fruit and vegetables
Neuss	J. Leuchterberg	Fruit and vegetables
Neuss	Neusser Sauerkraut Fabrik	Fruit and vegetables
Oldenburg	Nestle	Milk
Radebeul	Loessmitzer Fabrik	Fruit and vegetables
Roethe (Leipzig)	Freiherr V. Friessen	Fruit and vegetables
Ruehme	H. Hintze	Fruit and vegetables
Saarlouis	Fleischwerke Saarland	Meat
Salzdahlum	S. Muehlenkamp	Fruit and vegetables
Satrup	Reoletsen	Meat
Schoeningen	H. Benze	Fruit and vegetables
Seesen am Harz	Peter Thaden & Co.	Fruit and vegetables
Seesen am Harz	Sieburg & Pfoertner	Fruit and vegetables
Seesen am Harz	Illemann & Bosse	Fruit and vegetables
Seesen am Harz	F. Falke Gmbh	Fruit and vegetables
Schylde	A. Rollwaage	Fruit and vegetables
Siersee	Koenig & Hartung	Fruit and vegetables
Stuttgart	Fritz Wild AG	Meat
Tannhausen	Zimmerman	Meat
Thiede	Howi Gmbh	Fruit and vegetables
Schweitzingen	M. Bassermann & Co.	Fruit and vegetables
Vechelde	W. Oehlmann	Fruit and vegetables
Verl/Gütersloh	Fleischwaren Fa. Genossenschaft	Meat
Voelkenrode	Otto Ebermann & Co.	Fruit and vegetables
Voesfeld	Br. Cons. Fabrik	Fruit and vegetables
Wadenbuettch	H. Massberg	Fruit and vegetables
Wendeburg	Chr. Kruger	Fruit and vegetables
Wenden	Fr. Maghem	Fruit and vegetables
Wesermuende	Hartwig & Goedelen	Fish
Wesermuende	Wulst, Muller & Co.	Fish
Wesermuende	Kosmos Feinkost Gmbh	Fish
Wolfenbuettch	Busch. Barnewitz & Co.	Fruit and vegetables
Wolfenbuettch	S. Keune	Fruit and vegetables
Wolfenbuettch	H. Hamann	Fruit and vegetables
Wolfenbuettch	F. Mandel	Fruit and vegetables
Wolfenbuettch	A. Sapper	Fruit and vegetables

The German government's enforced policy of organizing the canning industry was responsible for the fact that Germany was more advanced than other countries in the development and use of:

A. Tinplate with thinner coatings of tin applied by electroplating rather than hot dipping;

B. in the development and use of lacquered instead of tinned steel plate;

C. aluminum and aluminum coated steel;

D. can lacquers made from synthetic resins containing no natural drying oils or resins;

E. synthetic rubber on non-rubber end seaming compounds, and other ersatz materials to replace or save important and scarce normal can making materials that Germany had to import.

In 1936-37 the German government pushed an increase in production facilities for the various types of shallow-drawn and welded tin-less cans from lacquered black plate, aluminum, and aluminum-coated steel, steel electroplated with tin and zinc, and by the maximum use of all paper or composite paper and metal containers.

Canned food played an important role in the rations provided to the German soldier. In 1944 approximately 600 million black plate cans were produced for packing non-acid vegetables, meat, fish, and milk products. The majority of these cans went to the Wehrmacht, but any cans in excess of government requirements were sold to the public. Home canning was very popular during the war. One of the interesting aspects discovered during home canning was cans with a welded lap seam could be reused several times by cutting off the end, reflanging the can body, and applying a new double seamed end. In fact, the Allied reports state that the Germans did not perfect the technique of soldering a lock- and lap-seam type of black plate can in order to continue the production of welded lap seam cans. Obviously black plate cans with a welded lap seam would have been in great demand by home canners. It's not known if black plate cans with welded lap seams were refurbished and reutilized by the military.

Canned meat played perhaps the most important part of all meat products in provisioning the Wehrmacht and Waffen SS. To quote the Allied reports:

A study of German canned meat products is impressive because of the extreme simplicity of their preparation. Very little seasoning was used in German canned meats. The salt content was kept at low levels. The spices and especially Maggi flavoring sauce must not predominate. Pre-cooking before canning was not practiced except for a few specialties. Products inclined towards juiciness were thickened by the inclusion of pork skin, gelatin or potato meal. Soya bean and other meat extenders were not commonly used. When used, soya beans were partially sprouted (for better flavor and additional Vitamin C), cooked, and used in paste form.

According to Allied analysts, fifty-eight canned meat products were listed in the *Bedingungen der Wehrmacht* (Military Requirements), which they were quick to point out was not a complete listing of all meat products. The most common of the canned meat products were: Canned Beef, Canned Pork, Canned Beef and Pork, Canned Veal and Pork, and Canned Veal and Beef, all in natural juices. All were made from the same formula (excluding meat selection) and were considered to be of excellent quality.

Three canned products were worthy of special mention by Allied analysts:

A. Canned whole hams prepared for the Wehrmacht and Waffen SS were especially popular with the troops. By United States standards the German hams were considered under processed, and by logic would not have kept very well unless refrigerated. However, the evidence was clear that German hams kept up to two years in non-refrigerated warehouses. The only explanation provided in the reports was that the German methods of dry curing and long smoking made the German cured meats more adaptable for Army use than the American counterpart. Hams, as well as other meat products manufactured for hot climates, were treated with sodium benzoate. Hams were packed into white metal tins (tin plate) in a variety of shapes (pear shaped was popular before the war), with welded or soldered side seams and with an average filled weight of 12-16 lbs. The lid of the can was marked with the product (ham with added benzoate = Schi-Benz), date of manufacture, firm name, and net weight.

B. Canned pork kasseler (cutlet) represented a German Army specialty which, next to ham, has the distinction of being the most prized German canned meat. Only small quantities were packed for the U-Boat and for special service use. Pork kasseler was packaged in a special (99 mm/diameter and 25 mm/high or 4" diameter x 1 1/8" high) can and the standard kilo can (99 mm in diameter and 122 mm in height). Gelatin (aspic dish) was sometimes added to the smaller can so that it could be served cold. The larger cans contained no gelatin.

C. Another very important canned meat product was Schmalz, Schmalzfleisch, or lard meat. It was produced in large quantities for the Wehrmacht. There was no equivalent in the United States military. Schmalzfleisch in finished form contained 50% lard and 50% lean pork meat. German soldiers spread the rendered fat on bread. It was viewed as a multiple purpose raw material for soups, stews, and various other potato and vegetable dishes. This product would not have appealed to Allied troops.

The most universally used size of can manufactured for Wehrmacht use was the 1/1 can, also known as the liter or kilo can. *(Author's note: I call it the 850 gram can.)* It is approximately 99 mm in diameter and 122 mm in height. Dr. Nehring and his laboratory staff at Braunschweig were food canning consultants for the canning industry, as well as the Wehrmacht. They were responsible for the Wehrmacht adopting the 99 mm diameter, kilogram, tin-less can as the standard can for Wehrmacht canned goods. These cans were produced from all types of plate, but the most dominant style was black plate with welded side seam. By 1944 over 90% of the kilo cans manufactured in Germany were made from black plate. The terms "A2", "Lema", or "Sila Can" were also used in describing the black plate can. The 99 mm diameter can was made in other heights for special usage (sausage, meat products); the half or "halb" size (99 mm in diameter and 63mm in height); and a special drawn or two piece can manufactured specifically for the military was manufactured (99 mm in diameter and 25 mm height) from enameled black plate. This style of can could be easily slipped into the uniform pocket. A third size of double seamed three piece can made from hot-dipped tin plate was also seen and measured (approximately 75 mm in diameter by 63 mm in height); this can was also used for meat and fish and is called the 200 gram can. This style of can was a component of the Half-Iron ration. A 99 mm x 180 mm can was also seen. Dented cans were not considered a problem by the German consumer, and in extreme cases severely dented cans were given to factory personnel. In the immediate postwar Germany black plate cans were widely used to feed the civilian population.

As mentioned, the black plate can was the most important style of can manufactured for use by the Wehrmacht. A detailed discussion of the

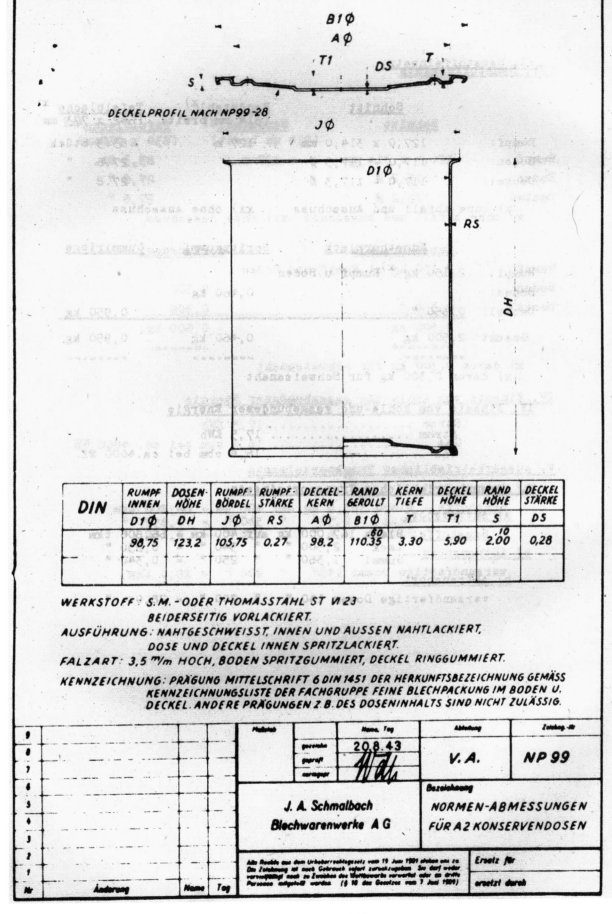

DECKELPROFIL NACH NP99-28.

DIN	RUMPF-INNEN	DOSEN-HÖHE	RUMPF-BÖRDEL	RUMPF-STÄRKE	DECKEL-KERN	RAND GEROLLT	KERN TIEFE	DECKEL HÖHE	RAND HÖHE	DECKEL STÄRKE
	D1Ø	DH	JØ	RS	AØ	B1Ø	T	T1	S	DS
	98,75	123,2	105,75	0,27	98,2	110,35 .60	3,30	5,90	2,00 .10	0,28

WERKSTOFF: S.M.-ODER THOMASSTAHL ST VI 23
      BEIDERSEITIG VORLACKIERT.
AUSFÜHRUNG: NAHTGESCHWEISST, INNEN UND AUSSEN NAHTLACKIERT,
      DOSE UND DECKEL INNEN SPRITZLACKIERT.
FALZART: 3,5 ᵐ/m HOCH, BODEN SPRITZGUMMIERT, DECKEL RINGGUMMIERT.

KENNZEICHNUNG: PRÄGUNG MITTELSCHRIFT 6 DIN 1451 DER HERKUNFTSBEZEICHNUNG GEMÄSS
      KENNZEICHNUNGSLISTE DER FACHGRUPPE FEINE BLECHPACKUNG IM BODEN U.
      DECKEL. ANDERE PRÄGUNGEN Z.B. DES DOSENINHALTS SIND NICHT ZULÄSSIG.

9					Maßstab		Name, Tag	Abteilung	Zeichng.-Nr
8						gezeichn.	20.8.43		
7						geprüft		V. A.	NP 99
6						verlager			
5					J. A. Schmalbach			Bezeichnung	
4					Blechwarenwerke A G			NORMEN-ABMESSUNGEN	
3								FÜR A2 KONSERVENDOSEN	
2								Ersatz für	
1									
Nr	Änderung		Name	Tag				ersetzt durch	

Technical sheet for the A-2 can.

139

black plate can was included in Volume I. Black sheet cans were of the drawn or open top sanitary style (bonderised or unbonderised), which are described as follows:

A. Shallow drawn black plate steel cans were produced for fish and meat with high bake phenolic lacquer; one coat on the outsides and two inside coats. Drawn cans have no side seam or bottom seam, which makes for greater safety in production. These shallow drawn, steel plate cans were manufactured in a variety of shapes: round, oval, and oblong being the most common. They were used to pack fish and meat in oil.

B. For non-acid vegetables, meat, fish, and milk products they used welded black plate cans, which were bonderised and dip lacquered on both sides in one operation, with one coat of high bake phenolic lacquer after the plain steel bottom end was double seamed to the plain steel welded can body, using closing ends prepared by the same method. These cans had a service life of one year.

C. For non acid-vegetables, meat, fish, and milk products they also used non-bonderised, welded black plate cans, produced from dual sided lacquered black plate sheet, the inside and outside welded side seam spray lacquered and the inside of the can with the bottom end attached spray lacquered with one coat of a high bake phenolic lacquer. The closing ends were prepared by the same method.

Until the end of the war the dull-grey, matt-finished, electroplated tin plate cans were reserved for fruits and acidic foods produced for the Wehrmacht. According to Allied intelligence, the Germans began stockpiling tin several years before the outbreak of war. Sufficient reserves of tin were set aside to support the canning industry through the 1945 canning season. The Allied analysts were surprised by the number of 1/1 cans made from electrolytic tin plate, hot dipped tin plate, or mixed tin plate being used for peas and beans. Occasionally, composite plate cans with tin plate bodies (soldered side seams) were found to bear enameled black plate ends. A modest amount of milk packing for government (probably Wehrmacht) contracts was also done in tin plated cans.

Germany succeeded in making fairly satisfactory can lacquers using synthetic resins, fatty acids, and solvents produced from raw materials available in Germany. The Sila and Lema black plate cans are distinguished by the lacquers used to coat the cans. The following descriptions are a bit awkward, but are taken almost verbatim from *A Survey of the Practices of the German Can Industry during the Second World War*:

A. The Schmalbach Factory tin less "Sila" can was made from 2 sides flat lacquered black plate strip or sheet, by inside and outside side seam lacquer striping and inside spray lacquering the welded flat lacquered steel body with the compound lined, double seamed, bottom end attached, using double seamed closing ends prepared by the same methods and materials. This can was guaranteed for one year for all types of non acid vegetables, meat, fish, and milk products. A "Sila Special" can was approved in early 1944 for fruit and acid products. The Sila Special cans have an additional coat of lacquer sprayed on the inside of the can. All but 3 canning firms in Germany were capable of producing the Sila cans. Sila is derived from the term sinter lacquering. The outside lacquer was light brown to brown golden in color.

B. The Zuchner Factory tin less "Lema" can was made from plain, untreated, deoxidized, steel strip or sheet, by bonderising and dip lacquering the welded, plain, steel body with the double seamed bottom end attachments, using double seamed closing ends prepared by the same methods and materials. This can was guaranteed for one year for all types of non acid vegetables, meat, fish, and milk products. Lema cans were generally manufactured for the civilian market.

Allied intelligence analysts found no indication of the development and substitution of low-tin or tin-less solders for the high tin-lead solders used in pre-war Germany. The three most common solders used on tin cans are described below. Black plate cans were manufactured using tin-lead soldered side seams or electrically welded side seams, which didn't use any solder.

An example of the shallow drawn black steel can for fish and meat in oil.

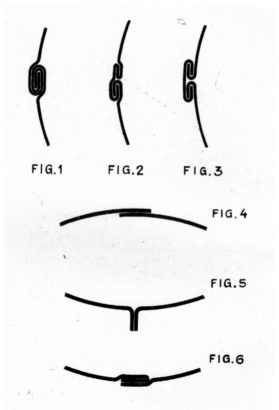

FIG.1   FIG.2   FIG.3

FIG. 4

FIG.5

FIG.6

Some examples of folded side seams that could have replaced welded side seams.

A. *50% Tin-50% Lead Solder*: This solder was used for hot dipped or electrolytic tinplate, lap seam can bodies.

B. *40% Tin-60% Lead Solder*: This solder was used for the high speed soldering of hot dipped and electrolytic tinplate can bodies with the lock and lap style side seam.

C. *60% Tin-40% Lead Solder*: This solder was used whenever hand soldering was being performed.

The Germans explored the option of manufacturing food cans with folded side seams instead of welded seams. The advantages were that the folding process was fully automatic, could be carried out with a high degree of output, and could be used for every type of material. Unfortunately, only cans produced from heavier materials worked when using folded side seams because of issues with can pressure. This increased the requirement for steel sheet, which outweighed all its other advantages.

In Volume I the authors devoted a lot of effort to trying to explain what the DIN stampings on the cans meant. Despite new information covering every technical aspect of the German canning industry, there was still no explanation for the DIN stampings. There doesn't appear to be a connection between the materials, lacquers, manufacturing standards, etc., and the DIN stampings. The theory that the DIN stamps are somehow tied to the packing of the cans still seems plausible; however, it's still nothing more than a theory. After the canned products were sterilized by boiling and cooling, samples of the product were evaluated prior to acceptance. The cooked items were removed from the can and weighed. The can lot was rejected if the weight of the product fell short, if the cans were not air tight, if the cans were dirty or rusty, if the closures were defective, or if the inspector identified any glaring defect. Cans were shook to test how noisy they were. Noisy canned products, except for mixed canned goods, which often were noisy, were stored in a cool room for a few days and retested. The following information was found in a document called the *Einsatzplan für die Fertigung von Konserven Dosen nach DIN*, or the *Operational Plan for the Manufacturing of Cans according to DIN*. On the line directly below the title it states Zahlenangaben 0/00 Packungen, which means to add the DIN Number in place of the 0/00 for type of *packaging* or *packing*. If you look at the picture of the A-2 Sila can technical sheet you will see this statement:

Kennzeichnung: Prägung mittelschrift 6 DIN 1451 der herkunftsbezeichnung gemass kennzeichnung liste der Fachgruppe Feine Blechpackung in boden und deckel. Andere prägungen z.b. des doseninhalts sind nicht zulässig. This roughly translates as: Markings: The top and bottom of the can will be embossed in medium letters in accordance with "6 DIN 1451" and the identification list of the Trade Group for Fine Metal Sheet Packing. Other imprints for example the content of the containers is not permitted. *(Author's note: DIN 1451 is a realist sans-serif typeface widely used for business applications since 1936.)*

So what does that mean? I believe that the Trade Group for Fine Metal Sheet Packing maintained a list explaining the generic information and codes that could be placed on a lid, for example Din Packung, Din 66, WEHRM, etc. This list may be the key to understanding the DIN codes and explain why there is no reference to these codes in any of the standard DIN references. Again, this is just a theory. Additional information including dates, contents, factory codes, etc., was added as determined by the requiring agency i.e. Wehrmacht.

All cans underwent strenuous quality control checks to ensure that they met or exceeded industry standards before they were accepted for use. The technical standards on materials, seaming, coatings, etc., were

Einsatzplan

für die Fertigung von Konservendosen nach DIN
(Zahlenangaben o/oo Packungen) Stand: 1.9.1943.

Another piece of the DIN puzzle, a statement from the *Operational Plan for the Manufacturing of Cans according to DIN*.

exacting and certainly beyond my capability to explain. The Germans designed a series of rapid tests for Sila cans which are set out below. Similar tests probably existed for all styles of cans.

A. *Appearance*: Evenness of coating and absence of blisters, uniformity of color. Adequacy or completeness of side seam stripes.

B. *Can Sealing*: Resistance without leaks to 2.5 atmospheres air pressure.

C. *Porosity*: 10 seconds current flow under 24 Volts (Duffek) must fall between 0.4 to 0.7 amperes.

D. *Lacquer Coating*: Total spray and base coat must fall between 8-12 grams per square meter. This test is made by boiling in Sodium Hydroxide (NaOH). Sections of the can may be cut out for coating weights on specific portions.

E. *Taste Test*: Made on water sealed in the cans and processed 30 minutes at 121^0 Celsius. The taste should not be too pronounced of lacquer, or bitter or medicinal.

F. *Corrosion Test*: Made by processing 1% acetic acid in the sealed can for 30 minutes at 121^0 Celsius. No corrosion, lifting of lacquer, or blistering must be present.

G. *Elasticity Test*: Made by use of the Erichsen 20 mm ball cup test. A 5 mm penetration must be made without hair lines or fracture on the enamel.

H. *Cover Testing*: Completeness of coating, uniformity, evenness of compound, and weight of compound (230-240 mg).

All canned foods manufactured for the Wehrmacht were designated by punching the lid. The lid stamping must contain the following: contents, number of the manufacturing firm, month of manufacture, year of manufacture, and net weight (not necessary with mixed preserved goods). The punches must not have sharp edges in order to avoid damaging the can. The lid stamping must be easy to read. If technically possible (if the stamp colors are resistant to fat), the designation may be made by rubber stamps. If there is no possibility to punch the net weight, the net fill will be done according to the standards established for the particular can type. It should be noted that stamping the cans affected its porosity, or the ability of a material to allow fluids to pass through.

In order to avoid confusion, preserves intended for civilian use or for POWs *must not be marked* as stated above. Preserves intended for the Navy will bear the additional marking "KM".

The German Ministry over meat production on occasion designated non-Wehrmacht products to be produced as Tax Free, or "Freibank". These cans will bear the mark "Freibank".

Many of the product codes found on cans were listed in Volume I. Here are a few additional codes that were either missed during our research, were not correctly annotated, or conflict with the codes in Volume I:

B schi A-Beer ham for hot zones
Bw S-Beer sausage with cerealia
Blw S-Black pudding with cerealia
Gr. Bo. R-Green beans with potatoes and beef
Gr. Bo. S-Green beans with potatoes and pork
Fl Ra-Red meat sausage for hot zones
G B-Roast goose
Hu Gr-Chicken with peeled barley and tomato
Jw S-Jadg sausage with cerealia
Lw S-White liver sausage with cerealia
 Lw A-White liver sausage for hot zones
Schi Benz-Boiled ham for hot zones
SA-Pork for hot zones
SK S-Pork jellied head
Wü Benz-Small sausages for hot zones

A very unusual 850 gram self sealing can. The can allowed products to be canned without the use of special tools to seal it. A special opener was required to open the can.

Another widely manufactured metal container was the 10 kilo pail made with a doped side seam, with or without handle, and with ring seal or lug seal closure. This type of pail is also made in the composite style with metal ends and fiber body, both lacquered and unlacquered. It was widely used for marmalade and jam. It was manufactured in various sizes.

The German military consumed large quantities of smoked, cooked, canned, and dried sausages. It was estimated that 40-45% of Germany's total meat supply was consumed as sausage. For the most part the Wehrmacht Butcher units supplied the military with fresh meats and sausage. These units were also capable of freezing meats and sausage. Commercial firms were called on to supply canned, cured, and special frozen meats. Certain dried sausages were coated with lacquers or other coating in order to protect them. One of the largest cellophane and sausage casing factories was Kalle and Co., located in Wiesbaden. During the war the company operated eight machines that produced sausage casing from viscose. Viscose is generally known as a form of wood cellulose acetate used to make rayon for the textile industry. However, the process was also used to manufacture cellophane used to wrap sausages. In their best year (1943), the Kalle Co. produced 12,000,000 meters of casings per month, equivalent to 180 tons.

A 1935 advertisement for vegetables and fruit packed in standard 1/1 cans (kilo dose).

25mm

99mm

Special Can For Wehrmacht Products

The special drawn or two piece can manufactured specifically for the military, measuring 99 mm in diameter and 25 mm high. It could hold 150-200 grams of product and was made to fit in the tunic pocket.

Bundesarchiv, Bild 1011-748-0090-24A
Foto: Kempe | 1942/1943

Nicely posed
picture
showing
meat in
gelatin,
cigarettes,
and bread.
*Courtesy
OSTFRONT
Militaria.*

Members of the
Grossdeutschland Division
unloading rations. *Bundesarchiv
Bild 1011-748-0090- (24A) and
(28A)/ Foto: Kempe/ License CC-
BY-SA 3.0.*

Bundesarchiv, Bild 1011-748-0090-28A
Foto: Kempe | 1942/1943

This 850 gram
can of Schmalz is
stamped with a generic
Wehrm and 54, but
lacks any product code.
This may indicate it was
manufactured for the
civilian market or POWs.

Veterinarians routinely checked meat
products to make sure they were free of
disease.

Sausage, bread, and maybe some Red Wine. *Courtesy OSTFRONT Militaria.*

Canned products were a very important part of the soldiers' diet. *Courtesy OSTFRONT Militaria.*

143

Can Name	Style	Diameter Long Axis	Diameter Short Axis	Height	Miscellaneous Notes	Standard Yes or No	Reference
Milk	3 Piece	63.5 mm		60.3 mm		NA	VI PG 51
Italian Can	3 Piece	71.3 mm		68 mm		NA	VI PG 75
200 g Can	3 Piece	75 mm		63 mm	For Half Iron Ration	Yes	BIOS
200 g Can	3 Piece	76 mm		66.6 mm		Yes	VI PG 184
Canned Roast	3 Piece	76 mm		58.7 mm	RST 200 g	Yes	VI PG 77
Buttermilk	3 Piece	76 mm		122 mm	Friction top powder	NA	VI PG 45
Milk	3 Piece	76 mm		109.5 mm		NA	VI PG 51
Milk	3 Piece	76 mm		98.4 mm		NA	VI PG 51
Pork	3 Piece	76.2 mm		122 mm		NA	VI PG 88
Canned Beef	3 Piece	90.5 mm		61.9 mm	French	NA	VI PG 74
Butter sweet	3 Piece	99 mm		74.6 mm		NA	VI PG 44
850 g Can	3 Piece	99 mm		122 mm	Most common style	Yes	x
Special	2 Piece	99 mm		25 mm	Lard & Kasseler	Yes	BIOS
Meat tin	3 Piece	98 mm		31.75 mm			VI PG 100
Half size	3 Piece	99 mm		63 mm		Yes	x
1 1/2 to 1	3 Piece	99 mm		180 mm		Yes	x
2 to 1	3 Piece	99 mm		240 mm		Yes	x
Sanitary	3 Piece	106 mm		131.7 mm	Danish butter	NA	VI PG 43
2 to 1	3 Piece	113 mm		184 mm		Yes	x
		4.45"		7.24"			
2 1/2 to 1	3 Piece	113 mm		228 mm		Yes	x
3 to 1	3 Piece	113 mm		260 mm		Yes	x
Butter	3 Piece	117.5 mm		127 mm		NA	VI PG 44
Butter spread	3 Piece	120.6 mm		104.7 mm		NA	VI PG 44
Ham		228.6 mm	330 mm	127 mm	Pear Shaped	NA	VI PG 84
Sardines	2 Piece	41 mm	90 mm	152 mm		NA	VI PG 89
Aluminum	Drawn	105 mm	73 mm	16 mm	1/8 L	Yes	BIOS
Aluminum	Drawn	105 mm	73 mm	22 mm	1/6 L	Yes	BIOS
Sardines	3 Piece	106 mm	65 mm	30 mm	Portugese Oblong	NA	VI PG 63
Aluminum	Drawn	123 mm	76 mm	30 mm		Yes	BIOS
Aluminum	Drawn	148 mm	81 mm	34 mm	281-369 g	Yes	VI PG 64
Sardines	2 Piece	152 mm	84 mm	136.5 mm	Drawn Oblong	NA	VI PG 64
Aluminum	2 Piece	58.7 mm		74.4 mm	Milk	Yes	BIOS
Aluminum	2 Piece	58.7 mm		73 mm	Milk	NA	VI PG 51
Aluminum	2 Piece	73 mm		56 mm	Round	Yes	BIOS
Aluminum	2 Piece	87 mm		76 mm	Round	Yes	BIOS
Aluminum	2 Piece	99 mm		33 mm	Round	Yes	BIOS
Aluminum	2 Piece	135 mm		33 mm	Round	Yes	BIOS
Aluminum	2 Piece	160 mm		46 mm	Round	Yes	BIOS

This chart highlights a selection of cans identified in wartime references. VI PG = Page number in Volume I. BIOS = British Intelligence Reports. Depending on how the can is measured there can be a variance of 4-5 mm.

A wartime receipt from the Dörffler company. A can from this company is shown in Volume I. *Courtesy OSTFRONT Militaria.*

Various views of drawn steel cans used to pack oily fish and meat products.

Sausages were also packed in Aluminum tubes similar to those used for cheese. This rare ground-dug example from Hans Bär is the only evidence they were actually distributed. *Courtesy Andreas Grote.*

V

FRUIT AND VEGETABLE PRODUCTS

In addition to the references cited in Annex I, the following reports were consulted in writing this Annex: *Some Aspects of the German Glass Industry in 1946* and *German Glass Industry*.

Glass was a popular means of packaging for numerous products like fruit, marmalades, jams, honey, etc. The use of glass was not without its disadvantages, as the Germans continually sought to balance the weight of glass against its resistance to breakage. The loss rate due to breakage was estimated at 5% during the years 1943-1945. Generally the use of glass as a packing material for the military was discouraged, but never eliminated. Since glass is almost immune to the ravages of time, ground dug examples are common. This may serve to exaggerate the importance of glass as a packaging product when compared to other materials.

Dehydrated foods played a key role in German ration supply because of their compact size and light weight. The state of the German dehydration industry was assessed as considerable by Allied intelligence personnel. Good marketing practices, the necessities of feeding the civilian and military population, and the shortage of metals were given as the main reasons why this industry grew so quickly. By 1945 the chief limiting factors on food dehydration appeared to be the ability of German agriculture to produce food for dehydration and the manpower shortage in the dehydrating plants to operate the machinery. The products produced in the greatest volume were: cabbage, potatoes, peas, carrots, plums, blueberries, bananas, cherries, beef, beef goulash, onions, sauerkraut, beans, celery, parsley, beets, red peppers, tomatoes, spinach, mushrooms, lentils, apples, rosehips, raisins, peaches, and chestnuts. Other dried items produced in Germany, but not regarded strictly as "dehydrated foods" in the usual sense of the word, included dried milk and eggs. Many methods of packaging were used for dehydrated foods: aluminum foil, laminated papers (ECO packages), heavy moisture-vapor-proof cellophane, lightweight Kraft paper, large size bags made of heavy paper, and small barrels. Dehydrated foods were generally disliked by German soldiers when used as a standalone product, but were acceptable in stews or soups.

The initial reports from Allied combat troops who captured German dehydrated foods indicated that American industry might learn much from Germany in this field. Further investigations narrowed down the list of acceptable dehydrated foods to a few products. Dehydrated eggs proved to be of excellent quality. They were produced on a small scale for the Wehrmacht, especially for submarine crews and specialty areas, like hospitals. The shortage of eggs was the major reason why this industry failed to grow. One very important manufacturer of dehydrated eggs was Kaffee Hag, Bremen. Dehydrated smoked ground beef, a flavorful dehydrated cabbage or sauerkraut, as well as dehydrated potatoes all ranked high on the quality scale.

Standard Normalkonserve 900 cc bottle in white glass used to pack fruit and vegetables.

Commercial can of peas from the Max Koch Factory.[1] *Courtesy OSTFRONT Militaria.*

A tin of Zentis marmalade. *Courtesy OSTFRONT Militaria.*

Sarotti dehydrated apple slices in a pulp paper carton.

A can of strawberries distributed by the Hamburg Import Company.[2] *Courtesy Zeugmeister.*

Generic jar marked "Nur für Nahrungsmittel" and Schwartauer Ovalglas.

Oka plum spread.[3] *Courtesy OSTFRONT Militaria.*

Soldiers were given hints on the proper way to send food home through the Feldpost to avoid breakage and spoiling.

The Hohenlohe company also manufactured pea soup in the shape of a sausage.

Large shipping container for Knorr pea soup. *Courtesy Maciej Tylec Collection.*

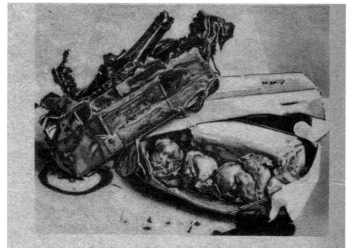

„Liebesgaben" von der Front

Leider nicht so ausgefallen, wie es gedacht war ...! Da hatte man im Osten das schöne Sonnenblumenöl und Butter kaufen können und wollte damit Mutter zu Hause eine freudige Überraschung bereiten. Statt dessen ärgert sie sich nun, und das mit Recht!

Noch wichtiger beinahe als der Inhalt eurer Päckchen ist eine ausreichende und sachgemäße Verpackung — ist die nicht aufzutreiben, laßt lieber das Schicken ganz sein, denn über ein paar fettige Flaschenscherben und einen Klumpen ölgetränktes Papier empfindet niemand Freude, sondern — Ärger. Flaschenverschlüsse immer noch besonders festbinden — Knüllpapier, Heu oder dergleichen zum „Polstern" nehmen! Ein kleines Päckchen, das heil zu Hause landet, ist bestimmt besser als ein großes, das unterwegs ausläuft und sich verflüchtigt, weil es mit der Verpackung haperte.

500 gram package of dehydrated Sauerkraut, which was a popular food item.

These soldiers have taken up residence in a private home. *Courtesy OSTFRONT Militaria.*

A carton of vegetable preservative.[4] *Courtesy OSTFRONT Militaria.*

A 2/1 can of cut beans from the firm H.L. Krone, which was mentioned in the Allied reports.

Two cans of vegetables from Konservenfabrik Gr. Lafferde, Ernst Arend. The company is still in business as Ernst Arends Fleisch- und Wurstwaren e. K. *Courtesy OSTFRONT Militaria.*

A nice prewar display of food products. *Courtesy OSTFRONT Militaria.*

ENDNOTES

[1] Max Koch founded his factory in 1881. By 1905 they were producing 7 million cans of food a year. Initially specializing in canned asparagus and vegetables, they branched out into game, poultry, sausages, soups, and a meat extract "Kochil". The company moved to Karl Schimidt Strasse in the 1950s. In 1964 the company moved to Wolfsburg. Here is their listing in the 1929 Mosse Register of Firms.

[2] No history was found on the Hamburg Import Company. Here is their listing in the 1929 Mosse Register of Firms.

Hamburger Import-Ges. Baresel & Blumenberg (O. Baresel), A H 2 El. 6280, Kolonialwarengrosshdlg., Spaldingstr. 62. Ps 4471. RMC.

[3] No history was found on the Oka Plum Spread Factory. Here is their listing in the 1929 Mosse Register of Firms.

Otto Klaus
„Oka"-Pflaumenmus-Fabrik
Hamburg 22
Alter Teichweg 33|35
Bankkonto: Deutsche Bank, Filiale Hamburg. Depositenkasse C
Telegr.-Adr.: „Okamus"
Tel.: H 3 Alst. 3485. H 4 Nords. 3867, H 5 Merk. 825
für Ferngespr. H 5 Merkur 6030

[4] No history was found on the firm. Here is their listing in a wartime Vienna phone book.

Rector Karl (Leopoldine) Erzeugung v. Konservierungsmitteln Betrieb VII/62 Seideng 27
B 3 24 34

VI

COFFEES, TEA, AND OTHER BEVERAGES

I n addition to the references cited in Annex I, the following report was consulted in writing this Annex: *Report on the German Soft Drink Industry with Special Reference to the Study of Ascorbic Acid in Fruit Beverages.*

I deviated from the format in Volume I by incorporating all discussion of beverages into this annex. The Allied intelligence reports did not contain any new information about the use or manufacture of coffees and tea. The Allies did conduct a limited survey on the German soft drink and bottled water industry which is discussed below.

In general terms the factories that bottled natural mineral water had higher standards than those concerned with table waters. Table water is an artificial mixture of tap water and other ingredients, such as saltwater or mineral water. Since table water is not bound to a specific spring it may be produced and bottled anywhere. The Germans stressed the medicinal benefits of natural mineral water. The Allies were complementary about the high percentage of recycled bottles used in the industry. A frequently encountered bottle was the 1/3 liter size (approximately 12 fluid ounces). Screw, swing top, and crown cork were all commonly used as closures. The crown corks were often made from tin less and unlacquered metal. The following water bottling firms were visited by the Allies after the war: Elbschlossbrauerei-Hamburg, Hinrich Woerdemann-Hamburg, Kirdorf & Co.-Dusseldorf, Apollinaris Brunnen Aktiengesellschaft-Bad Neunenahr, Brohler Mineralbrunnen G.m.b.h.-Brohl am Rhein, Bronni Mineralbrunnen-Niederbreisig am Rhein, Rhenser Mineralbrunnen-Rhens am Rhein, and Tonissteiner Sprudel-Brohl am Rhein.

Fruit beverages were generally confined to those that could be produced from home grown materials. Fruit squashes like lemon, orange, etc., never gained wide popularity in Germany. The current definition of a fruit squash (also called cordial) is a non-alcoholic concentrated syrup that is usually fruit-flavored and usually made from fruit juice, water, and sugar. On the other hand, fruit juices produced in Germany from apples, grapes, raspberries, etc., were considered as very palatable and refreshing. The fruit juice industry ranged in size from "one man" businesses to large factories. The German fruit juice industry originated in the cider making industry. The production of unfermented beverages then followed as a natural development when means of preserving them became known and a public demand became evident. The juices were placed in bottles which were closed with corks or crown corks. As a special note, the Germans produced a beverage rich in Vitamin C known as Sanddornberry. The Sanddorn plant is more commonly known as Sea-buckthorn, which has dense, stiff, and very thorny branches. The Wolfra A.G. firm in Munich was one firm involved in producing Sanddornberry juice. Sanddornberry juice is still being produced in Germany. The following fruit juice bottling firms were visited by the Allies after the war: Plöner Süssmosterei-Plön I Holst, Sudfrucht Verwertung-Hamburg, Essenzenfabrik und Fruchtpresserei-Hilden Rhein, F. Blumhoffer Nachfolger-Köln, Wolfra A.G.-Munich, Kondima Werk-Karlsruhe, Frankfurter Grosskellerei-Frankfurt a.M, Dr. Baumann-Obererlenbach, and Kreuznacher Fruchtsaftkellerei G.m.b.h.-Bad Kreuznach.

Bag of coffee substitute made from figs from the firm Andre Hofer.[1] *Courtesy OSTFRONT Militaria.*

Inside an Air Force Kantine. *Courtesy Bill Petz.*

A package of Ersatz tea manufactured in Warsaw, Poland. It weighs 1/2 a Decagram, or 5 grams.

Königs brand coffee manufactured in Dresden.[2] *Courtesy OSTFRONT Militaria.*

Mauxion brand cocoa. *Courtesy OSTFRONT Militaria.*

A package of ABEA coffee. *Courtesy Ruelle Frédéric Collection.*

Package of Emil Seelig coffee.[5] *Courtesy Kevin Barrett.*

A can of instant coffee distributed by the HEYO Vertrieb.[3]

Package of Kascha tea manufactured from cocoa shells.

An energy product called Kola 100. The use of African Kola meal was popular in the 1920s.

A package of Jacobs Coffee.[4] *Courtesy Militaria-Versand Emig.*

Dividing up the tobacco and alcohol ration. *Courtesy Bill Petz.*

Coca-Cola was widely available during the early years of the war. *Courtesy Paul Gromkowski.*

Alcohol was popular with the German soldier.
Courtesy OSTFRONT Militaria.

Nescafe instant coffee is one of the most recognized brands in the world.[6] *Courtesy Rich Prandoni.*

A package of coffee from Kaffee Hag. *Courtesy Militaria-Versand Emig.*

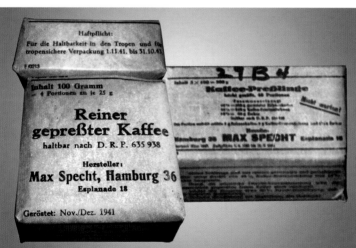

Package of pressed coffee from the Max Specht firm, along with the photograph in the U.S. Army Ration Report. *Courtesy Chris Karr Collection.*

Beer being stored. *Courtesy OSTFRONT Militaria.*

A can of Nestlé brand NESCAO along with an ad from 1934.

Ersatz coffee manufactured by Heida Werk, Müller, and Company. *Courtesy Kevin Barrett.*

Herva, a wartime soft drink.[7]

ENDNOTES

[1] The Andre Hofer company was founded in 1759. It was in business at least until the 1960s. Here is their listing in the 1929 Mosse Register of Firms.

[2] The Paul König Malt Factory was founded in 1889. No postwar history was located. Here is their listing in the 1929 Mosse Register of Firms.

[3] After two decades of research I still haven't determined with absolute certainty whether this can is wartime or not. Trying to track down the product and firm proved fruitless, so I researched the address and phone number. The street name is written as Thalstrasse or Talstrasse. In 1887 the famous Jewish lithographer Adolf Friedländer set up his shop at Thalstrasse 83-85; the same address on the can. Adolph Friedländer passed away on 7 July 1904, and after his death his sons Louis and Max Otto operated the company. As best I can determine they would occupy Thalstrasse 83-85 until 1935.

According to the information in the 1929 Mosse Register of firms, the street was spelled Talstrasse. By 1941 it was spelled Thalstrasse, according to the 1941 Hamburg phone book. It would continue to go by Thalstrasse until at least 1950, when it was named Talstrasse again. Given the level of destruction inflicted on Hamburg during the war it's unlikely that a new business sprung up at Thalstrasse 83 after the war.

A check of the 1941 Hamburg phone book indicated that the telephone prefixes 42 and 4211 were in use during the war. Based on the available evidence I believe the can is pre-1945.

[4] The Jacobs Kaffee roasting plant was opened in Bremen in 1906. Over the next 20 years the company rapidly expanded, including a successful mail order operation. By 1930 they were advertising in the U.S. The factory was destroyed in October 1944. The company rebuilt after the war and is still in business. Here is their listing from the 1929 Mosse Register of Firms.

Jacobs, Johann, ℛ D. 25275, Kaffee, Obernstr. 20. Ps 46796 Hg.
Jacobs & Co., Joh. (Joh. J.), ℛ D. 25577, Kaffeehandlung, Bonspforte 2. Ps 46796 Hg.

[5] The Emil Seelig chicory factory was founded in 1859. It was transformed into an AG in 1892. In 1943 the firm acquired the Pfeiffer GmbH & Diller coffee essence factory, Horchheim b. Worms. The name of the company was changed from the Emil Seelig corporation to Seelig and Diller A.-G., Heilbronn.

[6] As discussed in Annex 2, the Nescafé brand name has been in existence since April 1, 1938. When it was actually introduced to the German market is debatable. As I stated in Annex 2, I believe that Nescafé was introduced to Germany between 1939 and 1941, not 1943 as many web sources state. The real question is what does a wartime German Nescafé can or collapsible tube look like? Unfortunately I haven't located a picture of any wartime German Nescafé products. I did obtain some pictures of pre-war cans and a collapsible tube from Switzerland and France. There was also a German Nescafé can reported to have been brought back by a U.S. veteran that was posted on the internet, but unfortunately I couldn't use it due to copyright issues. The appearance of the subject can is consistent with those cans except for the size, with the subject can appearing to be larger. However, Nescafé cans produced in the late 1940s, 1950s, and 1960s all look very similar to the pre-war cans and subject can. The Nestlé logo on the subject can was in use from 1938 until 1965, which doesn't help in trying to date the can. I have included a picture of the two logos that would have appeared on wartime Nestlé products. I also included a comparison of a known postwar can alongside the subject can. There are a number of differences. While I can't say with absolute certainty that the subject can is wartime, I have a strong belief that it might be.

The Deutsche Schulverein, or German School Association, label is interesting. The association was founded in 1880 with the goal of strengthening education, especially for Germans living abroad and on the border. It was disbanded on 13 March 1938.

[7] There was no history available on the firm that produced Herva. By 1942 much of the embossing was replaced by a paper label. Here is a wartime advertisement.

1940

1938

1875-1938   1938-1965

Postwar   Subject Can

VII

SPICES, BAKING AIDS, BOUILLON, AND MISCELLANEOUS

As the war escalated, German food specialists and logisticians were challenged with feeding the force in the face of declining raw materials and transportation. The watchword was "To Simplify". For some food products, universal or base recipes called "frame formulae" were distributed to manufacturers. Other products were discontinued for a variety of reasons to include the destruction of factories or vital equipment. Some products were discontinued in order to free up raw materials for other products. In certain cases foods were modified to improve quality and acceptance by the troops. Some of these attempts "To Simplify" during the 1944-1945 timeframe included the following:

A. As the food situation deteriorated the use of Bratlingspulver increased, although it was normally not a well liked product. Bratlingspulver had the advantage of taking food of good nutritive value but poor palatability and appearance and turning it into an acceptable product. A bratlingspulver concentrate was developed that reduced its volume.

B. Egg substitutes were discontinued.

C. Powdered sauces, such as tomato sauce, onion sauce, etc., were discontinued.

D. Hard marmalades were abandoned in favor of marmalade pastes.

E. Wet mustard was abandoned in favor of powdered mustard.

F. Pickles and mineral water were no longer shipped to the front because of weight and transportation.

G. Butter cakes and Kraft Keks were all produced under a single frame formula.

H. Fruit slices and fruit bars were simplified in favor of a sugar covered bar made to a frame formula developed by Sarotti. The coating was made of hard fat without cocoa and with sugar and ground roasted nuts. The filling was made mostly of dried fruits with just a little fat.

I. Studentenfutter, or food to be eaten out of the pocket made of raisins, dried apricots, plums, and nuts, were stretched by 50% with the addition of puffed and roasted cereals.

J. Marzipan was discontinued due to a shortage of nuts and seeds.

K. Evaporated milk was replaced by powdered milk.

L. Mixed canned foods were developed to save half of the cans required by evaporating 50% of the liquid before the cans were filled. This product was later dehydrated in order to eliminate the use of cans completely.

M. The "Marching Beverage", or Marsch Getrank, continued to be manufactured despite complaints of a terpeney flavor. A lack of citric acid and better packaging materials did not allow the pursuit of an adequate solution.

When a new food or replacement food material was developed, it was prepared and served in the research kitchens of the OKH and examined by the staff. It was then evaluated on a point system in which flavor, appearance, consistency, and other properties were considered. After being approved by the OKH, the item was tested on a large scale to include troop trials. All the results were returned to the OKH for their final decision. Towards the end of the war, products were fielded regardless of their acceptance by the troops. Some but not all of the interesting efforts to improve food quality or acceptance by the troops are discussed below. Even though the following products were fully developed and deemed as satisfactory, it's not known if they were all actually adopted due to shortages of raw materials, lack of packing materials, etc. I have offered my opinions on whether an item was fielded based on available evidence.

A. Fried meat paste for use as a bread spread. The product could be used cold as a bread spread or warmed with water and flour to make goulash. The product was packed in cartons and had a storage life of 3-5 weeks at room temperature. *(Author's note: Probably fielded.)*

B. Canned Whale meat was tried as a new source of protein. *(Author's note: It's unlikely that this product was ever fielded because of the need for immediate canning.)*

C.   Smoked meat baked in bread dough was an alternative to improve the acceptance of Pemmican. *(Author's note: Probably fielded.)*

D.   Fat free potato chips as an easily carried snack. *(Author's note: Probably fielded.)*

E.   Cold pudding, which eliminated the need for cooking. *(Author's note: Probably fielded. "Notverpflegung Süß", produced by the Bahlsen firm, could be eaten as a cold pudding.)*

F.   Muesli, made of oats, sugar, and milk powder, was developed for flyers. *(Author's note: Probably fielded.)*

G.   Self heating cans were developed with a separate compartment on the end which contained quick lime and water. These two materials were separated until the can was punctured, which caused a chemical reaction which produced heat. *(Author's note: No examples have surfaced.)*

H.   Partially cooked soups were developed to allow one person to feed a large number of troops with ease. The soup was made from partially dehydrated potato squares or strips with dry bacon strips and spices, or from rice mixed with dried plums and other ingredients. It was boiled in hot water for 20-40 minutes. *(Author's note: Probably fielded.)*

I.   A product called Flaedle (Dried Pancake Strips) was developed for Mountain troops. It consisted of pancakes sliced into strips and dehydrated. It was reconstituted by pouring hot broth, water, or milk over them. Its nutritive value was high and it was lightweight. *(Author's note: This product is mentioned as a component of certain emergency rations and was probably fielded.)*

J.   A concentrated Pancake powder and paste was developed for Mountain troops. It was made from flour, whole egg powder, whole milk powder, butter, sugar, and flavoring. It was reconstituted by mixing with water and frying it in its own fat. *(Author's note: Probably fielded.)*

K.   Marmalade powder and Apple powder were produced by dehydrating fruit pulp. It was reconstituted by mixing it with water and citric acid or lemon juice. *(Author's note: Probably fielded.)*

L.   A Marzipan like product was manufactured from pine nuts and plum seed kernels. It had a good flavor but short storage life. It was eaten as a fruit bar or candy filling. *(Author's note: Probably fielded.)*

M.   Dried herbs were compressed under high pressure into cone shaped forms that could be grated. *(Author's note: Probably fielded.)*

N.   Yeast flakes were developed that resembled chicken soup when placed in boiling water. *(Author's note: Probably fielded.)*

O.   A nougat like mass was manufactured from roasted wheat to replace the nuts in fillings for chocolates. It contained roasted wheat, hardened fat, sugar, and flavoring. *(Author's note: Probably fielded.)*

P.   Dry vinegar was produced in cubes or squares similar to sugar. The cubes were simply dissolved in water and used like normal vinegar. *(Author's note: Probably fielded.)*

Another baking product from the Mondamin firm. *Courtesy OSTFRONT Militaria.*

A package of Klein and Rindt spices.[1] *Courtesy Ruelle Frédéric Collection.*

160

A package of Diemer spices.[2]
Courtesy Ruelle Frédéric Collection.

A small ground dug bottle of TERWYENS apple Pectin.

A package of Alba fruit preparation endorsed by the Deutsche Frauenwerk.

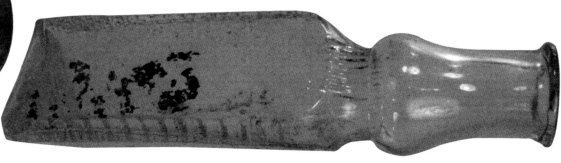

A small 4 inch high, ground dug bottle of vinegar.

A small bottle of baker's salt.[3]

Uvocal energy powder containing calcium, phosphorous, and grape sugar.[5]

A container of 100 Tricalcol tablets, which were a combination of calcium, egg white, and phosphorous. It was manufactured by Lecinwerk, Dr. Ernst Laves of Hannover, which operated from 1908 into the 1950s.

Knorr bouillon cubes.
Courtesy Kevin Barrett.

162

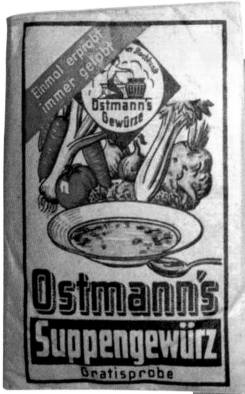

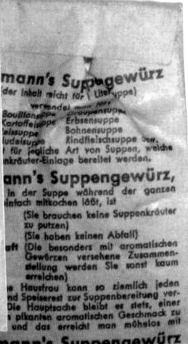

A package of Ostmann brand soup spices. *Courtesy Kevin Barrett.*[4]

Ground dug spice shakers are pretty common finds among German possessions.

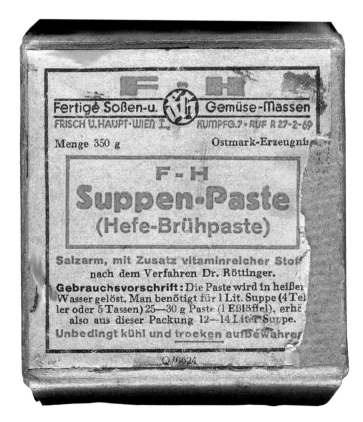

Soup paste.[6]

A jar of Quambusch mustard.

These RAD members had soup or stew for lunch. *Courtesy Paul Gromkowski.*

Large sack for salt. *Courtesy Zeugmeister.*

This officer has paused for a soup break. *Courtesy Paul Gromkowski.*

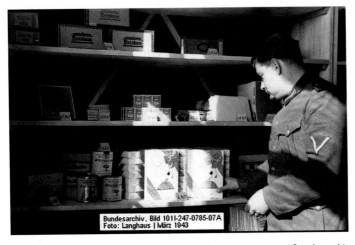

A soldier browsing the aisles of what may be a unit canteen. *Bundesarchiv Bild 1011-247-0785-07A/ Foto: Langhaus/ License CC-BY-SA 3.0.*

Package of baking powder from the Danish firm of W. Bahncke & Co. A / S.[7] *Courtesy Kevin Barrett.*

This package of baking powder from the Danish Graasten Chemical factory appears to be of wartime construction.

Liebig brand bouillon powder. *Courtesy Kevin Barrett.*

Baking powder manufactured by the Dr. Oetker firm. *Courtesy Kevin Barrett.*

UBENA brand artificial pepper with an expiration date of 1 October 1947. *Courtesy Andreas Grote.*

Baking powder from the Döhler firm. *Courtesy Kevin Barrett.*

Advertisement for Knorrox brand soup products.

Indu brand thyme from Fortkamp and Wiegers.[10] *Courtesy Kevin Barrett.*

Ground dug can of Karo Syrup.[13]

A package of Anise from the Alba firm. *Courtesy Kevin Barrett.*

Pickling powder from the Reese society.[9] *Courtesy Kevin Barrett.*

ENDNOTES

Boullo brand bouillon cubes.[8] *Courtesy OSTFRONT Militaria.*

[1] There was no history available on the Klein and Rindt spice Company. Jochen Rindt, the son of the owners, became a famous Formula 1 driver and Grand Prix winner after the war. He became heir to the firm after his parents were killed in 1943 during an air raid in Hamburg. The company did continue to operate after the war. Here is their listing in the 1929 Mosse Register of Firms.

[2] There was no history available on the Diemer spice company. Here is their listing in the 1929 Mosse Register of Firms.

[3] There was no history available on E. Hagenmüller. Here is their listing in the 1929 Mosse Register of Firms.

> **Fleischgewürze.**
> ×**Hagenmüller, E.,** ℵ 67,Ps1627
> Le. *Fleisch-* und *Fischgewürz*
> „Allerlei".

[4] Pharmacist Karl Ostmann founded the Ostmann Spice Factory in 1902. He patented the first spice cabinet in 1928. "Ostmann-Gewürze – von der Mühle bis zur Küche" (Ostmann-Spices-from the Mill to the Kitchen) was a brand concept that prevailed in 1930s Germany. In 1938 Karl Ostmann moved from his house to a former grain mill on the Mark Brandenburg Road in Bielefeld. The company is still in business. Here is their listing in the 1929 Mosse Register of Firms.

> Ostmann, Karl. Gewürzmühle, ℵ
> 2956. Ⓖ. Ps 3633 Hn.

DOWA brand soup extract.[12] *Courtesy Marcin Jonczyk Collection.*

[5] No history was found on the Pharm. Laboratorium, Dr. Anton Dull, KG, Hamburg. Here is their listing in the 1941 Hamburg Phone Book.

> **Düll Anton** Dr. Bakteriologe u.
> Apotheker Techn.-bakteriol. Labor. Hmb 11 Kl Reichenstr 21-23
> **32 55 80**
> priv. Hmb 20 Heilwigstr 108
> **52 04 40**

All purpose spice from Gebr. Wichartz, Wuppertal.[11] *Courtesy Kevin Barrett.*

[6] No history was found on the Frisch and Haupt Konservierte Lebensmittel. It's believed the pictured item is military issue. Here is the firm listing in the 1943 Vienna Phone Book.

Frisch & Haupt konservierte Lebensmittel I/1 Kumpfg 7 R 2 72 69 + Erzeugung der F-H-Nährmittel XVIII/110 Schumanngasse 34 A 2 93 42

[7] The W. Bahncke & Co.'s factory A / S is a Danish mustard vinegar and canning factory originally founded in 1830 in Kiel, Germany. It relocated to Copenhagen, Denmark, in 1858. It is still in business.

[8] No history was found on the Boullo Factory, however, I did find references to Boullo cubes being used to make soup in 1944.

[9] The Reese Society was founded in the early 1900s and is still in operation. Here is a pamphlet from the 1930s.

Rmn Rezepte für die feine Küche u. Hausbäckerei

Den Hausfrauen gewidmet von der

REESEGESELLSCHAFT m. b. H. HAMELN a.d. WESER

[10] Fortkamp and Wiegers was founded in 1921 and is still in business. Here is their listing in the 1929 Mosse Register of Firms.

Nahrùngsmittel-Industrie GmbH, ℜ 745, Mühlen (Gewürz), Weststr. 2. Ⓖ, Ps 9870 Ess.

[11] No history was found on Gebr. Wichartz, Wuppertal. Prior to 1930 Wuppertal was called Barmen. They are still in business. Here is their listing in the 1929 Mosse Register of Firms.

Wichartz, Gebr. (Frz. u. Aug. W.), ℜ 6430–32, Gewürz – R., Wichlinghauser Str. 16/16A. Ⓖ, Ps 9877 Kn.

[12] Today's Wachter AG Company was founded in 1934 by Donatus Wachter as Dowa soup extracts, Wachter GmbH, Nuremberg. It produced "Dowa" and "Supex" brand meat bouillon, broths grained, chicken broth, foie gras, aspic, and salad dressings. During the Second World War the facilities in Nuremberg and those in the Oberpfalz were bombed. After the war the company moved to Schwaig. Here is the company listing in the 1938 Nuremberg phone book.

Wachter, Alois, Getreide und Futtermittel, Holz u. Kohlen. Linde's Kunsteis-Vertrieb, Oedenberger Str 58 5 06 87 Whg. Danziger Str. 17 (5 06 87) — Donatus & Sohn, Suppenextrakte u. Lebensmittelfabrik, Nbg.-S, Maffeipl. 15 4 25 51

[13] The Corn Products Refining Company of New York and Chicago was formed on May 13, 1902. It was renowned for the production of Karo Light and Dark Corn Syrup. The company is still in business. The company website makes no mention of production facilities in Germany. However, it certainly appears as if the subject can is associated with the U.S. firm that manufactured Karo Syrup. Here are some pre-war U.S. Karo advertisements.

VIII

SUGARS, CANDY, JAMS, AND OTHER DESSERT PRODUCTS

In addition to the references cited in Annex I, the following reports were consulted in writing this Annex: *Tartaric Acid Processes in Germany, Sugar Confectionary and Chocolate Manufacture in Germany, German Chocolate and Confectionery Machinery Design and Processing, Schoko-Buck Stuttgart, German Chocolate Cocoa and Confectionery Production Layout and Manufacturing Methods, Chocolate Products-Superior Keeping Qualities, Manufacture of Soya Flour and Soya Chocolate and Cocoa Combinations at Gartmann-Hamburg and Affiliated Plants Elsewhere, Scientific Background of the German Chocolate Industry,* and *Chocolate–Kola Formulae and Manufacturing Process Schoko-Buck G.m.b.H. Stuttgart.*

Candies, chocolates, and other sweets were very popular with the German soldier. Many of these products were mentioned in Allied intelligence reports; unfortunately not all of them were discussed in detail. I have included any mention of these products, in case examples show up on the collector market. Here are descriptions of the various sweets mentioned in the British intelligence reports:

A. Soya cocoa, consisting of 80% powdered cocoa and 20% powdered debittered Soya flour, was developed that used water instead of milk. It had a slight laxative effect. Cocoa was successfully extended by adding bits of Knäckebrot, roasted pea flour, barley flour, or pumpkin flour.

B. The Sprengel firm produced Mokka Bon Bons or Mokka Kugeln manufactured from coffee, vegetable oil, sunflower oil, debittered Soya flour, sugar, almond oil, and whole milk. It had a caffeine content of 0.13%. Twelve pieces (weighing 50 grams total) were packed in a parchment bag, 30 bags per shipping carton. The Sprengel firm probably developed the frame formula that was distributed to other manufacturers.

C. The Sprengel firm produced dehydrated grape jelly utilizing grape juice, concentrated apple puree, marmalade, sugar, and liquid pectin. Each piece was dusted lightly with talc and packed/sealed in cellophane bags. The bag is placed in a carton which is wrapped with cellophane. The finished product weighed 85 grams. Thirty cartons constituted a shipping case. The Sprengel firm probably developed the frame formula that was distributed to other manufacturers.

D. The Sarotti firm solved the problem of chocolate stability under tropical conditions, which resulted in the manufacture of a product initially named "Schokotropa" and finally "Tropolade". Schokotropa withstands the highest practical storage temperatures encountered in the hottest tropical regions without smelting or softening to a point of form distortion. It doesn't melt in the mouth and has a "bread like" consistency when chewed. The Schokotropa recipe consisted of 5% finely melted chocolate, 15% powdered cocoa, 15% anhydrous glucose, 15% invert beet sugar, 40% beet sugar, and 10% dried ground fruits. The mix is formed into bars, then wrapped in moisture proof cellophane and placed into an outer printed paper wrap. Schokatropa was discontinued after the African campaign ended, but was probably available for some time after that. The Navy approved Tropolade for tropical storage on 17 March 1944. The Tropolade recipe consisted of 41% cocoa mass, 5% anhydrous glucose, 5% freshly pressed cocoa butter, 20% beet sugar, and 30% dextrose. It had a good consistency, and the addition of orange peels improved its flavor. Both Schokotropa and Tropolade appear to have been packaged in 50 gram portions.

E. Dehydrated plums appeared to have been a popular ration item for the Wehrmacht and Waffen SS. The dehydrated plums were tough leathery products easily reconstituted with water. It was popular with Submariners and was chewed as a gum. The product was sweet but did not provoke thirst.

F. Stimulating foods similar to Scho-ka-kola, in the fact they used chocolate and kola as ingredients were produced. The brand names Hilkola, Koffinos, Mokka Kugeln, and Glykolade appeared to have been popular. Sometime in 1944 or 1945 Hilkola, Koffinos, and Mokka Kugeln were discontinued in order to utilize the raw materials for Scho-ka-kola and Glykolade.

G. The Rutli Schokoladenwerke, Herford, produced a unique chocolate covered fondant cream bar which supposedly had a particularly soft, with attractive consistency, cream center. The fondant cream center consisted of water, sugar, and glucose. The final composition was 42-43% chocolate covering and 57-58% cream filling. The bar measured 12 cm x 4 cm x 0.8 cm and weighed 50 grams. The majority of chocolate bars issued in Emergency/Special Rations weighed 50 grams. It was packaged in a double envelope wrap, glassine liner, and printed paper outer cover.

H. Towards the end of the war Weinsaurebonbons (Tartaric acid drops), peppermints, wheat dragees, and gums were eliminated due to a lack of sugar. A dragee is used to describe any sugar coated confection, including nuts, raisins, and chocolate. A wheat dragee, or weizen dragee, had a wheat center and had some medicinal properties. The individual portion rate for candies was generally 30 grams.

I. During the war the Kondima Werk in Karlsruhe produced a rose hip preserve containing Sanddornberries for U-Boat crews. It was produced in the form of a thick paste and was used as a spread.

Prior to the war the trade organization of the German chocolate industry was the Verband Deutscher Schokolade Fabrikanten, which was a voluntary organization. In 1934 all chocolate and sugar confectionary manufacturers were organized into the Fachgruppe Susswaren Industrie der Wirtschaftsgruppe Lebensmittel Industrie, Berlin W. 15, Kurfurstendamm 46, a compulsory organization. It was believed that the Berlin office was destroyed during the war. During the war the stocks of cocoa beans were divided among six firms in various parts of Germany. Only three of those firms were mentioned in the Allied reports: Schoko-Buck, B. Sprengal, and Fehleisen & Rickel. It's interesting that these three firms all produced Scho-ka-kola.

The Allies were especially interested in the manufacture of chocolate for the military. Three terms frequently encountered in wartime German publications are: Scho-ka-kola, Wehrmacht Schokolade, and Heeres Schokolade. I believe the term Wehrmacht Schokolade was used to describe chocolate products manufactured without milk for all branches of the military. Non-milk Scho-ka-kola, or Edelbitter Scho-ka-kola, was sometimes referred to as Wehrmacht Schokolade. I'm not exactly sure what Heeres Schokolade is, but by definition it was a chocolate product manufactured specifically for the army. I have not encountered any product that went by the name Heeres Schokolade. Could the term apply to chocolate manufactured using milk? I don't know.

After the war personnel from the B. Sprengal, Fehleisen & Rickel, Schule-Hohenlohe, C. F. Hildebrand, Schoko-Buck, Suchard, and Sarotti firms were interviewed as part of the Allied investigation of the industry. The German manufacturers emphasized the importance of storing chocolate under uniformly cool, dry conditions, avoiding sudden temperature changes. Chocolate, having a low fat content, will keep much longer, and the addition of whole or skimmed milk powder lessens storage life. German troops were issued a somewhat bitter chocolate to reduce the thirst provoking effects of chocolate, such as American milk chocolate. The German soldier generally preferred the bitter chocolate taste. These facts, together with the shorter storage period which the shorter German supply lines made possible, all contributed to avoid "bloom" difficulties. The caffeine content of the added kola paste gave an appreciable "lift" to fatigued troops. The Allies were impressed with the high speed automatic

Product Name	Packaging	Weight	Known Makers	Product Name	Packaging	Weight	Known Makers
Mokka Bon Bons or Mokka Kugeln	12 individual pieces in a parchment bag	50 g	Sprengel	Scho-ka-kola	Plain square carton.	50 g	Unknown
Fondant Cream Bar	double envelope wrap: glassine liner and printed paper outer cover	50 g	Rutli Schokoladenwerke	Scho-ka-kola	Wrapped in paper and placed in metal tin	90g or 100g	Hildebrand
Schokotropa	Unknown but likely a waxed paper box	50 g	Sarotti	Fruchtschnitten	Cardstock box wrapped in cellophane	80 g	Sarotti, Suchard, Hildebrand and Bahlsen
Tropolade	Unknown but likely a waxed paper box	50 g	Sarotti	Fruchtriegel	Wax Paper and cardstock	80 g	Reichelt-Röseler, Felsche
Glycolade	Wax paper box	50 g	Sarotti	Dehydrated Grape Jelly	cellophane bags	85 g	Sprengel
Wehrmacht Gefüllte Schokolade	Waxed Sulphite paper and Printed Bond Paper	50 g	Hildebrand	V Drops	5 pieces wrapped in wax paper with a paper outer wrap	22 g ?	Lobositz
Wehrmacht Schokolade	Printed Bond Paper	50 g	Manner	V Drops	Wax paper envelope	30 g or 50 g	Lobositz and Achenwall
HILKOLA	Paper carton	50 g ?	Hildebrand	Weinsäure Zucker	Candy wrapped in cellophane placed in box	55 g	Wissoll
Koffinos	Unknown	50 g ?	Unknown	Caramels	Waxed paper	4-5 g each?	Milupa
Scho-ka-kola	Round metal or paper carton	100 g	Fehleisen and Rickel, Sprengel, Hildebrand, Wilhelm Felsche, Schoko-Buck/Buck Aktiengesellschaft, and Manner	Dextrose or Grape Sugar	Outer paper carton.	Four 25 g rolls.	Erich Schumm
Dextrose or Grape Sugar	Cellophane and paper.	50 g	Maizena Werke	Kolamint	Round Metal Can	?	Laboratory "Leo"
Notverpflegung Süß	Cardstock Carton	300 g	Bahlsen				

A summary of selected candies and sweets available to the German soldier.

Ingredients	Cocoa Mass	Cocoa Butter	Sugar	Cola Paste	Whole Milk Powder	Skim Milk Powder	Caffeine Content	Lecithin	Vanillin
1939 Vollmilch Schokakola	14.25%	13.25%	38.00%	5.00%	19.00%	10.50%			
1940 Vollmilch Schokakola	13.95%	13.00%	37.20%	7.00%	18.60%	10.25%			
1940 Wehrmacht Chocolate	50.00%	2.00%	40.00%	8.00%				0.15%	0.13%
1942 Wehrmacht Chocolate	40.00%	2.00%	50.00%	8.00%				0.15%	0.13%
1942 Edelbitter Schokakola	40.00%	1.00%	51.00%	8.00%			0.20%		
1944 Wehrmacht Chocolate	40.00%	1.00%	51.00%	8.00%				0.15%	0.13%
1945 Skim Milk Schokakola	24.00%	9.50%	38.50%	9.50%		18.50%			
Milk Scho-ka-kola General	16.00%	12.00%	37.00%	7.50%	27.50%		0.20%		
Milk and Skim Milk Scho-ka-kola	14.00%	13.00%	37.00%	7.00%	19.00%	10.00%	0.20%		
Coating for Wehrmacht Chocolate Bars	Cocoa Mass	Cocoa Butter	Powdered Sugar	Chocolate Liquour	Lecithin and Vanilla				
Schoko-Buck	21.00%	20.00%	57.00%	2.00%	800 g				

Frame formulas for Scho-ka-kola, Wehrmacht Chocolate, and a coating for Wehrmacht Chocolate manufactured by Schoko-Buck.

packaging and sealing machines (cellophane) and the cocoa butter press, which operated on a continuous process basis and automatically ejected the cocoa cake. These machines were inspected at the Schoko-Buck and Suchard firms.

The Hildebrand firm is best known for its production of Scho-ka-kola. It was Mr. Rinne, the firm's technical director, who produced and patented Scho-ka-kola. Interestingly enough, Hildebrand was in negotiations with British authorities to either market or produce Scho-ka-kola in England before the war broke out.

The formulas/recipes for Scho-ka-kola and Wehrmacht Chocolate were modified from year to year during the war as raw material shortages demanded. The cocoa used was good fermented Accra and superior Arriba. The frame formulas or recipes are shown below:

Allied intelligence conducted a number of interviews and site visits with the Schoko-Buck firm in Stuttgart. The factory came through the war in pretty decent shape and large stocks of raw materials for making chocolate were on hand. During the war the plant remained in operation until April 20, 1945, when the Allies entered the city. According to interviews conducted with plant personnel, the company started manufacturing Scho-ka-kola for the military in 1936. Personnel from Schoko-Buck said they never produced any Scho-ka-kola products for the civilian market. If the statements are true, then it's likely that Schoko-Buck manufactured the early Reichsadler version shown in Volume I. The only known manufacturers identified on the Reichsadler cans are Hildebrand and Mauxion. I'm assuming that the Schoko-Buck firm produced the Scho-ka-kola chocolate but packed them into Hildebrand cans.

According to interviews with factory personnel, the decision to manufacture Vollmilch, or whole milk Scho-ka-kola, was done to save raw cocoa. It was reported that the production of bitter chocolate Scho-ka-kola was ceased for a short period of time. However, the popularity of the bitter chocolate Scho-ka-kola and the fact it was less prone to spoilage were factors which probably resulted in resuming its production. According to interviews:

The Scho-ka-kola container was highly regarded by the German soldiers, as the package readily fit the uniform pockets, was temperature resistant, and was not fragile. Later, due to shortages of tin and iron plate, laminated paper cartons were used for this ration. These also proved to be resistant against temperature conditions, but were not as good in respect to moisture, mold, and sweating conditions.

It was stated that Schoko-Buck's production of Scho-ka-kola may have outpaced all other manufacturers. During the early war years they produced 15,000 kilos of Scho-ka-kola per month and ultimately reached 35,000 kilos a month. It was thought that the Sprengel firm, with its yearly output of 300 metric tons, was the largest supplier of Scho-ka-kola. However, towards the end of the war Schoko-Buck was producing 425 metric tons of Scho-ka-kola a year. Records dated Jan. 1, 1944, from the firm indicate that they also produced coatings for Wehrmacht Chocolate bars, which contained a very high percentage of cocoa butter (Covertures chocolate).

The Kola-paste so important to the production of Scho-ka-kola was supplied by the Hildebrand firm in Berlin to its subcontractors. The paste consisted of kola nuts (50%), ground coffee (24%), cocoa butter (25.3%), and added caffeine (0.7%). It was stated that the Hildebrand Kola-paste was only supposed to be used for Wehrmacht products. There was no reference to Kola-paste being used in the production of any commercial Scho-ka-kola products or in the Red Cross version. After the war Schoko-Buck was the only firm which had any Hildebrand Kola-paste on hand, except for a small laboratory sample found in Leipzig. The paste was stored in 20 kg hermetically sealed cans. Scho-ka-kola was manufactured in accordance with a standard formula distributed by the OKH, but it appeared that Schoko-Buck made modifications to the base formula during the period 1939-1945. The modifications were minor and involved adding more cocoa beans during the period 1942-1945. Records also indicate that Schoko-Buck was producing Skim Milk Scho-ka-kola in 1945. *(Author's note: I am not aware of any 1945 dated Scho-ka-kola products in collector hands.)*

Schoko-Buck produced several non-Hildebrand brands of Scho-ka-kola type candies during its history. I have not been able to verify any of them as being of wartime manufacture. Schoko-Buck also made cast fondant cream centers for chocolate enrobing, various jellies, and marmalade confectioneries which were produced for the civilian and military market during the war.

The western Allies visited all the factories in their occupation zone that manufactured Scho-ka-kola. Only six firms manufactured Scho-ka-kola for the Wehrmacht: Fehleisen & Rickel, Sprengel, Hildebrand, Wilhelm Felsche, Schoko-Buck/Buck Aktiengesellschaft, and Manner. Schoko-Buck and Buck Aktiengesellschaft refer to the same company. The use of the name Buck Aktiengesellschaft preceded Schoko-Buck as the company name. The address for Buck AG and Schoko-Buck was Ostendstrasse 88, Stuttgart.

I've included a few tidbits of information on the postwar state of the various factories involved in producing Scho-ka-kola. The Fehleisen and Rickel firm in Hamburg was a small firm. It suffered about 20% damage during the war and was the only firm still producing chocolate in August 1945 when Allied investigators visited the plant. Several wartime pictures of Holsatia brand chocolate bars are shown in Volume I that were manufactured by Fehleisen and Rickel. The Sprengel firm in Hannover was a medium size firm which suffered some bomb damage during the war (15%), and in the immediate postwar period it produced jam. The Hildebrand firm in Berlin employed about 1,000 workers during the war. The factory was destroyed (only 12.5% of machinery salvageable), and those visiting the plant after the war indicated that it would be a while before they started producing chocolate again. As mentioned, Schoko-Buck survived the war in good shape and was the only factory which still had the ingredients necessary to produce Scho-ka-kola in the immediate postwar period. The Wilhelm Felsche and Manner factories were captured by the Soviets. The state of the Wilhelm Felsche factory is unknown, but it eventually became a state owned enterprise in the former East Germany. The Manner factory survived largely intact, but was dismantled and shipped to Russia. The firm would begin its resurgence starting in the late 1940s.

The Mauxion firm had a short lived association with Scho-ka-kola. They produced the Reichsadler version of Scho-ka-kola before the war. By 1939 they were no longer manufacturing Scho-ka-kola.

The quality control of Scho-ka-kola appears to have been exceptional. During the period 1936-1945 the Hildebrand firm only received one complaint involving two boxes of moldy chocolate. The Fehleisen and Rickel firm received one complaint in 1943 about molding on a portion of six boxes. In both cases the reasons were traced to poor storage conditions.

An interesting side story concerning chocolate and Pervitin was found in an article by Professors Defalque and Wright from the University of Alabama. The article, *Methamphetamine for Hitler's Germany: 1937 to 1945*, was a look at the German military's use of Pervitin during the war. Throughout history countries have searched for that special something that would give their soldiers an edge over their enemies. Chemicals that could enhance stamina, alertness, and performance with minimal side effects were certainly enticing. Combining the stimulating effects of these drugs with a popular candy product was not unheard of. After all, Scho-ka-kola was a marriage of chocolate and caffeine which continues today. While a discussion about Pervitin is beyond the scope of this book, there was an interesting passage in the article which is repeated here: "The pharmaceutical companies continued to encourage the Army's use of Pervitin. The medical Inspector denied the requests of two firms to add Pervitin to their products such as Energetika (dextrose tablets) and the firm Sarotti's Mokka Glykolade (cocoa, caffeine, and dextrose)." I found no information on any product called Energetika. It's possible that Energetika was a slang term for Dextro-Energen produced by Deutsche Maizena A.G., Hamburg. The firm made a product called "Dextrosin" which was sold to firms to be used as an ingredient in various products. It contained 70-75% dextrose.

Another interesting reference to German rations was found in an article by Manfred Reese on the website *1031-2006, 975 Jahre Gliesmarode*. In the article he wrote:

"On 10 April, 1945 I woke my mother to tell her that the supply dump was open. We gathered our bags. We were barely on the road when our neighbors advised us to take a cart. When we arrived at Karl-Hintze Way, people were arguing about who should go in and who should stay with the carts. My dear mother stayed with the cart and sent me into the fray. Without much difficulty I got to the bottom two levels and found stored in boxes Tilsiter cheese, hunting sausage, liver sausage, and beef in its own juice packed in 850 gram cans. In the basement my aunt Rosa Hartwich pointed out a boarded crate. With her help I opened it, and found boxes with bright red labels marked, 'Nur für Flieger und Panzerkampfwagenbesatzungen: Glykolade' or 'Reserved for Pilots and Crews of Armored Fighting Vehicles: Glykolade'. We removed three cartons, two for me and one for her. The others guarding the carts, had sensed our loot, and before we knew it, the steel band securing the carton was removed and dozens of chocolate bars were lying on the ground."

Tartaric acid is an organic acid that is present in plants to include grapes. The most common use of tartaric acid is as a food additive. During WWII it was widely used in the confection industry. Tartaric acid gives candy its sour taste. Today tartaric acids have been largely replaced by citric acid. The raw materials for Germany's tartaric acid industry were obtained as byproducts from the wine industry. The primary raw material was "Lees", or the deposits of dried yeast found at the bottom of wine vats after fermentation and aging. Of course, the Lees were processed so it could be used as a food additive.

Plastic containers and closures were widely used in the packing industry. Unfortunately Allied investigators did not spend much time investigating the plastic and resin industry as part of their overall investigation into Germany's food industry. They only visited one plant where they saw molded articles, mostly closures made from phenol formaldehyde and urea formaldehyde thermosetting resins, as well as from acrylic and vinyl thermoplastic type resins. For a more complete discussion of the German wartime plastics industry I would highly recommend *Kunststoffe: A Collector's Guide to German World War II Plastics and their Markings* by W. Darrin Weaver, Schiffer Publications.

This entry from the 1929 Mosse Register of firms shows that Buck Aktiengesellschaft was located at Ostendstrasse 88, the same address used on the 1954 bill from Schoko-Buck.

Several varieties of saccharin tablets.
Courtesy Militaria-Versand Emig.

A selection of Dr. Oetker's dessert products packed in paper cartons.
Courtesy OSTFRONT Militaria.

A selection of Dr. Oetker's dessert products packed in envelopes.
Courtesy Kevin Barrett.

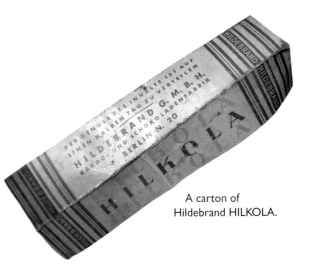

A carton of Hildebrand HILKOLA.

1.5 Kilograms of sugar from the Rositzer refinery. *Courtesy Zeugmeister.*

Sugar wrapper from the Ernst sugar factory.

Chocolate bar from Neisse and Co. which won a Gold Medal in 1932.

A cube of Erstein sugar.[2] *Courtesy Ruelle Frédéric Collection.*

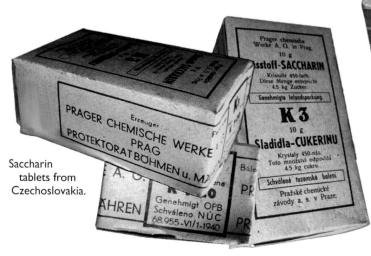

Saccharin tablets from Czechoslovakia.

A box of sugar from the Rositzer refinery. The firm may have continued to use these exact cartons until 1950.[1] *Courtesy OSTFRONT Militaria.*

The glass on this ground dug, 250 gram jar of honey is molded like a honey comb.[3]

A can of Biomalz.[4] *Courtesy OSTFRONT Militaria.*

A tin of Dallmann lozenges with original contents. *Courtesy Kevin Barrett.*

Chocolate wrapper from the Dr. Sperber firm.[6] *Courtesy Stanislav Kramsky.*

Kosa brand chocolate wrapper.[5] *Courtesy Zeugmeister.*

Estonian chocolate wrapper manufactured during the Soviet occupation of 1940. *Courtesy Stanislav Kramsky.*

Prewar Polish chocolate wrapper. *Courtesy Stanislav Kramsky.*

Prewar Stollwerck chocolate carton with what I believe is a postwar "Wehrmacht-Packung" stamp.

A tin of Wybert lozenges.

A tin of Promptin brand lozenges.[8] *Courtesy OSTFRONT Militaria.*

Artificial honey from the Walter Benedikt firm.[7] *Courtesy M.Sc. Stephan Haase.*

Cornelia brand pudding manufactured by Cornelius Stüssgen.[9] *Courtesy Kevin Barrett.*

This Maizena carton was recycled and used as emergency packing for German Pudding Meal DPM, made from potatoes, and a 1935 advertisement for DPM.

Süßstoff-Preise:

G-Packung, für Getränke,
  mit 100 Tabletten mit einer
  Süßkraft von ³/₄ kg Zucker
  kostet 10 Pfennig.

H-Briefchen, zum Mitkochen,
  Inhalt 1 ¼ g Kristall-Süßstoff, Süßkraft
  wie ½ kg Zucker, kostet 7 Pfennig.

Verwendungszweck:

G-Packungen enthalten Tabletten, die wegen der Dosierung mit Speisenatron versetzt sind. Sie eignen sich zum Süßen von Getränken usw., nicht aber zum Mitkochen, weil Natron das Kochgut geschmacklich beeinträchtigt.

H-Briefchen enthalten reinen Kristall-Süßstoff, der mitgekocht werden darf. Für Speisen, Kompotte, zum Einkochen (Sterilisieren) usw. nimmt man deswegen Kristall-Süßstoff der H-Packung.

Deutsche Süßstoff-Gesellschaft m.b.H., (1) Berlin W 35
24. 844. C1721   Potsdamer Straße 141

These saccharin tablets were produced in two styles. The "G" tablets were made for drinks and the "H" tablets were used for cooking.[10]

A shipping carton for 100 packages of saccharin. *Courtesy Chris Karr.*

Pre-1938 chocolate wrapper manufactured by Nestlé, Peter, and Kohler.

Chocolate bar from the Hartwig and Vogel firm. *Courtesy Kevin Barrett.*

Several containers of this type are shown in both volumes. *Courtesy OSTFRONT Militaria.*

Rare 1944 dated Scho-ka-kola container from the Wilhelm Felsche firm. *Courtesy Chris Pittman.*

Kaiser's Brust Caramellan.[12] *Courtesy Kevin Barrett.*

A chocolate wrapper from CHR. Storz.[11]

Cut out paper soldier advertisement for Trumpf chocolate.

A chocolate wrapper from the Premier-Werke, Leipzig.[13]

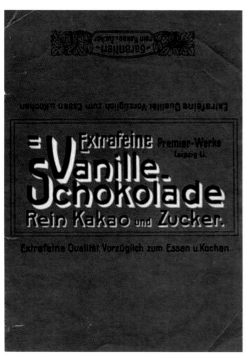

The Hildebrand Reichsadler Scho-ka-kola tin. Notice that the percentage of cocoa is expressed as 59 1/2% instead of the more normal 59.5%. *Courtesy Militaria-Versand Emig.*

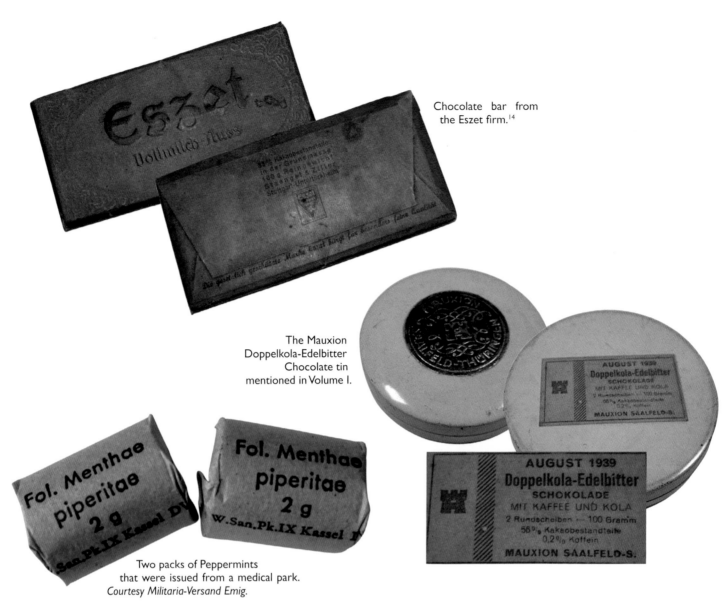

Chocolate bar from the Eszet firm.[14]

The Mauxion Doppelkola-Edelbitter Chocolate tin mentioned in Volume I.

Two packs of Peppermints that were issued from a medical park. *Courtesy Militaria-Versand Emig.*

A postcard from Atelier Binder, a Jewish firm which closed in 1938. It shows the Scho-ka-kola Plätzchen container. An example of the container is shown in Volume I.

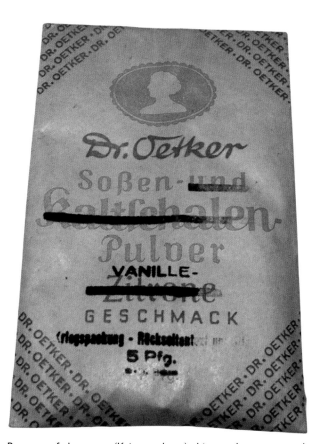

Because of shortages (Kriegspackung) this envelope was used for other than its intended product. *Courtesy Kevin Barrett.*

Rheika brand pudding manufactured by Cornelius Stüssgen. *Courtesy Kevin Barrett.*

ENDNOTES

[1] The Rositzer sugar refinery was founded in 1882. Carl Wentzel, who was executed in connection with the July 20th plot, was at one time the Chairman of the Supervisory Board for the refinery. It appears that the firm may have utilized the same cartons until at least 1950. Here is their listing in the 1929 Mosse Register of Firms.

Zuckerfabr. ×Rositzer Zucker-Raffinerie, AG (Dpf.), Ⅎ 30 u. (Altenburg 1028 u. 1038), Ⓖ, Ps 3692 Le.

[2] The Erstein sugar refinery was founded on December 27, 1883, in Erstein, France, near Strasbourg. It is still in operation.

[3] It's believed that the honey was manufactured by Alwin Franz of Leipzig, who used a bee hive as their logo. While difficult to see, there is a stylized bee hive with little bees flying around it on the front. On the bottom of the jar there is an M over V stamp. It may denote the firm of Muller and Co. from Vollstedt. The firm operated from 1907-1949, and is most famous for its decorative porcelain and figurines. The factory was destroyed during the war, and the company relocated to West Germany in 1949. They attempted to start up production in the west but failed. The logo used on their porcelain was an M over V with a crown above that. It's possible this was a simplified logo which dropped the crown.

[4] The Biomalz Company was founded on 1 April, 1907, as Biomalz-Gebr Patermann. In 1911 the factory in Teltow, Germany, was completed. The firm specialized in the production of malt extract, candy, and Biomalz. The factory was damaged in 1945. They resumed production after the war and are still in operation. Here are some war time advertisements.

⁵ No history was found on the Kosa Chocolate. However, it did survive the war and became part of the state run East German Chocolate industry. Here is their listing in the 1929 Mosse Register of Firms.

⁶ The Dr. Sperber firm was founded in 1922. It survived the war and became part of the state run East German Chocolate industry.

⁷ No history was found on the Walter Benedikt Food Factory. The address shown on the can is for the German Druggist Association, not the companies. Here is their listing in the 1943 Vienna Phone Book.

⁸ No history was found on the Garantol firm. Garantol is best known for its production of Egg preservatives. Here is their listing in the 1929 Mosse Register of Firms, as well as an invoice from 1933 listing Promptin lozenges.

⁹ Cornelius Stüssgen opened his first store in 1899. In 1903 the company was renamed the Rheinisches Kaufhaus für Lebensmittel. A year later there were twelve branch stores. He created the private label Cornelia. On 1 January 1928 the business was turned into an AG. By the end of 1933 there were over 150 Cornlius Stüssgen AG stores in the Rhineland, Westphalia, and Hesse-Nassau. During the war the headquarters in Cologne, as well as half the stores, were destroyed. Rebuilding began after the war, and the firm was still in operation in the 1950s.

Stüssgen A-G, Cornelius (Cornel.St.),
ℳ H. 91851, Kolonialwaren, Main-
zer Str. 32. Ⓖ, Ps 1916.

¹⁰ A wartime pamphlet with instructions on how to use the product.

¹¹ The Storz Chocolate Company was founded on 10 May 1884 in Tuttlingen. The company was initially located at Moehringer Strasse 11. Initially they produced gingerbread, macaroons, cookies, and fruit breads. The business was successful, so much so that they purchased the adjacent building and expanded in 1900. In 1972 the company relocated to Föhrenstrasse, in Tuttlingen. The firm is still in business. Here is a 1942 dated bill from the company. Note the RBN number.

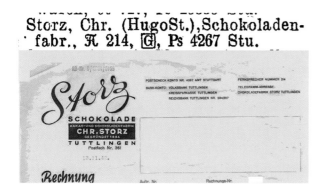

Storz, Chr. (HugoSt.),Schokoladen-
fabr., ℳ 214, Ⓖ, Ps 4267 Stu.

[12] The history of Kaisers Brust Caramellen trace back to 1889 with the "3 pines" being the oldest, officially registered German trademark. They are still in business. Here is a pre-war advertisement courtesy OSTFRONT Militaria.

[13] No history was found on the Premier-Werke, Leipzig. Here is a bill dated 1941.

✗ „Premier" Kakao- u. Schokoladen-
Werke **Schwarze & Röder,**
W 33, Demmeringstr. 49.

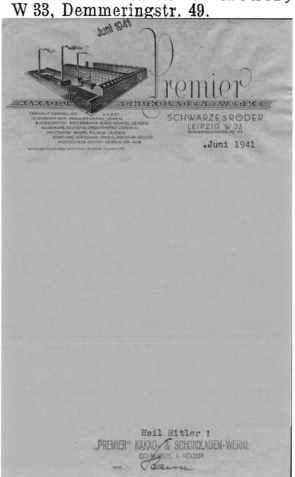

[14] The Eszet firm was founded in 1857. The term Eszet comes from the initials of its founders Ernst Staengel and Karl Ziller. In 1898 the company moved to Untertürkheim, near Stuttgart. In 1933 they started manufacturing its most famous product, the Eszet-Schnitten, or Eszet chocolate slices. In 1975 the firm was purchased by Stollwerck. The Eszet-Schnitten is the last remaining legacy of Ernst Staengel and Karl Ziller. Here is their listing in the 1929 Mosse Register of Firms.

Staengel & Ziller, Eszet-Schoko-
laden- u. Kakao-Fabrik — Unter-
türkh., Cannstatter Str. 98/100.

IX

Wartime Catalogs

artime catalogues are an excellent means of confirming if a product is wartime or not. Here are a few examples from some prewar or wartime catalogues.

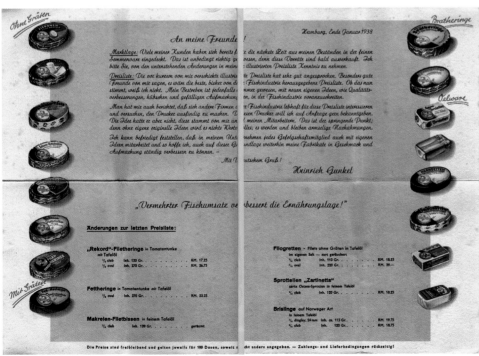

Pages from the Heinrich Gunkel fish industry catalogue. *Courtesy OSTFRONT Militaria.*

184

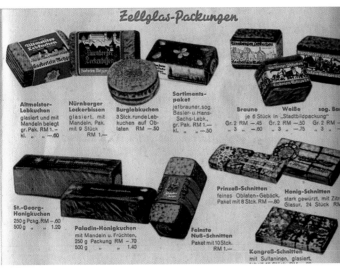

Pages from a wartime Haeberlein catalogue.
Courtesy OSTFRONT Militaria.

Fabrik-Nr.

				Gewicht	Packung	Einkauf
A 40	Nibelungen-Gold, herb			100 g	10 Tafeln	ℛℳ 0.52½
	Edelbitter-Schokolade					
	Nibelungen-Gold, Sahne			100 g	10 Tafeln	ℛℳ 0.52½ ℛℳ 0.75
80	Nibelungen-Gold-Täfelchen, herb			125 g	8 Schtln.	ℛℳ 0.87½ ℛℳ 1.25
82				250 g	4	1.75 2.50
81	Nibelungen-Gold-Täfelchen, Sahne			125 g	8	0.87½ 1.25
83				250 g	4	1.75 2.50
	Gold-Krone, extra zart, mildbitter			100 g	20 Tafeln	ℛℳ 0.49 ℛℳ 0.70

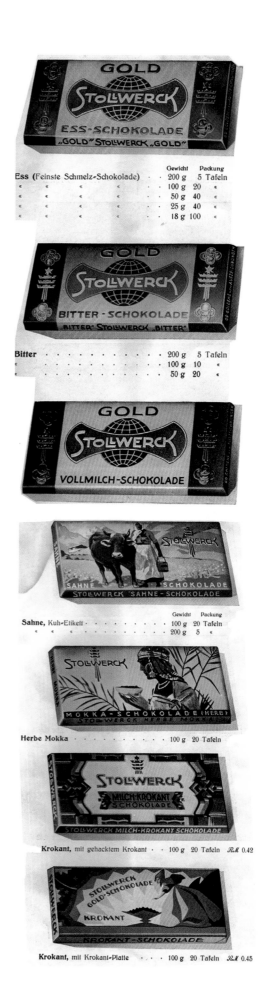

					Gewicht	Packung
Ess (Feinste Schmelz-Schokolade)					200 g	5 Tafeln
«	«	«	«		100 g	20
«	«	«	«		50 g	40
«	«	«	«		25 g	40
«	«	«	«		18 g	100
Bitter					200 g	5 Tafeln
«					100 g	10
«					50 g	20

Pages from a prewar Stollwerck catalogue.
Courtesy OSTFRONT Militaria.

				Gewicht	Packung
Mokka-Buntband				100 g	20 Tafeln
Mandel-Buntband				100 g	20 Tafeln
milch-Nuss-Buntband				100 g	20 Tafeln

				Gewicht	Packung
Sahne, Kuh-Etikett				100 g	20 Tafeln
				200 g	5
Herbe Mokka				100 g	20 Tafeln
Krokant, mit gehacktem Krokant				100 g	20 Tafeln ℛℳ 0.42
Krokant, mit Krokant-Platte				100 g	20 Tafeln ℛℳ 0.45

		Gewicht	Packung	Einkauf
70	**Gold-Ess-Täfelchen** · · · ·	200 g	5 Schtln.	*RM* 0.98
71		100 g	10 «	0.49
72		50 g	20 «	0.24

Gold-Bitter-Täfelchen · · · · 100 g 10 Schtln. *RM* 0.49
50 g 20 « 0.24

Gold-Vollmilch-Täfelchen, halbsüss · 100 g 10 Schtln. *RM* 0.49
50 g 20 0.24

		Gewicht	Packung	Einkauf
Ess-Taler · · · · · ·		100 g	10 Rollen	*RM* 0.49 *RM*
		50 g	20 «	0.24 1/2 «

Bitter-Taler · · · · · · 100 g 10 Rollen *RM* 0.49 *RM*
50 g 20 « 0.24 1/2 «

Vollmilch-Taler, halbsüss · · · 100 g 10 Rollen *RM* 0.49
50 g 20 « 0.24 1/2 «

		Inhalt	Packung
91	**Buntband-Täfelchen** · · · ·	5 versch. Täf.	20 Schtln.
	in Gelatine-Schiebeschachteln		

| 84 | **Napolitains**, gemischt · · · · | 14 versch. Täf. | 20 Schtln. |

		Gewicht	Packung	Einkauf	Verkauf
	...eater-Schokolade · · · · ·	125 g	8 Schtln.	*RM* 1.05	*RM* 1.50

Inhalt 12 Täfelchen
Eine vornehme Geschenkpackung. Farbe: Gold-Orange
Enthaltend: **Feinste Dessert-Schokoladen** in Golddamast-Stanniol
Milch-Krokant — Milch mit Apfelsine (Orange) — Sahne — Goldkrone

...Krokant-Täfelchen · · · · · · 100 g 10 Schtln. *RM* 0.56 *RM* 0.80

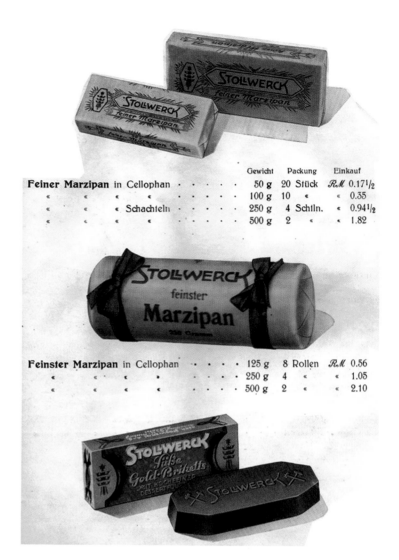

A 1930s advertisement for Knorr and Mondamin products. *Courtesy Zeugmeister.*

Anlage zur Preisliste

über

M a g g i ' s   Erzeugnisse

für

Wehrmacht und Reichsarbeitsdienst

Neben Maggi's Würze in Original-Flaschen führen
wir noch zwei billigere Qualitäten:

Maggi Flavoring Sauce in wicker bottles.

Spezial-Würze		A	F
in Korbflaschen mit 30 kg Inhalt das kg netto		RM 1.44	RM 1.10
" " " 12½ kg Inhalt das kg netto		" 1.62	" 1.28

Die Preise verstehen sich einschließlich
Korbflasche frei Bahnstation des Bestimmungsortes.

Maggi's Würze — **Maggi flavor sauce 1400g Bottle Nr. 6**

in Flaschen Nr.6 mit 1400 g Inhalt	die Flasche RM 5.10
bei Abnahme von mindestens 12 Flaschen auf einmal	" " " 4.85

Maggi's Gekörnte Fleischbrühe — **Meat Bouillon in cans.**

in Büchsen mit 4 kg Inhalt	die Büchse RM 20.-- (also das kg " 5.--)
" " " 10 "	die Büchse " 43.-- (also das kg " 4.30)

Maggi's Fleischbrüh-Paste (fettreich) — **Meat Broth Paste in Buckets**

in Eimern mit 4½ kg Inhalt	der Eimer RM 22.-- (also das kg " 4.89)
" " " 10 "	der Eimer " 43.-- (also das kg " 4.30)
" " " 25 "	der Eimer " 106.25 (also das kg " 4.25)

Maggi's Suppen, lose — **Maggi Soup Individual (Loose) packed in a Gold can with 5 to 10 Kg. total weight.**

in Goldblecheimern mit 5 oder 10 kg Inhalt.
1 kg ergibt je nach Sorte 12-14 Liter Suppe,
1 Liter stellt sich billigst auf ca. 6,7 - 11 Pfg.

	Das kg kostet	Wir gewähren 10% Rabatt. Das kg kostet also netto	In Eimern mit 25 kg ermäßigen sich die Brutto-Preise um 5 Pfg. Das kg kostet netto
Blumenkohl	RM 1.55	RM 1.39[5]	RM 1.35
Eierbuchstaben	" 1.60	" 1.44	" 1.39[5]
Eier-Nudeln	" 1.60	" 1.44	" 1.39[5]
Eier-Riebele	" 1.60	" 1.44	" 1.39[5]
Eier-Sternchen	" 1.60	" 1.44	" 1.39[5]

- 2 -

Maggi's Suppen, lose (Fortsetzung) — **Various flavors of loose soups identical to those described in the U.S. Army Ration Report.**

	Das kg kostet	Wir gewähren 10% Rabatt. Das kg kostet also netto	In Eimern mit 25 kg ermäßigen sich die Brutto-Preise um 5 Pfg. Das kg kostet netto
Erbs	RM 1.40	RM 1.26	RM 1.21[5]
Erbs mit Schinken zubereitet	" 1.60	" 1.44	" 1.39[5]
Erbs mit Speck zubereitet	" 1.50	" 1.35	" 1.30[5]
Familien (Feine Mehle,Gemü-se, Teigwaren)	" 1.40	" 1.26	" 1.21[5]
Frühling	" 1.50	" 1.35	" 1.30[5]
Gemüse (Gebundene Suppe)	" 1.45	" 1.30[5]	" 1.26
Gerstenflocken mit Gemüse	" 1.05	" -.94[5]	" -.90
Gerstengrütze mit Gemüse	" 1.05	" -.94[5]	" -.90
Graupen (Gersten)	" 1.15	" 1.03[5]	" -.99
Graupen mit Mager-milch	" 1.25	" 1.12[5]	" 1.08
Grieß mit Mager-milch	" 1.35	" 1.21[5]	" 1.17
Grünkern	" 1.45	" 1.30[5]	" 1.26
Hausmacher, (Erbsen, Kartoffeln, Ge-müse, Gewürze)	" 1.45	" 1.30[5]	" 1.26
Kartoffel	" 1.65	" 1.48[5]	" 1.44
Königin (Legierte Suppe)	" 1.20	" 1.08	" 1.03[5]
Linsen mit Speck zubereitet	" 1.50	" 1.35	" 1.30[5]

- 3 -

Maggi's Suppen, lose (Fortsetzung) — **Various flavors of loose soups identical to those described in the U.S. Army Ration Report.**

	Das kg kostet	Wir gewähren 10% Rabatt. Das kg kostet also netto	In Eimern mit 25 kg ermäßigen sich die Brutto-Preise um 5 Pfg. Das kg kostet netto
Mockturtle	RM 1.50	RM 1.35	RM 1.30[5]
Ochsenschwanz	" 1.65	" 1.48[5]	" 1.44
Pilz	" 1.55	" 1.39[5]	" 1.35
Reis mit Tomaten	" 1.20	" 1.08	" 1.03[5]
Rheinische (Grüne Erbsen mit Karotten)	" 1.50	" 1.35	" 1.30[5]
Rumford (Erbsen, Gerstengraupen Gemüse,Gewürze)	" 1.40	" 1.26	" 1.21[5]
Sago	" 1.55	" 1.39[5]	" 1.35
Spargel	" 1.30	" 1.17	" 1.12[5]
Tapioka	" 1.65	" 1.48[5]	" 1.44
Tapioka-Julienne	" 1.65	" 1.48[5]	" 1.44
Tomaten	" 1.25	" 1.12[5]	" 1.08
Windsor	" 1.40	" 1.26	" 1.21[5]

www.zeugamt.com

- 4 -

Maggi's price list for the military and labor front. *Courtesy Zeugmeister.*

Maggi's Bratensoße

1 kg Masse ergibt 10 Liter Bratensoße.

Gravy loose packed in paper sacks or Gold Cans

	Das kg kostet	Wir gewähren 10% Rabatt. Das kg kostet also netto
lose in Papierbeuteln mit 5 oder 10 kg Inhalt	RM 2.30	RM 2.07
lose in Goldblecheimern mit 25 kg Inhalt	" 2.25	" 2.02⁵

Maggi's Spezial-Eintopf — **Maggis special stew.**

Aus 1 kg Masse lassen sich etwa 9 Liter Eintopfessen zubereiten, 1 Liter stellt sich also auf etwa 13,5 Pfg.

Zusammensetzung: Feine Mehle, Gerstengraupen, Gemüse, Fett, Gewürze

	Das kg kostet	Wir gewähren 10% Rabatt. Das kg kostet also netto
lose in Goldblecheimern mit 5 oder 10 kg Inhalt	RM 1.40	RM 1.26
" 25 kg Inhalt	" 1.35	" 1.21⁵

Flour in sacks.

Maggi's Mehle

sind reine Naturprodukte ohne irgendwelchen Zusatz.

	In Säcken von	Das kg kostet	Wir gewähren 10% Rabatt. Das kg kostet also netto
Einbrennmehl	2½ kg	RM -.95	RM -.85⁵
	5 "	" -.90	" -.81₂
	10 "	" -.88	" -.79₂
	25 " +)	" -.85	" -.76⁵
Erbsmehl	2½ kg	RM 1.15	RM 1.03⁵
	5 "	" 1.10	" -.99₂
	10 "	" 1.08	" -.97₂
	25 " +)	" 1.05	" -.94⁵

+) Für größere Packungen (Säcke von 50 kg) verlange man Sonderangebot.

- 5 -

Maggi's Mehle (Fortsetzung)

	In Säcken von	Das kg kostet	Wir gewähren 10% Rabatt. Das kg kostet also
Gerstenmehl	2½ kg	RM -.83	RM -.74₇
	5 "	" -.78	" -.70₄
	10 "	" -.76	" -.68₄
	25 " +)	" -.73	" -.65₇
Grünkernmehl	2½ kg	RM 1.20	RM 1.08₅
	5 "	" 1.15	" 1.03₅
	10 "	" 1.13	" 1.01
	25 " +)	" 1.10	" -.99
Grünkerngrieß	2½ kg	RM 1.17	RM 1.05₃
	5 "	" 1.12	" 1.00₈
	10 "	" 1.10	" -.99₃
	25 " +)	" 1.07	" -.96₃
Grünkernschrot	2½ kg	RM 1.15	RM 1.03₅
	5 "	" 1.10	" -.99₂
	10 "	" 1.08	" -.97₂
	25 " +)	" 1.05	" -.94₂
Kartoffelmehl	2½ kg	RM -.88	RM -.79₂
	5 "	" -.83	" -.74₇
	10 "	" -.81	" -.72₉
	25 " +)	" -.78	" -.70₂
Linsenmehl	2½ kg	RM 1.15	RM 1.03⁵
	5 "	" 1.10	" -.99₂
	10 "	" 1.08	" -.97₂
	25 " +)	" 1.05	" -.94⁵

Die Preise verstehen sich brutto für netto, also ohne Berechnung des Sackes.

+) Für größere Packungen (Säcke von 50 kg) verlange man Sonderangebot.

Sämtliche Preise verstehen sich frei Post- bzw. Bahnstation des Bestimmungsortes.

- 6 -

Prewar advertisement for Perga paper. *Courtesy OSTFRONT Militaria.*

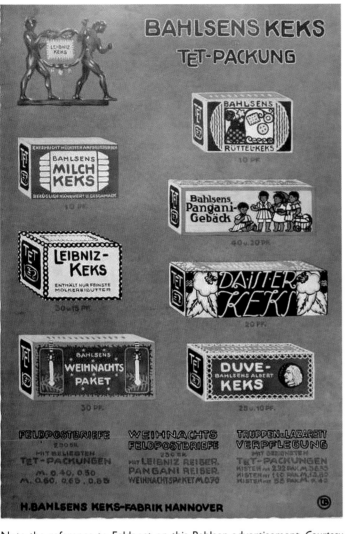

Note the reference to Feldpost on this Bahlsen advertisement. *Courtesy OSTFRONT Militaria.*

1934 advertisement for mustard. *Courtesy OSTFRONT Militaria.*

A 1937 price list for Dr. Oetkers products. *Courtesy Kevin Barrett.*

191

THE AUGUST GRILL STORY

In Volume I we showed several items which came from August Grill, a small chain of stores which operated from 1912 to 1965. There were ten store locations I could confirm, but there were never more than nine operating simultaneously. Around the year 2000 left over stocks from the store were sold on the open market. Their products are great examples of prewar and wartime packaging. Since the store continued to operate after the war and much of the packaging is undated, there was no easy way to determine which packaging was prewar, wartime, or postwar. I collected all the information I could find on the firm, analyzed it, and came to some conclusions which are discussed below. The few facts available were:

In 1929 the phone number for the store was 68. Other businesses in Schorndorf were using two and three digit phone numbers. This information was found in the 1929 Mosse Register of firms.

Mehlgrosshandlg. Grill, August, ℋ 68, Ps 11179 Stu.

1929 listing for August Grill. It shows that the phone number was 68.

In 1934 the store was offering 3% Rabatts (discounts) in accordance with the Discount Act of 1933, which limited discounts to 3%. This information came from the advertisement below. Note the dates of the wine offered in the advertisement.

With these few facts and pictures of actual packaging I built the two charts shown below. Town names, phone numbers, discount information, etc., was taken off store packaging and from the 1929 Mosse Register of firms.

From the available information I concluded that packaging with a 68 phone number are in fact wartime/prewar. Certain packages with a 68 number also carried a ships logo, so I figured the ships logo was also a characteristic of wartime/prewar packaging. The ships logo was also found on packages with a phone number of SA 368 and 468. I found no packages that had a combination of the ships logo and 3% Rabatt, so I concluded the ships logo was used between 1912 to November 1933. There were packages where the phone number 468 was used separately with either the 3% Rabatt or ships logo, so I also concluded that the use of the three digit phone numbers were also indications of wartime manufacture.

There is strong evidence to suggest that packaging with a 2468 phone number are also wartime. I compared two almost identical packages:

These charts attempt to trace the history of August Grill.

Name	Date	Phone	Sc.	Wel.	Gm.	Lo.	Wa.	Wi.	Plu.	Gru.	Schn.	Urb.	Ship Logo	3% Rabatt
AUGUST GRILL	1929	68	X		X		X		X	X			X	
AUGUST GRILL		68	X		X	X	X	X	X	X	X	X	X	
LEBENSMITTEL HAUS AUGUST GRILL		68	X	X										
AUGUST GRILL		SA 368	X		X	X	X	X	X	X	X	X	X	
A. GRILL		468	X											
GRILL SCHORNDORF		468	X		X	X	X	X	X	X				X
LEBENSMITTEL HAUS AUGUST GRILL		468	X	X	X	X	X	X	X	X				
AUGUST GRILL		468	X	X	X	X	X	X	X	X	X		X	
AUGUST GRILL		468	X		X	X	X	X	X	X		X		
GRILL SCHORNDORF		2468	X				X	X	X					X
AUGUST GRILL	1934		X											X

Sc.=Schorndorf	**Wel.**=Welzheim	**Gm.**=Gmund	**Lo.**=Lorch	**Wa.**=Waldhausen
Wi.=Winterbach	**Plu.**=Pluderhausen	**Gru.**=Grunbach	**Schn.**=Schnait	**Urb.**=Urbach

So billig und doch gut!

1 Pfd. neue gerasp. Kokosnuß (Mandelers.) nur 32 Pfg.
1 Pfund neue beste Haselnußkerne . . nur 68 Pfg.
1 Pfund prima neue Mandeln . . . . nur 88 Pfg.
5 Pfund Konfektmehl 0 . . . . . nur 90 Pfg.
5 Pfund Konfektmehl feinst 00 . . . nur 100 Pfg.
1 Pfund-Würfel Kunsthonig . . . . nur 42 Pfg.
1 Glas ca. 1 Pfd. gar. rein. Bienenhonig o Gl. nur 98 Pfg.
¼ Pfund Citronat und Orangeat 27,
      3 Vanillezucker 10 u. 3 Citronen zus. 45 Pfg.
1 Pfund gelbe Sultaninen 40 und 3 Kranz
      Feigen 27 . . . . zus. nur 60 Pfg.
2 Tafel à 1 Pfund reines Kokosfett . . nur 125 Pfg.
2 Pfund neue Walnüsse . . . . . nur 65 Pfg.
2 Pfund Zwetschgen 70 und 2 Kranz
      Feigen 18 . . . . zus. 88 Pfg.

1 Ltr. feines **Salatöl**, gar. reinschm. nur **98 Pf.**

3 Pfund prima Suppen- oder Gemüse-
      Nudeln oder Maccaroni oder
      Hörnle (leicht gefärbt) . . . . . nur 95 Pfg.
2½ Pfund Eier-Nudeln od Eier-Macca-
      roni oder Eier-Hörnle . . . . . nur 100 Pfg.
3 Pfund schönen ital. Tafel-Reis . . nur 57 Pfg.
2½ Pfd. sehr schönen Natur-Tafel-Reis nur 65 Pfg.
3 Pfund sehr schöne gutkochende Linsen nur 55 Pfg.
1 Pfund gelbe Erbsen 30 und 1 Pfund
      große Linsen 35 . . . . . . zus. 58 Pfg.
2½ Pfund Weizen-Gries . . . . . nur 55 Pfg.
6 Paar große Landjäger . . . . . nur 95 Pfg.
½ Pfund Bierwurst 50 u. 3 Paar Land-
      jäger 45 . . . . zus. nur 95 Pfg.
1 Pfd.-Laib Stangenkäse o. Rinde m. 20% nur 48 Pfg.

½ Pfund guten **Kaffee**, fr. Röstung nur **95 Pf.**

1 Pfd. Kaffee-Ersatz-Mischung mit 20%
      Bohnenkaffee . . . . nur 60 Pfg.
1 Pfd. Kaffee-Ersatz-Mischung mit 40%
      Bohnenkaffee (was ganz vorzügliches) nur 95 Pfg.
2 Pfund Malzkaffee 50 und ¼ Pfund
      Bohnenkaffee 50 . . . . . . zus. 85 Pfg.
2½ Pfund echten Malzkaffee . . . nur 55 Pfg.
3 Tafeln à 100 Gr. Block-Schokolade nur 50 Pfg.
3 Tafeln à 100 Gramm Milch-, Nuß- oder
      Mocca-Schokolade . . . . . . nur 60 Pfg.
6 Tafeln à 50 Gramm Speise- u. Milch-
      Schokolade . . . . nur 65 Pfg.

1 Pfund guten Kakao
1 Ltr.-Flasche 1933er Deidesheimer-Neu-
      berg-Rotwein o. Gl. . . . . . nur 110 Pfg.
1 Ltr.-Flasche 1933er St. Martiner-Berg-
      Weißwein o. Gl. . . . . nur 90 Pfg.
1 Flasche ¾ Ltr. guten alten Malaga o. Gl. nur 95 Pfg.
1 Liter-Flasche 1934 Ingelheimer Rot-
      wein o. Gl. . . . . nur 60 Pfg.

3000 Tafeln à 100 Gr. **Milchschokolade**
3 Tafeln nur 57 Pfg.

1 Emaileimer 10 Pfd. gelbe Schmierseife nur 185 Pfg.
1 schöner Sorghobesen 80 und 1 Bür-
      ste 22 . . . . zus. nur 95 Pfg.
2 Dosen à ca. 1 Pfund Bodenwachs oder
      Beize . . . . nur 75 Pfg.
1 Handtuchsack mit 5 Pfd. Seifenpulver nur 95 Pfg.
1 Kokos-Fußmatte 55 und 2 Putz-
      tücher 40 . . . . zus. nur 90 Pfg.
1 große Salon-Fußmatte . . . . . nur 110 Pfg.
1 großer Schrupper 40 und 1 doppelte
      Bürste 25 . . . . zus. nur 60 Pfg.
1 kleiner Schrupper 28 und 1 großes
      Putztuch 23 . . . . zus. nur 50 Pfg.
1 Karton 72 Waschklammern 45 und
      5 Kleiderbügel 40 . . . . . zus. nur 80 Pfg.
1 großer Staubbesen 75 und 1 Hand-
      besen 45 . . . . zus. nur 110 Pfg.
3 Liter prima Bodenöl . . . . . . nur 95 Pfg.
6 große weiße Porzellan-Tassen . . nur 100 Pfg.
6 große weiße tiefe Teller . . . . nur 95 Pfg.
1 Satz 6 weiße Schüsseln . . . . nur 100 Pfg.
1 grauer Emaileimer 2a . . . . . nur 70 Pfg.
1 großer schwerer Emaileimer . . . nur 125 Pfg.

● Sämtliche Waren sind von einwandfreier Qualität ●
Ein Versuch wird Sie befriedigen

Außer obigen billigen Preisen erhalten Sie 3% Rabatt.

August Grill

Obige Preise gelten soweit Vorrat reicht.

1934 advertisement for August Grill. Notice that they offered a 3% discount.

The store was also called Grill Schorndorf.

Lebensmittel Haus August Grill was another name used by the store.

A sack from August Grill.

A 1937 receipt from the Brinkmann tobacco company which accompanied a shipment of cigarettes to August Grill.

A package from the A. Grill store.

one with the phone number 468 and the other 2468. Both advertised a 3% Rabatt, and the construction of both sacks was the same. The major difference was there were eight stores listed on the 468 sack and only four on the 2468 sack. Since I didn't have a "known" postwar package to compare with, I can't rule out that 2468 might be a postwar phone number.

194

XI

HOW DO I KNOW IF IT'S MADE BEFORE MAY 8, 1945?

There is nothing more gratifying to the collector than adding a new item to his or her collection. On the other hand, nothing can be more frustrating than not knowing if the item you just picked up is pre-May 8, 1945. Rations are a difficult collecting area, because unlike uniforms and medals, many of the actual items aren't detailed in regulations or identified in photographs. Another problem is that most food items aren't dated. This annex provides a few pointers on what to look for when trying to date items as wartime or not. It's important to remember that just because an item displays one or more of the traits discussed below doesn't always make it wartime. Many wartime policies/procedures carried over into postwar Germany. This is especially true from May 9, 1945, till the early 1950s. During this period it was not uncommon for companies to reutilize left over wartime stocks, slightly modify wartime logos, etc., or use a combination of wartime and postwar components. So in the end there is no substitute for a wartime date, picture, or other reference to validate an item as wartime.

A. **Prices.** Prices during prewar and wartime Germany were often expressed in Reichmark (RM), Reichpfennig (Rpf), or simply as Mark or Pfennig.

B. **Expositions.** A common event in the prewar global economy was to hold Expositions where various products competed for prizes. Many of the prizes were expressed in terms of Gold, Silver, or Bronze Medals. Winning one of these prestigious medals was usually expressed on the product. I haven't encountered a postwar product with a reference to a pre-1945 exposition. However, it shouldn't be ruled out.

C. **Rationing.** Sometime around 1940 Germany started rationing critical items like meat, bread, sugar, etc. Many of these rationed items were no longer priced in monetary terms, but in Ration Stamp equivalents. Terms like Markenwert, Brotmarken, Marken Artikel, and Zuckermarken denoted a rationed item. Rationing was also continued in postwar Germany.

D. **Recycling.** Recycling of empty packaging materials was a common wartime practice. Phrases like "Verkauf nur gegen Rückgabe einer leeren Packung für die Altmaterial-Sammlung", "Verkauf nur gegen Rückgabe einer leeren Packung", and "Leere Packung muß zum Händler zuruck" indicate that empty packages had to be returned.

E. **Discounts.** During pre-Reich Germany it appeared that discounting prices by consumer cooperatives was a popular practice. As one of the NSDAP's measures to destroy the consumer cooperatives they passed the Discount Act of 1933, which limited discounts to three percent.

F. **Trade Marks.** Many pre-1945 products were identified by logos that were given some level of protection. This protection was sometimes identified in writing next to the brand's logo.

Ges. Gesch.-(Gesetzlich Geschützt) (Legally Registered)
Schutzmarke-Trademark.
Eingetragene Schutzmarke-Trademark.

V-Drops were sometimes identified with a *Reichsgesundheits Gutemark*, a proof of its health benefits. It's likely that other medicinal candies were so stamped. *Courtesy Zeugmeister.*

German rye bread products were sometimes identified as *Vollkornbrot, Volksgesundheit,* a proof of its health benefits.

The Reichsnährstand established standards for the growing, harvesting, storing, packaging, transporting, and pricing of all agricultural products. Many dairy products like cheese, milk, etc., carried the Reichsnährstand logo.

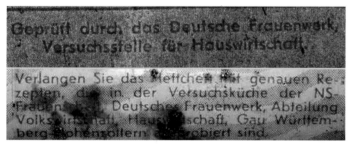

This shows product approval by the Deutsche Frauenwerk, one of many women's organizations during the Third Reich.

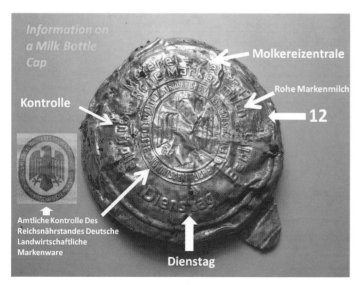

The Reichsnährstand seal on a milk bottle cap. *Courtesy Zeugmeister.*

WZ. Ges. Gesch.-(Warenzeichen Gesetzlich Geschützt) (Trade Mark Legally Registered)

Geschützt Fabriksmarke -Registered Factory Logo

D.R.G.M.-(Deutsches Reich Gebrauchsmuster) Not a patent, but a secondary protection for an item which by itself would not qualify for patent protection.

D.R.P.-(Deutsches Reichs-Patent) indicates patent protection in Germany.

D.R.P.u.A.P-(Deutsches Reichs-Patent und Ausländische Patente) indicates patent protection in Germany and in foreign countries.

D.R.W.Z.-(Deutsches Reich Warenzeichen) indicates a trade mark.

G. **Third Reich Agencies.** Sometimes products will show approval or administration by certain Third Reich organizations.

H. **Reference to Regulations**. Occasionally products make reference to certain regulations and their date, which helps to determine if the product is wartime. (A Herstellerliste is a list of manufacturers. This was done when certain items were produced by multiple factories but generically packaged.)

I. **Special Company Packaging.** As a marketing tool, companies would often advertise that their products were packed in some unique manner that ensured freshness, was moisture proof, etc., to distinguish their products from the competition. Many of the terms like TET Packung, Perga Packung, Frischbleibe-Packung, HO Packung, Ernst Packung, etc., were probably copyright protected, even though it wasn't always expressed on the product. It's likely that the Hildebrand firm held ownership over the terms Wehrmacht Packung and Rote Kreuz-Packung. Its use by other firms was probably contingent on Hildebrand's approval.

J. **Identifying Marks on Items Manufactured for Military Use**: The most desirable ration items are obviously those manufactured specifically for the military. The challenge is trying to determine if something is a commercial or military item. The German military used a variety of commercial products and foreign goods in addition to military production items. Many of the military products are rather unpretentious looking; plain cans with stamped information, paper and cellophane wrappings, plain glass jars, paper cartons, sacks, etc., with little information to suggest they were manufactured for the military. Commercial firms worked closely with the military to produce products that met their requirements. Popular names developed by commercial firms like Scho-ka-kola, Wittler Brot, Kossenbrot, Rosta, etc., were adopted by the military. Here are a few tips to help identify military products.

(1). *Jars and Bottles*. Jars embossed or otherwise marked as "Nur für Nahrungsmittel" (Only for food) are believed to be manufactured for the military. 900 ccm normal glass jars were widely used for fruit products issued to the military. It's likely that the 900 ccm jars weren't used until 1942, when they were approved as standardized packing. The *U.S. Army Ration Report* writes: "This applesauce was in a 900 cc glass bottle, sealed by a metal top. It was very good". Standard commercial jars and bottles were also distributed to the military.

(2). *Sanitary Top Cans*. There were generally four styles of sanitary open top cans used by the military: Weißblechdosen,

Examples of how dated regulations or other information is placed on a product, which assists in identifying if an item is wartime.

Sparverzinntdosen, Schwarzblechdosen WEHRM, and Schwarzblechdosen Lötrand. A detailed discussion on these cans is included in both volumes. The presence of a product code, factory code, date, etc., is confirmation that the product was manufactured specifically for the military. Standard off the shelf commercially canned products were also supplied to the military.

(3). *Drawn Aluminum or Steel Fish Cans.* Fish was supplied to the military packed in cans of various sizes and shapes. The most common style was the aluminum oblong, square, or oval shaped can. Many were standard off the shelf commercial products of the same design manufactured for the civilian market. Then there were cans made without any of the commercial designs or colors which were most likely produced for the military. These cans are generally manufactured from aluminum, but examples in aluminum coated steel or black plate steel were also used. In place of the product information, the cans were stamped with various letter and number codes. The information could include dates, manufacturer's code, DIN, country of origin, etc. Some meat products appear to have been packaged in drawn aluminum, aluminum coated steel, or black plate cans.

(4). *Production or Expiration Dates.* Many products produced for the military included either a manufacture date, expiration date, or both. Most commercial products did not adopt this practice. While most of the examples shown below are on paper labels, this information was also stamped or stenciled on canned products.

(5). *Marketenderwaren.* Marketenderwaren, also referred to as Kantine or PX items, were generally commercial off the shelf items. The author is not aware of any ration items except alcohol and cigarettes identified as a Kantine item. That does not mean that food items weren't available in unit kantines, only that they weren't marked as such. The Army procured and distributed alcohol products to the Army, Waffen-SS, and Air Force which are generally identified as Wehrmachts-Marketenderwaren. The sale of Marketenderwaren on the open market was forbidden. The SS and Air Force also procured Kantine items on their own. The Air Force items are generally marked as Eigentum der Luftwaffe, or Property of the Air Force. Items marked as Marketenderwaren der Luftwaffe have not been identified yet. SS items all appear to be contracted through the Zentral Marketenderwaren der Waffen-SS. How the Navy identified Marketenderwaren is not known.

(6). *Kriegspackung.* Some wartime food containers have been found annotated with the term Kriegspackung,

which means wartime packaging or wartime packed. This term could apply to commercial items, as well as items manufactured for the military. The term was common in WWI but saw limited use in WWII.

(7). *Wehrmacht Chocolate.* The Germans manufactured a variety of chocolate products for the military. Three frequent terms found in wartime German publications are: Scho-ka-kola, Wehrmacht Schokolade, and Heeres Schokolade. I believe the term Wehrmacht Schokolade was used to describe chocolate products manufactured without milk, for all branches of the military. I'm not exactly sure what Heeres Schokolade is, but by definition it would be a chocolate product manufactured specifically for the army. See Annex 8 for additional information on candy products.

(8). *Saccharin.* Saccharin was produced and packaged in a number of ways. Several examples have surfaced identified as Wehrmachts-Packung, a term similar to Hildebrand's famous Wehrmacht Packung.

A sampling of manufacture and expiration dates.

The Wehrmacht Carton Factory, Weisswasser, G.M.B.H. *Courtesy Zeugmeister.*

(9). *Using Wehrmacht in the Firm's Name.* Some companies may have incorporated the term Wehrmacht into their firm name to show that they specialized in production for the military.

(10). *Other uses of the term Wehrmacht.* Just how many products incorporated the term Wehrmacht into their packaging is unknown. It doesn't appear that there were any contractual requirements to incorporate the term "Wehrmacht" into ration products manufactured for the military. That decision was likely determined by the individual firm.

K. **Postal codes**: Sometimes ration items will contain the address of the firm, which could help date the item. However, it's probably one of the least accurate methods, because postal codes were introduced so late in the war. This is not a detailed history of the German postal system and is limited to its use as a collector tool for dating items. Prior to October 1943 mail was addressed to the person/firm, street address, town, and sometimes the state. Larger cities like Berlin were sometimes divided into geographic sectors like NW (North West) to assist in the quicker delivery of mail.

In July 1941 the German Postal Ministry introduced a zip code policy for packages. In October 1943 the two digit zip code was introduced for all mail, with full implementation anticipated by June 1944. There were 32 postal codes roughly corresponding to a district. The two-digit numeric code was sometimes followed by a small case letter to subdivide districts; for example, 12a for western Austria and 12b for eastern Austria. The two digit post code with modifications would remain in effect until 1962, when the four digit post code was introduced.

The East German Postal system was introduced in 1949. To be honest, I could not find a good explanation on how the East German Postal system operated. It appears a four digit system

Two ration products identified as being manufactured for the Armed Forces.

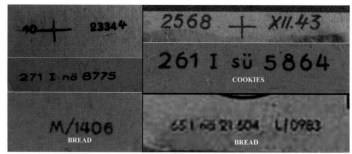

A sample of codes found on issue packaging for baked goods.

was implemented in the East. Sometimes the letters "O" (Ost) and "W" (West) were used to differentiate between East and West Germany. In 1999 Germany was reunited and a five digit postal code was introduced.

L. **Printers' Codes**: On some paper packaging the printer will place a series of numbers, letters, cross hairs, or bull eyes. These stamps are generally in very small print and don't interfere with the product information. It appears that these markings were found on commercial as well as military packaging. Most paper packaging for food items are not stamped with printer codes, or the stamps are hidden underneath a glued flap. It's clear that the bulls eyes and cross hairs were a means of aligning the packaging. The number and letter codes are a mystery. Even though the sample population was very small I could see some patterns. Paper packaging for select military rations might have required these special stamps/codes. However, there is no way to know what codes were required, when they were implemented, where they were to be positioned, and what type of items required them without the pertinent instructions to industry. So while the presence of these codes is a good sign of wartime manufacture, the lack of codes shouldn't be taken too seriously.

(1). *Bread Products.* The following codes were found on packaging for three issue bread items: Hecke Knäckebrot carton (271 I nö 8775), Heimatgrüss Cookies carton (261 I sü 5864), and Knäcke-Werke Knäckebrot carton (651 nä 21 504 L/0983). Heinis Knäckebrot (not shown) simply wrapped in paper is marked F/0368. The last two numbers on the Hecke Knäckebrot (40+ 23**344**) and Heimatgrüss Cookies (2568+ XII. **43**) denote the year. It appears that some combinations of codes were used on most paper packaging for bread products manufactured for the military.

(2). *Candy and Sweets.* The following codes were found on packaging for three dessert items: DPM restamped carton (271 II nä 2626), Grape Sugar carton (III 0023 384 I ch 8276), and Glykolade Chocolate Bar box (710 I sü 3864). It's believed all three items were manufactured specifically for the military. The code M/1406 was found on both the DPM carton and the Hecke Knäckebrot carton.

(3). *Miscellaneous Products.* The following codes were found on envelope type packages for spices and V Drops. The all number coded items are definitely commercial in nature. Numbers preceded by a letter or Roman numeral may signify military production. In Volume I there are two Wehrmachts-Packung Saccharin envelopes shown that are stamped with a letter/number or Roman numeral/number code.

A map of the 32 postal districts.

Postleitzahl 1 (Berlin), 2 (Mark Branden-burg, Stadtkreis Schneidemühl und die Landkreise Arnswalde, Friedeberg (Neum) und Netzekreis), 3 (Mecklenburg), 4 (Pommern), 5 a (Danzig-Westpreußen), 5 b (Ostpreußen), 5 c (Reichskommissariat Ostland), 6 (Wartheland), 7 a (General-gouvernement), 7 b (Reichskommissariat Ukraine), 8 (Niederschlesien und den Landkreis Grulich), 9 a (Oberschlesien), 9 b (Sudetenland Ost), 10 (Sachsen, Halle-Merseburg und v. Thüringen den Kreis Altenburg), 11 a (Sudetenland West), 11 b (Protektorat Böhmen und Mähren), 12 a (Wien, Niederdonau, Steiermark), 12 b (Kärnten, Oberdonau, Salzburg, Tirol-Vorarlberg), 13 a (Bayreuth, Franken, Mainfranken), 13 b (München - Ober-bayern, Schwaben u. den Bezirk Nieder-bayern), 14 (Württemberg-Hohenzollern), 15 (Thüringen), 16 (Hessen-Nassau, Kur-hessen), 17a (Baden), 17b (Elsaß), 18 (West-mark), 19 (Magdeburg-Anhalt), 20 (Ost-Hannover, Süd-Hannover-Braunschweig), 21 (Westfalen-Nord und Süd), 22 (Düssel-dorf, Essen, Köln-Aachen, Moselland), 23 (Weser-Ems und die Landkreise Bremervörde, Wesermünde, Verden, (Aller), Rotenburg (Hannover) und Oster-holz-Scharmbeck; Grafschaft Hoya und Diepholz), 24 (Hamburg, Schleswig-Hol-stein und die Landkreise Land Hadeln, Stade, Lüneburg und Harburg sowie Stadt Cuxhaven).

The postal zones as of 1946.

A sample of codes found on packaging for some dessert products.

These postwar codes found on a carton of Dextro-Energen are very similar to the codes on wartime cartons.

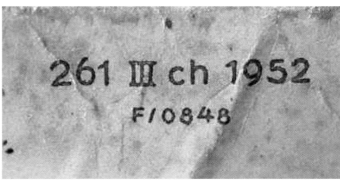

A sample of codes found on packaging for miscellaneous products.

These early Bundeswehr rations could easily be mistaken for wartime rations.

(4). *Over Printing of Packaging.* In order to conserve precious resources, recycling of packaging was a high priority during the war. This was especially true when it came to paper boxes and cartons. I assumed that the packaging was simply reutilized or repulped. However, it also appears that some packaging was over printed to eliminate unnecessary or incorrect information, or so it could be utilized for a completely different product. There were examples cited in the *U.S. Army Ration Report* where the package did not match the contents.

A Maizena box over stamped with the term "Emergency Package" or "Emergency Packed".

XII

CHANGES AND ADDITIONS TO RATIONS OF THE GERMAN WEHRMACHT IN WWII

TABLE OF CONTENTS

ACKNOWLEDGMENTS
Page 6, right hand column, bottom of the page, add the following contributor: Bundesarchiv - Federal Archives, Potsdamer Str. 1, D-56075 Koblenz

INTRODUCTION
Page 8, right hand column, line 19, paragraph to read:

The requisite supplies to keep the field kitchens operating came from three sources....There is a common misconception that in order for a food item to be for military issue, it must be marked "Wehrmacht Packung". The only undisputable original ration item the authors can confirm as being marked "Wehrmacht Packung" is Scho-ka-kola. There is no evidence to suggest that the military or any civil authority established that phrase as a contract specification for manufacturers to follow. It is possible it was simply a marketing phrase by the Hidebrand firm, over which they held proprietary rights. **All** the non Scho-ka-kola items the authors have seen over the years marked "Wehrmacht Packung" are of dubious authenticity if not outright fakes. There are other original wartime sugar products worded Wehrmacht(s) Packung, with the addition of an "s", as if to avoid any legal issues. That doesn't mean there weren't specific types of packaging used for the military; it's just that it's not as clearly identified as many collectors believe. The rations provided to the German soldier came from three major sources:

CHAPTER 1
CEREAL AND BAKED PRODUCTS
Page 14, left hand side, line 1, paragraph to read:

Bread was one of the major ration components of the Wehrmacht food supply. A wide variety of bread products were supplied to the German soldier. Until 1942 bread was delivered to the soldier in loaves, in paper cartons, or wrapped in various types of paper. Canned bread was common within the Navy, but doesn't appear to have been distributed to ground formations prior to 1942. Canned bread for the Navy was stamped with "KM". Surviving examples of canned bread verify that the Schwarzblechdosen WEHRM and Schwarzblechdosen Lötrand were used to package bread in. All surviving cans are dated 1944 and identified with a code stamped on the can. It's likely that cans with stenciled information were also produced. The lack of a "KM" stamp on those cans indicate they were not manufactured for the Navy. The ration report also mentions one can where "*Dark Dour Brot*" was spelled out. I believe this was a label placed on the can by the U.S. Army personnel who captured it.

Page 18, left hand side, first caption to read:
This package of Knäckebrot was taken off a German POW. Knäckebrot Werke Murten is a Swiss firm which started producing Knäckebrot in 1939.[3A] *Courtesy Kevin Barrett.*

Page 19: Picture captioned "Knäckebrot manufactured by Hecke and Company, Hamburg.[4]" should be at the top of the page.

Page 26, right hand side, line 23, paragraph to read:
    5. **Cookies.** Two samples were evaluated.

        A. (Sample 1). Approximately four pounds of sugar cookies ….The cookies had a relatively high fat content and were neutral in flavor.[16]

Page 27, middle of the page, the following photograph and caption, item is postwar:

The authors believe this item ….We believe it's actually some type of cookie.

Page 29, right hand side, the caption at the bottom of the page to read:
A small box of Feurich brand Keks.[18A] *Courtesy Kevin Barrett.*

Endnotes Chapter 1 Cereal and Baked Products
Page 39, right hand column, additional endnote, photographs, and captions:

[3A] The firm was founded in 1938 by Leopold Schoffler in the town of Murten/Morat, situated near the French and German borders. During our research, it appears that there were two product lines being simultaneously manufactured. One line features the word "Roland", or features a knight on the product. The firm name is written as Roland Morat SA in French, and the German version is Roland Murten AG. The other variation, which we've only seen on Knäckebrot, features the word "Singer". The firm name is written in French as Fabrique De Pain Croustillant SA Morat and in German as Knäckebrot-Werke Murten AG. In 1941 the company produced its first product; pains croustillants or Knäckebrot. Both "Singer" and "Roland" brand Knäckebrot were produced. It has been suggested that it was Dr. Wilhelm Kraft that initially suggested the idea of opening a Knäckebrot factory in Switzerland. It's possible that Knäckebrot-Werke Murten was a separate operation within the Roland Murten firm. Roland Murten AG started producing Zwieback in 1941. A receipt from Knäckebrot-Werke Murten AG dated April 1946 is shown below. The Murten Knäckebrot carton is very similar to wartime cartons manufactured by Dr. Wilhelm Kraft; to include the way various flavors like "H" for "Home" were identified.

Knäckebrot-Werke Murten AG receipt dated 1946. The cross bow logo does not appear anywhere on the receipt. The terms Singer and Roland are both printed on the receipt.

Page 41, left hand column, additional endnote and picture:
[18A] Despite the popularity of Feurich brand Keks, there is almost no information available on their history. What is certain is the company survived the war, and in February 1960 it was acquired by Melitta. Here is their listing in the 1929 Mosse Register of Firms.

Page 42, left hand column, line 1, endnote to read:
[26] The Loeser and Richter firm …. Here is their listing in the 1929 Mosse Register of Firms.

Page 42, right hand column, replace following photograph:

Knäckebrot-Werke Murten AG advertisement from 1939-1940, notice the use of the crossbow.

Replace it with the following photograph:

CHAPTER 2
DAIRY PRODUCTS
Page 47, right hand side, line 1, caption to read:
Two lids for canned cheese products (500 grams). The ADA lid (above) is for Tilsiter cheese.[4] The lid (below) is for a soft cheese.[5] Picture on the bottom *Courtesy of Chris Pittman.*

Page 52, right hand side, line 1, caption to read:
A small can similar to the aluminum milk cans shown below.

CHAPTER 3
FISH, FATS, AND POULTRY PRODUCTS
Page 59, left hand column, line 10, paragraph to read:
> **Fish.** Fish products were a key component.... Product information could take the form of simple codes stamped into the can or colorfully printed commercial cans. …

Page 59, left hand column, bottom of the page, additional picture above the caption:
Wooden crate used to transport Schmalzkonserven. *Courtesy Ruelle Frèdèric.*

Page 60, right hand column, line 1, paragraph to read:
1. **Lard.** Two samples were tested.

A. (Sample 1). Seven hundred and fifty grams of lard was packaged in a hermetically sealed open top style metal can, 4 x 4.875 inches in size…

Page 60, left hand side, bottom of the page, caption to read:
An aluminum lard container stamped for military use. It's possible the stamp is a postwar addition.

Page 67, right hand side, middle of the page, caption to read:
A can of smoked salmon.[19]

Endnotes Chapter 3 Fish, Fats, and Poultry Products
Page 72, right hand column, additional endnote and picture:
[19] While there are numerous references to Heinrich Strentz on the internet, there was no history of his company. The evidence suggests it is still in operation. On the can the firm is listed as being in Bremerhaven-F. The address from the 1929 Mosse Register of Firms shows the address as Wesermünde. Bremerhaven was founded in 1827. In 1845 the kingdom of Hanover founded a rival town directly beside Bremerhaven and called it Geestemünde. In 1927 Geestemünde and some neighboring municipalities were united to become the new city of Wesermünde. In 1939 Wesermünde and Bremerhaven were merged.

> **Heinr. Strentz**
> **Wesermünde, Fischereihafen**

CHAPTER 4
MEAT PRODUCTS
Page 79, bottom left, caption to read:
A 200 gram of pork, measuring 3 inches in diameter and 2.312 inches high. This style can is identical to the can discussed in paragraph 13.A. Its stamped S-36 (Pork-1936), GW (unknown), and R.St.14. (code for a type of galvanized steel).

Page 85, right hand column, line 7, caption to read:
30. **Head Cheese.** Approximately 1.5 pounds of head cheese was packaged in a hermetically sealed open top style metal can 4 x 4.875 inches in size…

Page 93, bottom of the page, caption to read:
German soldiers organizing rations for distribution. The chocolate bars shown on the bottom left are Holsatia brands from the Fehleisen and Rickel firm. *Courtesy Mike Hamady.*

CHAPTER 5
FRUIT AND VEGETABLE PRODUCTS

Page 102, right hand column, line 12, paragraph to read:
> 25. **Vegetables, Assorted.** Approximately two pounds of assorted vegetables were packed in a round hermetically sealed can, having outside dimensions of 4 x 4.875 inches.…

Page 102, bottom of the page, caption to read:
Issue can similar to those pictured in the ration report. In addition to the paper label it is stamped "GR. KO" for large cabbage.[7A] *Courtesy OSTFRONT Militaria.*

Page 110, right hand side, bottom of the page, caption to read:
A package of Wehrmacht pea soup manufactured by FINO-WERKE. *Courtesy Ruelle Frèdèric Collection.*

Page 110, left hand side, bottom of the page, caption to read:
Wehrmachts Suppenkonserven labels as described in the ration report. The manufacturers on these examples are C.H. Knorr and Schüle-Hohenlohe. *Courtesy Zeugmeister.*

Endnotes Chapter 5 Fruit and Vegetable Products
Page 116, left hand column, additional endnote and picture:
[7A] The Jentsch and Sohn, Konservenfabrik was founded in 1877. No postwar history was found. Here is their listing in the 1929 Mosse Register of Firms.

> Jentsch & Sohn, H. C. (Alex. Neumann. ℜ 110, Konservenfabrik, Kreuzstr. 17/18. Ps 1240 Hn., ℛℐ𝒞.

Page 117, right hand column, line 4, change to endnote and additional pictures:
[18] Switzerland openly traded with Germany until 1944. Conservenfabrik St.Gallen, AG was registered on January 16, 1931. Sometime after the war it became part of the HERO food corporation. The factory closed in 1989 and is currently a real estate firm. No postwar products marked "Conservenfabrik St.Gallen AG" have been observed. A can of the same exact construction (powdered cheese, different manufacturer) was observed on eBay and was dated to 1935. It was not uncommon for products manufactured in Switzerland to have information printed in German and French. On this can Tomato extract is written in French, German, and Italian. Here is a 1944 address label from the firm and a picture of the bear logo on the can.

From 1944

Conservenfabrik St. Gallen AG. St. Gallen 15
Telephon 3 81 21 - 23 - Bahnstation St. Gallen-Winkeln

CHAPTER 6
COFFEES, TEA AND OTHER BEVERAGES
Endnotes Chapter 6 Coffees, Tea and Other Beverages
Page 131, right hand column, additional photograph after endnote.
[16]

CHAPTER 7
SPICES, BAKING AIDS, BOUILLON, AND MISCELLANEOUS
Page 141, right hand side, bottom of the page, caption to read:
A package of paprika from the Saba Mühle, Nürnberg.[19A] *Courtesy Kevin Barrett.*

Endnotes Chapter 7 Spices, Baking aids, Bouillon, and Miscellaneous
Page 145, right hand column, line 1, additional endnote:
[19A] Sabamühle GmbH was founded in 1933 in Nürnberg. It is still in operation today as Ferdinand Kreutzer Sabamühle GmbH.

CHAPTER 8
SUGAR, CANDY, JAMS, AND OTHER DESSERT PRODUCTS

Page 153 The following photographs and caption are postwar:
A chocolate bar manufactured by the Meybona Chocolate Factory.[21]

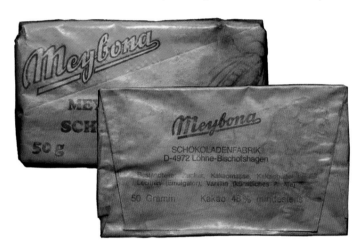

Endnotes Chapter 8 Sugar, Candy, Jams, and Other Dessert Products
Page 167, right hand column, line 8, change the paragraph to read:
[21] Not used.

CHAPTER 10
EMERGENCY AND SPECIAL RATION ITEMS

Page 183, left hand column, line 1, change the paragraph to read:
Authors' notes. The U.S. Army ration study …. See Annex 3 for additional discussions on Emergency, Supplemental, and Special Rations.

Page 192, right hand side, top of the page, change the caption to read:
The top locking Front Line Assault Ration (L) carton and a recreation (R).

Page 198, right hand column, line 25, change the paragraph to read:
1. **Emergency Ration for Air Force and Naval Personnel.** Specialized Emergency Ration containers were developed for use by the German Navy and Air Force. There were two basic types of containers: one style that looks like a rifle cleaning kit, held 90-100 grams of product and the other style had a latch closure for easy replenishment an held 300 grams of emergency rations. Both types of cans were waterproof. The compact size makes it convenient for a person to carry with them. According to Mick Prodger's excellent book *Luftwaffe vs. RAF: Flying*

Equipment of the Air War, 1939-45, the contents of the can consisted of Scho-ka-kola, chewing gum, Pervitin tablets, Dextrose or Grape Sugar tablets (Weinsäure Zucker and a small metal box with Dextro written on it, are shown in the book), and sunburn/frostbite ointment. The author states the blue cans were for flights over water and the green cans for flights over land. Mr. Prodger also discusses a special high calorie ration for flights over wilderness/sparsely populated areas. We're assuming the can was identical to the green, flights over land container except that the contents consisted of high protein soy bread, dried meat (Pemmican), and additional caffeine tablets. The contents of the Navy version were probably similar to the Air Force flights over water can. It's rumored that there are photographs of Fallschirmjagers using this style of can. To the authors' knowledge, no cans with Heer or SS markings have been found. There is also a picture of the Zwieback Seenotpackung container on page 95 of *Luftwaffe vs. RAF: Flying Equipment of the Air War, 1939-45.* It is shown along with a tube of cheese. It's not clear what this ration was used for.

Additional photographs and captions near page 201:

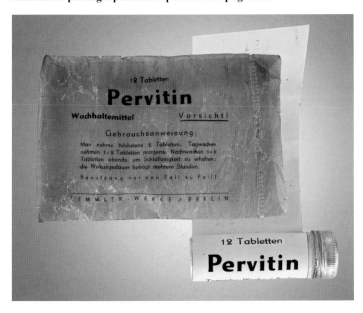

Pervitin tablets. *Courtesy Ed Stroh.*

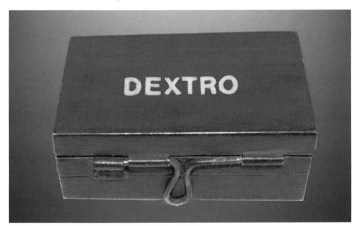

A recreation of the dextrose container shown in *Luftwaffe vs. RAF: Flying Equipment of the Air War, 1939-45.* This multi-use box does indeed fit inside the Emergency Ration Container for Air Force and Naval Personnel.

Page 206, left hand column, line 10, paragraph to read:
The crackers were packed in a cloth bag (Zwiebackbeutel) .... In the book *Der Feldkochunteroffizier* (*The Field Cook NCO*), the author states that when the regular food supply was exhausted that the *full* iron rations could be distributed. ...

Page 212, right hand column, line 1, paragraph to read:
The 1939 Special Allowance for Motorized Troops portion consisted of the following:

A. **1 can of mixed vegetables and meats** *(probably 850 grams)*
B. **600 grams of Dauerbrot or 500 grams of Knäckebrot**
C. **100 grams of Chocolate**
D. **5 grams of Lemon powder**

Page 212 left hand side, the following photograph and caption are replaced:

A recreation of the 1939 special allowance for armored forces. The ration consisted of the following items: 1. Shipping container 2. Chocolate 3. Mixed canned goods 4. Knäckebrot, and 5. Lemon powder.

Replacements for preceding photograph and caption:

A recreation of the 1939 special allowance for armored forces. The ration consisted of the following items: 1. Can of mixed meat and vegetables 2. Lemon powder. 3. Knäckebrot (Four Packages total) and 4. Chocolate.

Page 212, bottom of the page, caption to read:
Vitamin supplements in the form of candy or chocolate were issued to the troops to combat scurvy and other diseases. The container contained 100 Vitamin A and D tablets. [12]

Endnotes Chapter 10 Emergency and Special Ration Items
Page 213, left hand column, line 3, endnote to read:
[2] T he example shown is either an original variant example of Knäckebrot …. Our analysis leads us to believe this variant is a new improved, high tech fake.

Page 213, bottom of the page, caption to read:
In her book *Reducing Diets,* by Sabine Merta, the author ….

ANNEX 1
THE SUPPLY OF WEHRMACHT RATIONS
Page 216, right hand column, line 1, paragraph to read:
1. **General.** Subsistence was provided by the Army for the Army, Air Force, and Waffen SS. At the start of the war the Navy had its own independent food procurement organization but during the course of the war this power was largely transferred to the OKH. The Air Force undertook only one function, the storage of special flying rations. These rations were procured by the Army. Later in the war the direction of food for other organizations such as the RAD and Hitler Youth was incorporated into the OKH. It was the aim of the Germans to ship supplies forward to the troops, with a minimum of handling. The theoretically perfect, but almost never achieved system of supply was to ship whole trains right to the troops, leaving reserves untouched except in an emergency. If, for instance, supplies could be shipped on the same train in which they left the Zone of the Interior directly into division dumps, an effort was made to do so.

ANNEX 4
THE WEHRMACHT RATION CAN
Page 249, bottom of the page, caption to read:
A typical lid with stamped markings used on meat or mixed meat cans. The code on this example indicates it contained schmalz/lard.

Page 257, left hand column, line 9, paragraph to read:
Now what do the markings on sanitary cans used for rations mean? The following chart shows a sampling of markings used on ration cans. The stand alone numbers stamped on the cans are probably the "Kurz-zeichen" for a yet unidentified DIN. The term DIN Packung was not referenced in the 1942 or 1956 *"DIN Normblatt-Verzeichnis",* however from surviving examples we know that this term was used prior to 1942. Following the logic of other DIN categories with special identifier, there's little doubt that Packung/Packing refers to the packing of the product and not to the actual manufacturing techniques in constructing the can.

ANNEX 5
THE SCHO-KA-KOLA STORY
Page 269, right hand column, line 31, paragraph to read:
E. (Conclusion). Several unopened Hybrid cans were posted on a militaria forum for the authors to review. The chocolate wrapper was postwar which ends any speculation that the product may have been wartime. However the chocolate could have been wartime or at least manufactured using a wartime mold. It was most likely produced sometime right after the war, utilizing excess stocks of wartime front covers and other postwar components. There are reports that in the immediate postwar years Hildebrand distributed Scho-ka-kola in Berlin.

It's important to remember that the Hildebrand factory was destroyed and would lack any manufacturing capabilities for years after the war's end. The only Hildebrand sub contractor which still retained any capability to manufacture Scho-ka-kola after the war was Schoko-Buck.

ANNEX 6
PERSONAL COOKERS
Page 278, right hand side, caption to read:
This is an accessory piece issued with the steel carbide lantern accessories kit. It would be filled with petroleum and used instead of carbide. It's possible that some ingenious soldiers figured out that it could be used to warm up rations.

ANNEX 9
MISCELLANEOUS PRODUCTS
Page 287, left hand column, line 11, subject in bold:
   3. **Marsch Getränk Container.**

Page 290, right hand column: Paragraph 4 starts on a separate line.

Page 293, right hand side, top of the page, caption to read: WHW members sorting through food items. *Bundesarchiv Bild 102-17313/ Foto: o.Ang. / License CC-BY-SA 3.0.*

BIBLIOGRAPHY

Additional reference on page 297:

Prodger, Mick J., *Luftwaffe vs. RAF: Flying Equipment of the Air War, 1939-45,* Schiffer Military/Aviation History, 1998

Additional references on page 302:

138. Bremerhaven, http://en.wikipedia.org/wiki/Bremerhaven (8 August 2010)

139. Konservenindustrie in Braunschweig, http://de.wikipedia.org/wiki/Konservenindustrie_in_Braunschweig (8 August 2010)

140. Andre Hofer Feigenkaffeefabrik, http://www.salzburg.com/wiki/index.php/Andre-Hofer-Feigenkaffeefabrik (8 August 2010)

141. Carl Wentzel, http://de.wikipedia.org/wiki/Carl_Wentzel (8 August 2010)

142. Erstein, http://www.sucre-erstein.com/ (8 August 2010)

143. Jochen Rindt, http://de.wikipedia.org/wiki/Jochen_Rindt (8 August 2010)

144. Ferdinand Kreutzer Sabamühle GmbH, http://www.sabamuehle.de/home.html (8 August 2010)

GLOSSARY

Automatic Square Bottom Bag - Essentially the modern paper bag.

AG - Aktiengesellschaft is a German term that refers to a corporation that is limited by shares, i.e., owned by shareholders. It may be traded on a stock market.

Bonderising or *Bonderizing* - A chemical process to help prevent the corrosion of iron, steel, and other metals. The surface is sprayed with or immersed in a hot phosphate solution, and a superficial insoluble phosphate layer is formed. The metal is then usually painted or lacquered.

Cellophane - Cellophane is a thin, transparent sheet made of regenerated cellulose. Also known as viscose foil.

Chipboard - A type of paperboard generally made from reclaimed paper stock.

D.R.G.M. - (Deutsches Reich Gebrauchsmuster) Not a patent, but a secondary protection for an item which by itself would not qualify for patent protection.

D.R.P. - (Deutsches Reichs - Patent) indicates patent protection in Germany.

D.R.P.u.A.P - (Deutsches Reichs - Patent und Ausländische Patente) indicates patent protection in Germany and in foreign countries.

D.R.W.Z. - (Deutsches Reich Warenzeichen) indicates a trade mark.

Duplex Satchel Bottom Bag - The satchel - bottom bag is a flat bag that has a diamond - shaped, preformed bottom that allows the bag to stand up on its own.

Eco - packing - Aluminum foil between 2 water repelling impregnated cellulose layers.

Foil Sheet - In the late nineteenth century and early twentieth century, tin foil was in common use. Tin foil is much stiffer than aluminum foil and gave a slight tin taste to the food wrapped in it.

Fondant - A cream confection used as a filling or coating for cakes, pastries, and candies or sweets.

Friction Plug Can - A can with a removable cover consisting of a plug, which fits into a ring in the top end of can

Ges. Gesch. - (Gesetzlich Geschützt) (Legally Registered) A general lesser legal notice that the item is protected by one or more of any number of legalities such as a DRGM, trademark, design patent, or copyright.

GmbH, GesmbH, Ges.m.b.H. - Gesellschaft mit beschränkter Haftung - (GmbH) is a type of legal entity created in Germany in 1892. It literally translates as a company with limited liability.

Greaseproof Glassine Paper - or Parchment Sheet, which is a specially treated, very dense, and hydrated sheet, which provides a barrier to grease or oily ingredients

Kossenbrot - From what little information was available, Kossenbrot was invented by Dr Richard Bruhn. Kossenbrot is better known today as WASA - Knäckebrot.

Kraft Paper - Strong paper made from unbleached, wood pulp that is naturally brown but may be dyed another color. It is frequently used for large envelopes, paper bags, wrapping papers, and toweling. A lighter grade of Kraft paper is used for newspapers and food packaging.

Manila Paper - Paper originally made from Manila hemp, today many fibers are used. It is beige, buff or light brownish yellow in color, and the fibers are usually visible to the naked eye. It is a semi - bleached chemical sulfate paper with a smooth finish. It is not as strong as Kraft paper, but has better printing qualities. Today it's commonly used to make file folders.

Parchment Paper - Paper that is coated with silicone, making it moisture and grease resistant. It can withstand exposure to temperatures up to 420°F in the oven. It will brown when exposed to direct heat, but won't burn.

Reverse Tuck Carton - A very common style of box. The end tuck flaps are extensions of opposite carton faces. There are numerous styles.

Soda Pulp Paper - A chemical wood pulp produced by high temperature digestion of papermaking material with sodium hydroxide. The soda pulp method is used in making paper from poplars, birches, oaks, and other deciduous trees. Papers containing a high proportion of soda pulp are very white and soft, and possess high bulk and opacity but low strength. Soda pulp is frequently used to give a soft finish to a sulfite - pulp base paper.

Sulfite Paper - Sometimes referred to as sulphite paper, it is an often elegant and useful type of paper that has a number of uses. In the production process it starts out as sulfite pulp. Sulfite pulp is made by treating wood pulp with peroxide or hypochlorite, and ran through an operation that yields a thick paper product, that has lost the natural hue of the wood pulp and has begun to take on a lighter shade. Repeated applications of the chemical compounds will result in an even lighter shade, until the end product has taken on a brilliant white appearance. From there, the sulfite paper can be further processed to any thickness that is desires, depending on how the end product is to be used. One of the most common uses for sulfite paper is with the development of photographs.

Waxed Paper - Tissue paper which is coated with a paraffin wax.

BIBLIOGRAPHY

Books

Absolon, Rudolf. *Die Wehrmacht im Dritten Reich, Band VI. 19 Dezember 1941 bis 9 Mai 1945.* (Harald Boldt Verlag, Boppard Am Rhein, 1995).

Der Adler. (Magazine Various Issues).

Amtliches Fernsprechbuch fur den Bezirk der Reichspostdirektion Berlin 1941.

Amtliches Fernsprechbuch fur den Bezirk der Reichspostdirektion Berlin 1943. (CD Version).

Amtliches Fernsprechbuch fur den Bezirk der Reichspostdirektion Hamburg 1941. (CD Version).

Amtliches Fernsprechbuch fur den Bezirk der Reichspostdirektion Nurnberg 1938. (CD Version).

Amtliches Fernsprechbuch fur den Bezirk der Reichspostdirektion Potsdam 1941. (CD Version).

Amtliches Fernsprechbuch fur den Bezirk der Reichspostdirektion Wien 1943. (CD Version).

Bahlsen 1889-1964. (H. Bahlsens Keksfabrik KG Hannover).

Bein, Fritz. *Der Feldkochunteroffizier.* (Verlag Bernard und Graefe Berlin SW 68, 1943).

Buckner, Alex. *The German Infantry Handbook 1939-1945.* (Schiffer Military History, 1991).

Cellophane and Sausage Casings Made at Kalle and Co. Wiesbaden. (British Intelligence Objectives Sub-Committee-B.I.O.S., Final Report No.553, Undated).

Certain Aspects of the German Herring Canning Industries. (British Intelligence Objectives Sub-Committee-B.I.O.S., Final Report No. 1071, Undated).

Chocolate Kola Formulae and Manufacturing Process. (British Intelligence Objectives Sub-Committee-B.I.O.S., Misc.Report No. 38, 30 July, 1945).

Chocolate Products-Superior Keeping Qualities. (B.I.O.S. Misc.Report No.15, 5 July, 1945).

Classified List of OTS Printed Reports PB 81500. (Department of Commerce, October 1947).

Cole, Hugh M. *The Ardennes: Battle of the Bulge.* (Office of the Chief of Military History, United States Army, Washington, D.C., 1965).

DAMALS-Erinnerungen An Grosse Tage Der SS-Totenkopf-Division Im Franzosischen Feldzug 1940. (Chr. Belser Verlag, Stuttgart).

Defalque, Ray J. MD., Wright, Amos J. MLS. *Methamphetamine for Hitler's Germany: 1937 to 1945.* (Bulletin of Anesthesia History, Volume 29, Number 2, April 2011).

Dekofei.(Magazine Various Issues).

De Lagarde, Jean. *German Soldiers of World War Two.* (Histoire Et Collections, Poole, Dorset, UK).

Deutsche A.G. fur Nestle Erzeugniss Kiel Milchewerke Angeln. (Item NO. 22, File No.XXX-99, 3-4 July 1945).

Das Deutsche Mädel. (Magazine Various Issues).

Dickson, Paul. *Chow: A Cook's Tour of Military Food.* (A Plume Book, New York 1978).

FAS Herbst und Winter. (1936/37).

Filmwoche. (Magazine Various Issues).

Feldkochbuch, H.Dv.86. (Erich Zander Druck und Verlagshaus, Berlin, 1941).

FM-E 101-10 Staff Officers' Field Manual Enemy Forces Organization, Technical, and Logistical Data. (United States Government Printing Office, Washington: 1942).

Frauen-Warte. (Magazine Various Issues).

Gaul, Roland. *The Battle of the Bulge in Luxembourg, Volume 1: The Germans.* (Schiffer Military/Aviation History, 1995).

Gemeinschafts-Verpflegung in Lager und Werksküchen. (Verlag der Deutschen Arbeitsfront, Berlin, 1940).

German Chocolate, Cocoa, and Confectionery Production Layout and Manufacturing Methods. (British Intelligence Objectives Sub-Committee -B.I.O.S., Final Report No. 1077, Undated).

German Chocolate and Confectionery Machinery Design and Processing. (British Intelligence Objectives Sub-Committee-B.I.O.S., Final Report No. 1115, Undated).

German Confection Rations. (U.S.Army Intelligence Bulletin, Undated).

German Clothing, Equipment and Rations. (Office of the Quartermaster General Military Planning Division Research and Development Branch, 5 September 1945).

The German Fishing Industry. (British Intelligence Objectives Sub-Committee-B.I.O.S., Final Report No. 493, Undated).

German Glass or Enamelled Lined Equipment on Mild Steel and Cast Iron for Chemical-Food-Drink and Allied Industries. (B.I.O.S Final Report No.569. Item Nos.21, 22 and 31, Undated).

German Glass Industry. (B.I.O.S Final Report No.403. Item No.22, Undated).

The German Ham Canning Industry. (British Intelligence Objectives Sub-Committee-B.I.O.S., Final Report No. 299, Undated).

The German Herring Curing and Herring Canning Industries. (British Intelligence Objectives Sub-Committee -B.I.O.S., Final Report No. 804, Undated).

German Light Metal Industry-Fancy Goods. (British Intelligence Objectives Sub-Committee-B.I.O.S., Final Report No.836. Item No.36, Undated).

German Milk Can Industry. (B.I.O.S., Final Report No.1473. Item No.31, 1946).

German Mountain Warfare. (Special Series, NO. 21, 29 February, 1944. Prepared by Military Intelligence Division War Department).

German Papermaking Industry. (Final Report No.312. Item No.22, Undated).

German Papermaking Industry. (B.I.O.S., Final Report No.1041. Item No.22, 27 April, 1946).

German Rations and Subsistence Items. (Quartermaster Food and Container Institute for the Armed Forces, May 1947).

German Ski Training and Tactics. (Special Series, No. 290 January 31, 1944. Prepared by Military Intelligence Division War Department).

The German Synthetic Sausage Casings Industry. (Field Information Agency Technical-F.I.A.T., British Intelligence Objectives Sub-Committee Final Report No. 1118).

German Tinplate Industry. (B.I.O.S Final Report No.610. Item No.21, February 1946).

Gesetze und Verordnungen Deutsches Reich. (Various issues).

Haeberlein Metzger sales brochure. (undated).

Handbook on German Military Forces TM-E-30-451. (United States Government Printing Office, Washington, 1945).

Heer, Jean. *Nestle 125 Years 1866-2001.* (Nestle 1992).

Heiss, R. *Fortschritte der Lebensmittelforschung Band I-IV.* (Theodor Steinkopff, Dresden u. Leipzig, 1942-1944).

Hoffman, Eleanor. *Feeding Our Armed Forces.* (Thomas Nelson and Sons, Edinburgh, New York, Toronto 1943).

Höhne, Günther Dr. *Der Feldverpflegungsbeamte.* (Verlag Bernard and Graefe Berlin SW 68, 1939).

Internationales Militaria-Magazine. (Verlag Heinz Nickel 66482 Zweibrucken, Various issues).

Investigation of Certain German Paper and Board Mills with Particular Reference to the Production of Leatherboard, Carton and Shoe Board and Coated Papers. (B.I.O.S Final Report No.838. Item No.22, Undated).

Jaddatz, Bruno. *The Luftwaffe Guide Book to Basic Survival at Sea.* (Schiffer Military/Aviation History, 2002).

Johannes, Jeff. Article for Der Erste Zug. *German Rations at the Front: A snap of what the German Soldier consumed during the Battle of the Bulge.*

Kittel, Walther Dr., Schreiber, Walter Dr., Zigelmayer, Wilhelm Dr. *Soldatenernährung und Gemeinschaftsverpflegung.* (Theodor Steinkopff, Dresden u. Leipzig, 1939).

Koehler, Franz A. *Special Rations for the Armed Forces, 1946-53.* (QMC Historical Studies, Series II, No. 6, Historical Branch, Office of the Quartermaster General, Washington D.C. 1958).

Das Lebensmittelfenster. (Magazine, Various Issues 1936-1941).

Light Alloys. (British Intelligence Objectives Sub-Committee-B.I.O.S., Final Report No.981. Item No.21, Undated).

Maier, Curtis E. *A Survey of the Practices of the German Can Industry During the Second World War.* (Combined Intelligence Objectives Sub-Committee, Item No. 21 and 22, File No. XXX-85, London-HM Stationary Office, Undated).

Manufacture of Pulp Paper and Related Products from Wood in Western Germany. (FIAT Final Report No.487. 9 November, 1945).

Manufacture of Soya Flour and Soya Chocolate and Cocoa Combinations at Gartmann-Hamburg and Affiliated Plants Elsewhere. (B.I.O.S. Misc.Report No.17, 2 July, 1945).

Meyer, Reiner. *Die Reklamekunst der Keksfabrik Bahlsen in Hannover von 1889-1945.* (Doctorate Dissertation Georg-August-Universität zu Göttingen, Münster, 1999).

McGuirk, Dal. *Rommel's Army in Africa.* (Motorbooks International, 1993).

Merkblatt 18a/17 Taschenbuch für den Winterkrieg. (1943).

Military Improvisations During the Russian Campaign. (Department of the Army Pamphlet NO. 20-201, August 1951).

The Modern Ration of the German Armed Forces (Translation), (U.S.Army Infantry School, February 1941).

Mosse, R. *Deutsches Reichs-Adressbuch für Industrie, Gewerbe, Handel und Landwirtschaft.* (Druck und Verlag Rudolf Mosse, Berlin, 1929, Five Volume CD Version).

Oberkommando des Heeres, GenStdH/Ausb.Abt. (I) Nr. 10/44: Waldkampf. (2 February, 1944).

Otte, Alfred. *The HG Panzer Division.* (Schiffer Military/Aviation History, 1989).

Paper Pulp Moulding Industry in Germany. (B.I.O.S Final Report No.1589, undated).

Pool, Jim and Bock, Tom. *Rations of the German Wehrmacht in WWII.* (Schiffer Military/Aviation History, 2010).

Prodger, Mick J. *Luftwaffe vs. RAF: Flying Equipment of the Air War, 1939-45.* (Schiffer Military/Aviation History, 1998).

Production of Flour and Bread in Germany. (British Intelligence Objectives Sub-Committee-B.I.O.S., Final Report No. 111, Undated).

Rath, Ingeborg. *Das Einmachen in Weissblechdosen.* (Braunschweig, 1934).

Reichsnährstand Taschenkalender 1943. (Reichsnährstandverlag G.m.b.h., Berlin N4, Linienstrasse 139-140).

Report on the German Soft Drink Industry with Special Reference to the Study of Ascorbic Acid in Fruit Beverages. (B.I.O.S Final Report No.1265, 19 September, 1946).

Sáiz, Agustín. *Deutsche Soldaten.* (Casemate Philadelphia and Newbury, 2008).

Schoko-Buck Stuttgart. (Field Information Agency Technical-F.I.A.T., British Intelligence Objectives Sub-Committee Final Report No. 125, 1 October, 1945).

Scientific Background of the German Chocolate Industry. (B.I.O.S Final Report No.57. Item No.22, Undated).

Signal. (Magazine Various Issues).

Some Aspects of the German Glass Industry in 1946. (B.I.O.S. Final Report No.1780, Item No.22, undated).

Stollwerk Preisliste. (1929-30).

Struppe Proviant Geschäfte Wien. (undated).

Sugar Confectionery and Chocolate Manufacture in Germany. (British Intelligence Objectives Sub-Committee-B.I.O.S., Final Report No. 406, Undated).

Summary of Field Investigations, Fats, Oils, and Oilseeds. (F.I.A.T. Final Report No.213, 8 October, 1945).

Summary Report on German Research and Technology in Food. (Field Information Agency Technical-F.I.A.T., British Intelligence Objectives Sub-Committee Final Report No.82).

A Survey of German Wartime Food Processing, Packaging and Allocation, Parts I and II. (British Intelligence Objectives Sub-Committee-B.I.O.S., Final Report of the Food Commission. 27 September, 1945).

Tartaric Acid Processes in Germany. (F.I.A.T. Final Report No. 1049, 31 January, 1947).

Technical Aspect of Pectin Manufacture in Germany. (B.I.O.S Final Report No.388. Item No.22, Undated).

Thiele-Rieger-Klas. *Die Preissvorschriften bei Lieferung von Lebensmitteln an die Wehrmacht.* (Verlag Franz Vahlen, Berlin 1941).

Taschenbuch für den Verpflegungs-Lagerbeamten. (Druck und Verlag der Reichsdruckerei Berlin 1942).

Thompson, Scott L. *Gulaschkanone: The German Field Kitchen in World War II and Modern Reenactment.* (Schiffer Military/Aviation History, 2011).

Vorschrift für die Verwaltung Der Truppenküchen, H.Dv. 43a, 11 März 1922. (Mittler und Sohn, Berlin).

Weaver, W. Darrin. *Kunststoffe: A Collectors's Guide to German World War II Plastics and their Markings.* (Schiffer Military/Aviation History, 2008).

Wehrmacht-Verwaltungsvorschrift IV. (Druck und Verlag der Reichsdruckerei, Berlin 1939).

Die Woche. (Magazine Various Issues).

Yelton, David K. *Hitler's Home Guard: Volkssturmmann Western Front, 1944-45.* (Osprey Publishing, Westminster, MD., 2006).

Websites Used

1. "Manner," http://www.manner.com/ (7 March 2008).

2. "Bernhard Brunner, Deutsche Postleitzahlen,Postgeschichte und Poststempel 1944/45," 3 Nov 2007, http://www.plz-stempel.de/4559.html(1 March 2008).

3. "The Chocolate Wrappers Museum," http://mujweb.cz/www/chocolate/en /index.htm (29 February 2008)

4. "Sarotti" from Wikipedia, the Free Encyclopedia, 7 November 2007, http://en.wikipedia.org/wiki/Sarotti (2 February 2008).

5. "Stollwerck since 1839," http://www.stollwerck.de/en/frameset/index1.php? content=../unternehmen/geschichte&navi=unternehmen&unavi=g eschichte (4 March 2008).

6. "Bahlsen," http://www.bahlsen.com/root_bahlsen_anim_en/index.php (1 March 2008).

7. "Haeberlein-Metzger," http://www.haeberlein-metzger.de/ (5 March 2008).

8. "Nestle-History," http://www.nestle.com/AllAbout/History/HistoryList.htm (13 March 2008).

9. "Dr.Oetker," http://www.oetker.de/wga/oetker/html/default/twaa-664d7m.de.html (3 February 2008).

10. "Maggi" 22 February 2008, http://en.wikipedia.org/wiki/Maggi (3 March 2008).

11. "Milei," http://www.milei.de/en/01_unternehmen/01_1_geschichte.php (18 February 2008).

12. "Army and Air Force Exchange System Historical Highlights," http://www. aafes.com/pa/history_page.htm (12 March 2008).

13. "SCHO-KA-KOLA," http://www.scho-ka-kola.de/1.1.Unternehmen.html (6 April 2008).

14. "Brandt Zweiback-Schokoladen," http://brandt-gmbh.de/ (15 April 2008).

15. "WEPU Brot," http://www.wepu-brot.de/index.html (16 May 2008).

16. "Images from the German Federal Archive by Year," http://commons. wikimedia.org/wiki/Category:Images from the German Federal Archive by year (23 December 2008).

17. "Biomalz," http://www.biomalz-back.de/ (20 February 2011).

18. "Max Koch," http://de.wikipedia.org/wiki/Konservenindustrie_in_Braunschweig (20 February 2011).

19. "Krafts Foods," http://www.kraftfoods.de/kraft/page?siteid=kraft-prd&locale=dede1&PagecRef=2613&Mid=2613 (20 February 2011).

20. "Gottfried Friedrichs," http://www.gottfried-friedrichs.de/ (20 February 2011).

21. "K-ration," http://en.wikipedia.org/wiki/K-ration (20 February 2011).

22. "C-ration," http://en.wikipedia.org/wiki/C-ration (20 February 2011).

23. "Niedersedlitz Malz Fabrik," http://wikimapia.org/11461315/de/Ehemaliger-Malzfabrik-Niedersedlitz (3 March 2011).

24. "Lebkuchen Schmidt," http://ww2.lebkuchen-schmidt.com/eng_index.php (30 March 2011).

25. "Delitzscher," http://www.delitzscher-schokoladen.de/ (30 March 2011).

26. "Burger Knäcke Gmbh + Co. KG," http://www.burger-knaecke.de/ (1 April 2011).

27. "Ostmann," http://www.ostmann.de/Unternehmensgeschichte_80851.html (2 April 2011).

28. "Yoghurt," http://en.wikipedia.org/wiki/Yoghurt (11 April 2011).

29. "Hammerbrotwerke," http://de.wikipedia.org/wiki/Hammerbrotwerke (20 May 2011).

30. "1031-2006, 975 Jahre Gliesmarode," http://www.gliesmarode1031.de/1.html (6 June 9, 2011).

31. "Liste der Unternehmen," die im Nationalsozialismus von der Zwangsarbeit profitiert haben, http://zinelibrary.info/files/NS-Zwangsarbeit.pdf (29 June 30 2011).

32. "Deutsche Schulverein," http://de.wikipedia.org/wiki/Deutscher_Schulverein (1 July 2011).

33. "Andra Hörtnagl," http://www.hoertnagl.at/index.php?id=38 (1 August 2011).

34. "Wichartz Gewürze," www.wichartz.de (19 August 2011).

35. "Pionier-Bataillon 39," http://www.pionier39.pl/index.html (August 27, 2011).

36. "Karo Syrup," http://www.karosyrup.com/ (1 September, 2011).

37. "Story About Brands," http://www.marcasconhistoria.com.ar/detalle_nestle.php (27 November, 2011).

38. "Cremilk," http://www.cremilk.com/ (27 November, 2011).

TRADEMARK INFORMATION

Most of the items and products in this book may be covered by various copyrights, trademarks, and logotypes. Their use herein is for identification purposes only. All rights are reserved by their respective owners.

The text and the products pictured in this book are from the collection of the author of this book, its publisher, or various private collections. The book is not sponsored, endorsed, or otherwise affiliated with any of the companies whose products are represented herein. They include the products or firms listed below, among others.

In certain cases companies allowed me to use pictures or information from their archives. These firms are fully credited in the book.

I attempted to research the trademarks of all the companies and products discussed in the book. The results are shown in the list below. This list should not be taken as gospel. Over the years trademarks have been renewed, firms have merged, were reorganized, went out of business, or changed names, making it difficult to confirm the accuracy of the list. For that reason I have not annotated every product with the ® or ™ symbol. This was only done in those instances where the research showed that a trademark symbol of a particular product or firm was integral to the name.

Alba Gurkendoktor is a registered trademark of Gehring & Neiweiser GmbH & Co KG, 33611 Bielefeld.

Alete is a registered trademark of Société des Produits Nestlé S.A., Vevey, CH.

Bahlsen appears to have a registered trademark for all their products under Bahlsen GmbH & Co. KG, 30163 Hannover.

BIOMALZ is a registered trademark of Gebr. Patermann, Kirn/Nahe.

Brandt products all appear to have registered trademarks with Brandt, Carl-Jürgen, 58135 Hagen.

Chocolade Manner Wien is a registered trademark of Josef Manner & Comp. A.G., Wien, AT.

Dr.Oetker and products is a registered trademark of Dr. August Oetker Nahrungsmittel KG, 33617 Bielefeld.

Eduscho is a registered trademark of Tchibo Markenverwaltungs GmbH & Co. KG, 19258 Gallin.

ESZET was a registered trademark of Eszet Kakao-und Schokolade-Fabrik Staengel & Ziller.

Frigeo is a registered trademark of Katjes Fassin GmbH + Co. KG, 46446 Emmerich.

KAFFEE HAG is a registered trademark of HAG AKTIENGESELLSCHAFT, 2800 Bremen,1.

KARO is a registered trademark of ACH Food Companies, Inc., Cordova, TN 38016.

Kola Dallmann macht Müde mobil is a registered trademark of Fabrik chem. pharm. Präparate Dallmann & Co., 65201 Wiesbaden.

Knorr products all appear to have registered trademarks with Knorr-Nährmittel AG, Thayngen, CH.

Libby's was a registered trademark of Corlib Brand Holding LTD, Tortola.

Maggi products have registered trademarks with Société des Produits Nestlé S.A., Vevey, CH.

MAIZENA is a registered trademark of Unilever Supply Chain, Inc, Clinton, CT. 06413.

Milei was a registered trademark of Südmilch AG, 70191 Stuttgart.

Nestle is a registered trademark of Societe des Produits Nestle S.A. in Vevey, 1800.

Nescafe® is a registered owned by the Societe des Produits Nestle S.A., Case Postal 353, 1800 Vevey, CH.

OSTMANN is a registered trademark of Karl Ostmann, Bielefeld 17, D-4800.

Perga and *Perga Packung* is a registered trademark of the PKL Verpackungs systeme GmbH, 52441 Linnich.

RAHMA is a registered trademark of International Foodstuffs Co. in P.O. Box 4115 Sharjah.

Sarotti is a registered trademark of Société des Produits Nestlé S.A., Vevey, CH.

Scho-Ka-Kola is a registered trademark of SCHO-KA-KOLA GmbH, 10719 Berlin.

Sprengel is a registered trademark of Barry Callebaut AG, Zürich, CH.

Suchard is a registered trademark of Kraft Foods Deutschland Holding GmbH, 28199 Bremen.

Ubena is a registered trademark of Fuchs Gewürze GmbH, 49201 Dissen.

Velveeta is a registered trademark of Kraft Foods Global Brands LLC in Northfield, IL, 60093.

Waldbaur is a registered trademark of Barry Callebaut AG, Zürich, CH.

Wittler Brot was a registered trademark of August Wittler Brotfabrik KG, 13347 Berlin.

Wrigley is a registered trademark of Wm. Wrigley Jr. Co., Chicago, Ill., US.

XoX is a registered trademark of XOX Gebäck GmbH, 31789 Hameln.

ZENTIS is a registered trademark of ZENTIS GmbH & Co. KG in 52070 Aachen.